The Future of Russian Gas and Gazprom

The Future of Russian Gas and Gazprom

JONATHAN P. STERN

Published by the Oxford University Press
For the Oxford Institute for Energy Studies
2005

OXFORD

UNIVERSITY PRESS

Great Clarendon Street, Oxford OX2 6DP

*Oxford University Press is a department of the University of Oxford.
It furthers the University's objective of excellence in research, scholarship
and education by publishing worldwide in*

Oxford New York

*Auckland Cape Town Dar es Salaam Delhi Hong Kong Karachi
Kuala Lumpur Madrid Melbourne Mexico City Nairobi
New Delhi Shanghai Taipei Toronto*

with offices in

*Argentina Austria Brazil Chile Czech Republic France Greece
Guatemala Hungary Italy Japan Poland Portugal Singapore
South Korea Switzerland Thailand Turkey Ukraine Vietnam*

*Oxford is a registered trade mark of Oxford University Press
in the UK and in certain other countries*

*Published in the United States
by Oxford University Press Inc., New York*

*British Library Cataloguing in Publication Data
Data available*

*Library of Congress Cataloguing in Publication Data
Data available*

*Cover designed by Clare Hofmann
Typeset by Philip Armstrong, Sheffield
Printed by The Alden Group, Oxford*

ISBN 0-19-730031-6   978-0-19-730031-2

For Judy, Rebecca and Daniel with my Love

TABLE OF CONTENTS

LIST OF TABLES, FIGURES AND MAPS

Tables

Figures

Maps

NOTES ON SOURCES AND UNITS

Sources

Important sources of information on which this study has relied are:

The Gazprom website – www.gazprom.ru – has become an increasingly rich source of information during the 2000s. Several different sources of information are used in this study, some of which are only available in Russian:
- Company press releases are published in English (with a delay of some days) but the translation can be of variable quality. Quotes from press releases are as published on the site unless specifically noted.
- Some interviews with senior management are published in the 'interviews' section of the English-language site. Many more are published in the 'Briefingi i Press Conferentsii' and 'Pryamaya Rech' sections of the Russian site. Other speeches are stored in the 'Spravochnyi Materiali' section. Where material from these sources is used, the section of the website from which it is taken is noted in the source.
- Articles from the company's house journal 'Gazprom'.
- Annual reports and financial (audit) accounts according to international accounting standards (IAS)

The Gazexport website – www.gazexport.ru – which also has improved considerably during the 2000s but with much material only available in Russian.

Major periodicals and journals:

This study uses *Interfax Oil and Gas (previously Petroleum) Report* extensively because it is one of the few sources to carry interviews with key individuals and primary data from a range of government and company sources.[1] Many (if not most) English language services use Interfax as their main source of information on Russia.

---

1 The change of name from *Interfax Petroleum Report* to *Interfax Oil and Gas Report* took place at end November 2004.

Gas Matters, Gas Briefing International, Gas Matters Today, all published by Economatters: www.gas-matters.com

European Gas Markets published by Heren: www.heren.com

International Gas Report and *UK Gas Report* published by Platts (McGraw Hill): www.platts.com

Russia Energy Monthly (formerly *Eastern Bloc Energy*), *Central Asia Energy Monthly*, *Caucasus Energy Monthly*, all published by Eastern Bloc Research Ltd: www.easternblocenergy.com

Units

All natural gas units in the book are expressed in Russian billion (thousand million) cubic metres (Bcm) or trillion (thousand billion) cubic metres (Tcm). Where figures needed to be converted, the International Energy Agency's figure for gross calorific value of Russian gas of 38231 kilojoules per cubic metre has been used.[2]

Prices are generally quoted in Rubles (RR) or US$ per thousand cubic metres (mcm)

---

2 International Energy Agency, *Key World Energy Statistics 2004*, IEA/OECD: Paris, 2004, p.59.

ACKNOWLEDGMENTS

My first debt of thanks is to everybody at the Oxford Institute for Energy Studies, and especially Robert Skinner, for cheerfully bearing with the expanding time scale and general hassles which seem to accompany any significant publication. Next I want to thank the sponsors of the Natural Gas Research Programme at the Institute whose generosity has enabled us to create an independent academic research unit focusing specifically on natural gas. This gives those of us who work for the Programme the very rare luxury of writing what we believe, unencumbered by negotiating positions or concerns that we may upset our current or future 'clients'. This does not of course mean that what we write is correct, only that it is a genuine reflection of what we believe.

Many people have provided comments on the text and access to information which I either could not have obtained myself, or would not have known about without their help. Most of these kind people would not want either themselves or their organisations to be named. I would particularly like to thank John Grace of Earth Science Associates for preparing Appendix 1.2 on the geology of gas basins in West Siberia. The review meeting at the Oxford Institute in January 2005 provided me with additional valuable insights. Understanding the locational and geographical dimensions of the subject has been immeasurably enhanced by Anita Gardiner's maps. Judy Mabro's editing has made a similar contribution to the clarity and readability of the text. My grateful thanks to all concerned; the result is solely my responsibility.

PREFACE

The publication of this book comes just over 30 years since I started studying the Soviet natural gas industry, and 25 years after my first book on the subject. At that time, natural gas was of very little interest even to students of fossil fuel industries, and the Soviet gas industry was a particularly esoteric choice of subject for a British researcher. My subsequent research on natural gas has ranged over a wide geographical area, but I continued to monitor developments in the Russian gas industry because of a conviction about its importance for the entire Eurasian energy space; a conviction which I hope I have expressed more strongly and coherently in this study than in previous work.

Having spent such a long time studying the industry, and published a number of works on Soviet and Russian gas, it can reasonably be asked: why publish yet another book and why now? The reason can be found in the title of the study which is intended to suggest that *the future* of both the Russian gas industry and Gazprom will be substantially different from *the past*, both domestically and internationally.

This book does not cover the Soviet and immediate post-Soviet history of the domestic industry or export markets in any detail, as I have written about this period in other publications, not least in two other books published by the Oxford Institute for Energy Studies. The aim of this study is to provide a detailed picture of market developments in the late 1990s and early 2000s, and a look forward through the 2010s. When looking ahead, the principal intention has not been to develop numerical scenarios, but rather to look at:

- problems and choices facing market players – especially Gazprom – in terms of field, pipeline and export developments;
- prospects for industry reform, restructuring and evolution of the industry.

Given the pace at which developments are moving, this has proved to be a much more difficult task than I anticipated when I embarked on the study. Readers should bear in mind that the text was largely written in 2004 and completed with information available up to May 2005.

Jonathan Stern
Oxford, May 2005

INTRODUCTION

From the late 1980s through the immediate post-Soviet era, Russian domestic and export markets in the western CIS and Europe were supplied by Gazprom, largely from three super-giant fields in Western Siberia. During the late 1990s and early 2000s that picture began to change with the emergence of other suppliers, sources of supply, and potential export markets. Over the next ten to fifteen years, Russia will begin to supply Asia and North America with liquefied natural gas (LNG) and, in the case of Asia probably with pipeline gas as well. The theme of this book therefore is that the future of Russian gas and Gazprom is likely to be substantially different in comparison with the past. In terms of the domestic gas industry *the future* has already started with independent companies supplying a growing proportion of the Russian market. In terms of export markets, *the future* will take a little longer to arrive, but is in sight in terms of LNG exports to Asia and North America and (in a longer time frame) pipeline gas to Asia.

The book is arranged in five chapters. Chapter 1 deals with the Russian gas market under the broad headings of supply and demand, the resources, physical assets and the commercial actors. It looks forward to 2020 laying out the challenges facing both Gazprom and independent gas companies, of which the most difficult is to know whether Russian gas customers will be willing and able to pay prices that are sufficiently high to make profitable the development of new gas fields and, assuming the answer to that question is positive, what effect this will have on their demand for gas.

Chapter 2 looks at Russian gas trade and transit with CIS countries divided into three main groups: Central Asia (Turkmenistan, Kazakhstan and Uzbekistan), the Caucasus (Azerbaijan, Georgia and Armenia) and the western CIS (Ukraine, Belarus and Moldova). In the post-Soviet period, the management of interdependence relationships with these countries has been extremely difficult for Gazprom. These countries sell gas to, buy gas from, and provide transit routes for Gazprom, with many playing two of these roles. The importance of gas in general economic and political relationships means that prime ministers and presidents are automatically involved in what would normally be considered commercial agreements.

Chapter 3 describes the evolution of Gazprom's export strategy in Europe and looks at the prospects for pipeline gas and LNG exports to

Asia and North America. It shows how developing downstream marketing operations and 'transit-avoidance' pipelines dominated Gazprom's European strategy starting in the 1990s. At the same time, the European Union dimension of gas trade has become increasingly important for Russia and Gazprom both institutionally and commercially, with the liberalisation and competition initiatives, the Energy Charter Treaty, negotiations for accession to the WTO, and the EU-Russia Energy Dialogue. The second part of the chapter examines the prospects for gas trade with Asia, and LNG trade with North America over the next decade.

Chapter 4 deals with reform, restructuring and liberalisation of the Russian gas industry from the late 1990s to the mid-2000s. With the replacement of the Soviet-era management post-2001, the influence of the government and president over Gazprom has become increasingly evident. Reform of prices is well under way and third party access to networks has advanced further than is often realised. But the major issue to be resolved is structural reform. Corporate restructuring of Gazprom is under way, but 'break-up' of Gazprom is not on the agenda. Also to be resolved is the extent to which Gazprom will become a major player in the oil sector in the wake of the collapse of the merger with Rosneft. At the end of each of these chapters there is a summary and conclusions for those less inclined to plough through the detailed analysis.

Chapter 5 assesses the future of Russian gas and Gazprom using some simple scenarios to demonstrate that the correct methodological approach to the subject starts with prices and leads back through demand to supply and resources. It illustrates the need for Gazprom's management to make clear strategic decisions regarding the domestic and international challenges that face them over the next decade. Finally it questions whether the company can continue to operate successfully as a domestic Russian gas utility while at the same time fulfilling its apparent ambition to become a global gas company.

CHAPTER 1

THE RUSSIAN GAS MARKET

Resources and Reserves[1]

The birth of the modern Russian natural gas industry is generally held to be the building of the first long distance (845 km) natural gas pipeline (between Saratov and Moscow) commissioned in 1946. The industry established itself over the following two decades with production of around 100 Bcm by the mid-1960s and 10.4 million dwellings were either converted to natural gas from town gas, or newly supplied with natural gas.[2]

A number of 'supergiant' fields – Medvezhe, Urengoy, Yamburg, and Zapolyarnoye – were discovered in Western Siberia and at Orenburg (in southern Russia) in the mid to late 1960s. These were followed in the 1970s by the Yamal Peninsula fields (in particular Bovanenko and Kharasevey) which firmly established Western Siberia at the centre of Russian gas production for decades to come. Map 1.1 shows this region with the major fields and pipelines taking the gas west to markets in Russia, CIS countries and Europe. Two specific regions are worth noting from this map: the Nadym Pur Taz (NPT) region (shaded on the map) in which most of the currently producing gas fields are located; and the Yamal-Nenets Autonomous Region (YNAO) which encompasses all the gas fields shown on the map including those of the Yamal Peninsula.

There are many pitfalls in citing figures for the Russian gas resource base. Differences between reserves according to Russian and international classifications have traditionally been a problem. That problem was exacerbated in the 1990s by the increasingly urgent need to distinguish between Gazprom reserves and Russian reserves owned by other companies or yet to be allocated. The Russian Energy Strategy gives a figure of 127 trillion cubic metres (Tcm) for gas 'resources'.[3] But this is a much smaller number than the 236 Tcm given by the Ministry of Natural Resources for the beginning of 2003, divided into 160.3 Tcm onshore and 75.8 Tcm offshore including:[4]

- 12.8 Tcm of cumulative production
- 46.8 Tcm of $A+B+C_1$ (roughly equivalent to proven, probable and some possible) reserves

1

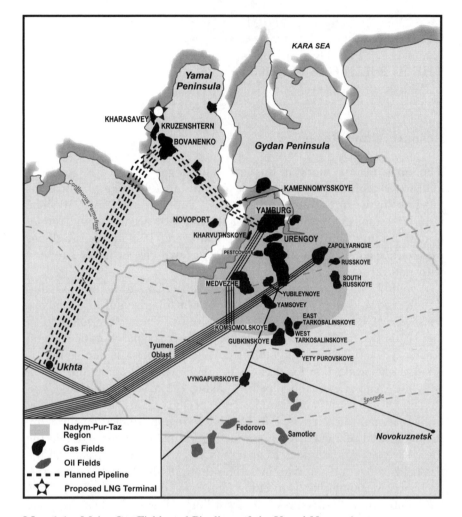

Map 1.1: Major Gas Fields and Pipelines of the Yamal-Nenets Autonomous
Region

- 14.2 Tcm of C_2 (possible) reserves
- 162.3 Tcm of $C_3+D_1+D_2$ (inferred and yet to be discovered) reserves

But without substantially more detail as to their location, it is not
possible to judge the significance of these aggregated figures in terms
of commerciality.

Much of the resource base with immediate commercial significance is
owned by Gazprom. In 1997 Gazprom engaged the well-known interna-

tional company DeGolyer and McNaughton to re-evaluate the reserves in its most important fields according to the Society of Petroleum Engineers' (SPE) classifications 'proven and probable'. (Appendix 1.1 contains definitions of Russian and SPE reserve classifications.) Table 1.1 shows the reserves in these fields, evaluated by Gazprom according

Table 1.1: Gazprom's Gas Reserves Estimated by Russian and International Classification** at December 31, 2004 (Bcm)

	$A+B+C_1$	Proved	Probable	Proved and probable*
WESTERN SIBERIA				
Urengoiskoye	5294	2517	226	2742
Urengoiskoye Achimov		569	320	889
Urengoiskoye Oil		0.5	1	1.6
Yamburgskoye	3988	2644	304	2948
Zapolyarnoye	3414	2615	160	2775
Medvezhye	523	269	28	298
Komsomolskoye	438	390	22	413
Gubkinskoye		286	4	290
North Urengoiskoye		196	21	217
Vengapurskoye		22	0	22
West Tarkosalinskoye		206	3	209
Yamsoveiskoye		360	6	366
Yen-Yakhovskoye		171	14	185
Yeti-Purovskoye		297	3	299
Yubilyeynoye		237	28	265
Yuzhno-Russkoye		580	6	586
Vynga-Yakhinskoye		86	5	91
Pestsovoye		7	29	36
YAMAL PENINSULA				
Bovanenkovskoye	4375	3270	292	3562
Kharaseveyskoye	1259	1082	303	1385
Novoportovskoye		0	195	195
BARENTS SEA				
Shtokmanovskoye	2536			
SOUTHERN RUSSIA				
Astrakhanskoye	2506	209	47	256
VOLGA REGION				
Orenburgskoye	787	343	21	364
TOTAL FOR NAMED FIELDS*	25121	16357	2133	18490

* totals may not add due to rounding ** for definitions see Appendix 1.1.

Source: *Loan Notes 2005* p.111.

to the Russian A+B+C$_1$ classification, and by DeGolyer according to SPE proven and probable classifications for 2004.

The difference of 6.6 Tcm (more than one quarter of A+B+C$_1$ reserves) is striking.[5] These fields account for around 90% of the proven and probable reserves owned by Gazprom, estimated at 28.9 Tcm for 2004. While the international estimates are significantly lower than the Russian classification for all the major fields – 2.6 Tcm for Urengoy, 1.0 Tcm for Yamburg, 0.6 Tcm for Zapolyarnoye, 0.8 Tcm for Bovanenko; for Kharasevey the international estimates are slightly higher. The biggest discrepancy between the two sets of figures is that the international classification fails to register most of the 2.5 Tcm of A+B+C$_1$ reserves at Astrakhan in south west Russia near the Caspian Sea.[6] The international estimates for Orenburg are also substantially lower than Russian estimates. This is significant given that the locations of the Astrakhan and Orenburg fields are substantially closer to potential markets than Siberian reserves. Another interesting issue is the very low international estimate for Pestsovoye given that Gazprom is expecting substantial production from the field in the late 2000s (see Table 1.4 below).

Possibly the most significant observation about Gazprom's reserve position is that if the fields on the Yamal Peninsula and the Shtokman field – neither of which are yet in production – are excluded, the total reserve figures reduce to 20.5 Tcm of A+B+C$_1$ and 13.3 Tcm of proven and probable reserves. While this still gives a reserves-to-production ratio of 24–38 years at the 2004 level of production, it assumes that all of the remaining reserves are recoverable (which is not necessarily the case in relation to A+B+C$_1$ reserves or SPE probable reserves). This is not to suggest that Gazprom is short of reserves but it does indicate the importance to the company of commercialising the reserves of both the Yamal Peninsula and the Shtokman field, to which we return below.

Although Gazprom's reserves comprise the vast majority of those with immediate commercial significance, the vertically integrated oil companies and the independent gas companies (whose only business is producing and marketing gas) are also becoming important; Table 1.2 is an attempt to summarise the gas reserves of those companies. It is intended to make the point that although no single company comes close to rivalling Gazprom in terms of resources, the gas resources held by individual companies are very significant, particularly in terms of Western Siberia where NPT gas accounts for more than 90% of Russian production and where new fields in the YNAO are relatively close to established infrastructure currently transporting gas to markets. The majority of the resources are located in Western Siberia and are therefore oriented towards the markets of western Russia and export markets in the CIS and Europe. However, there are also substantial gas fields in Eastern Siberia and the Far East which are the subject of export projects in East Asia (see Chapter 3). Table 1.2 gives figures for the YNAO reserves of the independents of 3.3 Tcm for $A+B+C_1$ and 4.6 Tcm for C_2+C_3, while the Union that represents them has total figures of 5.46 Tcm of proven (2.4 Tcm) probable (1.64 Tcm) and possible (1.42 Tcm) which probably relate to total $A+B+C_1$ reserves, suggesting that 2.13 Tcm of their reserves are outside Siberia.[7]

Table 1.2: Gas Reserves in Russia and YNAO by Company, 2002 (Tcm)

COMPANY	$A+B+C_1$ *Reserves in Russia*	$A+B+C_1$ *Reserves in YNAO**	C_2+C_3 *Reserves in YNAO**
Gazprom	26.3	17.2	3.8
OIL COMPANIES			
Lukoil		0.4	2.4
Yukos		0.4	0.8
TNK		0.5	0.8
Rosneft		1.2	0.4
Slavneft		0.08	0.6
INDEPENDENT GAS COMPANIES			
Novatek		1.4	1.7
Itera		0.7	0.3
Others		1.2	2.6
TOTAL NON GAZPROM		5.88	9.6

*   Western Siberia not including the Yamal Peninsula

Sources: S.V. Gmyzin, *Yamal-Nenets Autonomous Region: the core of Russian gas security.* Paper to the 2nd International Conference on: Energy Security, the Role of Russian Gas Companies, International Energy Agency, Paris, November 2003.

Domestic Supply Options

The data in Table 1.1 are Gazprom's reserves in fields which are either in production or which are in the process of being prepared for production at some point over the next two decades. There are important distinctions between:[8]

- fields which are in decline: Urengoy, Yamburg, Medvezhe and Orenburg;
- those which in 2004 were close to plateau production levels: Zapolyarnoye and Astrakhan;
- those which had not yet been developed: Yamal Peninsula fields
  (onshore and offshore) and Shtokman in the Barents Sea.

There is substantial uncertainty about future production from these
different groups. As we shall see below, there are some very difficult

Table 1.3: Russian Gas Balance 1999–2004

	1999	2000	2001	2002	2003	2004
SUPPLY						
Russian TOTAL	618.2	633.5	630.6	637.1	674.1	687.4
Gazprom total production	545.6	523.2	512.0	521.9	540.2	545.1
Gazprom's delivery into the pipeline network[1]	534.1	510.1	499.0	510.6	524.9	529.1
Independent supply including gas bought by Gazprom and Central Asian purchases[2]	30.2	68.2	77.4	79.6	95.5	105.2
Pipeline shrinkage	1.4	1.2	5.2	5.9	10.2	11.4
Withdrawals from storage[3]	52.5	53.3	48.3	40.4	42.8	41.1
DELIVERIES TO:						
Russian customers	299.8	308.4	317.5	319.1	327.0	333.5
Exports to Europe	126.8	129.0	127.0	129.4	134.7	148.9
Exports to FSU Countries	87.2	87.1	88.0	88.8	94.2	97.1
including:transit deliveries from Central Asian countries	9.5	23.4	34.7	36.6	44.1	
Own use and losses[4]	50.8	47.1	45.7[5]	47.7	51.3	52.0
Changes in linepack	1.0	1.6	5.6	6.4	10.6	10.4
Injections into storage	52.6	60.3	46.8	45.7	56.3	45.4

1 Gas which enters the high pressure network (UGSS) which is less than total
  annual production because of gas used in cities near the fields
2 Includes Purgaz even though Purgaz was consolidated into the group in April
  2002
3 Includes gas of independent suppliers
4 Includes gas used for compression plus losses including gas lost during repair
  work
5 of which 86% (39.3 Bcm) was used as fuel in compressor stations and the rest
  (6.4 Bcm) was lost through leaks and repairs.

Sources: *Loan Notes* 2003 p.106, *Loan Notes* 2004 p.115; *Loan Notes* 2005 p.121; *Gazprom
         Annual Report 2003*, p.48; *Razvitie sotrudnichestva v gazovoy sfere so stranami
         bivshevo SSSR*, Gazprom Briefing, June 15, 2004, www.gazprom.ru.

choices to be made given the importance to Gazprom of achieving the lowest cost solution for delivering secure supplies to its major markets.

Table 1.3 presents a total gas balance of supply, demand and trade for the period 1999–2003. We shall return to individual elements of this picture throughout this study but the total picture is important in order to appreciate the degree of complexity of Russian supply and demand options and the degree of precision required in differentiating between:

- Russian production and total supply available in Russia – the difference being Central Asian imports;
- Gazprom production and Russian production;
- Deliveries to each market: Russia, CIS countries, Europe and (in the future) Asia and North America (as LNG).

Decline at Existing Fields

Table 1.4 shows Gazprom's major fields in production indicating when production started, when it peaked and at what level. It also shows the degree of depletion of the field's resources at the end of 2003. There

Table 1.4: Major Gazprom Gas Fields in Production

	Year of First Production	Year of Peak Production	Peak Production) Level (Bcm)	% Degree of Depletion 2003
Urengoyskoye	1977	1987	304.5	48.7
Including Yen-Yakhinskoe	2003	2008*	5.0	
Yamburgskoye	1985	1994	179	39.0
Including Kharvutinskoye	1996	2009	25.0*	
Medvezhe	1971	1983	75	75.8
Zapolyarnoye	2001	2005*	100*	3.2
Komsomolskoye	1993	2003	31.9	39.7
Pestovoye	2004	2007	27.5	
Yubilyeinoye	1993	2004	21.2	
Yamsoveiskoye	1997	2003	22.2	
West Tarkosalinskoye	1996	2005*	15.8	
Vynga-Yakhinskoye	2003	2004	5.8	
Yeti-Purovskoye	2004	2006*	15.0	
Astrakhanovskoye	1987	2006*	12*	4.0
Orenburgskoye	1970	1985	49.4	56.9

* estimated

Source: *Loan Notes 2005*, p.117; *Gazprom Annual Report*, p.38.

has been much speculation about the rate of decline at Gazprom's three main fields – Urengoy, Yamburg and Medvezhe. Table 1.5 shows production from gas fields currently in production which, since 1999, have accounted for more than 90% of Gazprom's output.[9] Of these fields, in 2005 six were in decline, including the three largest; six were still increasing production including Zapolyarnoye reaching its plateau production of 100 Bcm/year. Of the fields in decline, Medvezhe has been producing for more than 30 years and is at around half of its peak production, which was achieved more than 20 years ago; the Orenburg field is at a similar stage in its life. Urengoy has been producing for more than 25 years and by 2003 was at less than 60% of its 1987 peak. Yamburg has produced gas for only 20 years and in 2003 was still at more than 90% of its peak level.

The 2003 Russian Energy Strategy acknowledged that three fields are in the decline phase having produced the majority of their reserves: 75.8% in the case of Medvezhe, 65.4% of Urengoy and 54.1% of Yamburg.[10] The key issues are how fast the decline will continue and whether, with further investment, it would be possible to slow the rate. Decline at the Urengoy field has been more rapid than anticipated with the annual rate in the range 11.8–15.8 Bcm per year during the period 1996–2003 (with the exception of 1998). If this rate of decline continues, the Urengoy field could cease to produce significant quantities of gas within a decade. By contrast, production at Yamburg fell at a slower and more uneven rate with marginal declines in some years interspersed with falls of up to 9 Bcm in other years; the increase in production of 10 Bcm in 1998 is not readily explicable (unless it relates to a technical problem at the field in the previous year).

The extent to which production decline, particularly at Urengoy, can be slowed is uncertain. Crucial to this may be the ultimate recoverability factor of the reserve figures which are quoted and we return to this issue below. Shortage of capital in the industry during the chaotic years of economic transition in the 1990s was one reason why investment to prevent rapid decline, which was successfully practised at Medvezhe, was not replicated at the other fields. Gazprom investment plans for the next decade do not seem to be specifically targeted at slowing production decline at existing fields. Production declines at the three fields that have sustained the Russian gas industry over the past two decades, have averaged more than 22 Bcm/year over the period 1999–2004, and this indicates how much new capacity needs to be brought on stream every year just to maintain production at current levels.

Along with the actual decline in production, the depletion of the shallow (up to 1500 metres depth), easily accessible (and therefore

Table 1.5: Production at Gazprom's Major Fields* (Bcm)

	1995	1996	1997	1998	1999	2000	2001	2002	2003	2004
Urengoyskoye	242.9	242.2	227.2	223.8	209.1	193.3	180.4	166.9	152.4	140.6
including Yen-Yakhinskoye										3.4
Yamburgskoye	177.8	176.5	169.3	179.6	175.9	168.0	166.0	157.1	153.4	146.3
including Kharvutinskoye									7.9	8.1
Medvezhe					39.0	35.8	33.4	30.9	28.3	25.6
SUB TOTAL					424.0	397.1	379.8	354.9	334.1	312.5
Zapolyarnoye	N/a	N/a					7.1	36.8	67.5	94.8
Komsomolskoye	N/a	N/a	N/a	N/a	30.5	30.5	31.0	31.1	31.9	30.6
Yubilyeynoye			N/a	N/a	N/a	N/a	17.4	17.6	19.5	21.3
Yamsoveiskoye			N/a	N/a	N/a	N/a	20.6	21.1	22.2	21.9
West Tarkosolinskoye										3.5
Vynga-Yakhinskoye									0.9	5.8
Pestsovoye										2.2
Yeti-Purovskoye										2.5
Astrakhanovskoye					8.7	9.8	10.5	10.9	11.4	11.5
Orenburgskoye					24.8	24.1	22.8	21.5	20.1	18.6
TOTAL					488.0	461.5	489.2	493.9	507.6	525.2
% total Gazprom production					91	90	94	95	94	96

* These are production figures from the fields, which do not correspond to those of the production associations – Urengoygazprom, Yamburggazodobycha, etc – which include production from more than one field.

Source: Loan Notes 2003, pp. 100–101; Loan Notes 2004, p. 107, Loan Notes 2005, p 117, 1995–98 figures from IEA, *Russia Energy Survey 2002*, Table 5.1.

low-cost) gas reserves at existing fields is also very important. The Russian Energy Strategy makes clear that of the 10.3 Tcm of gas in fields yet to be brought into production, 1.7 Tcm are in larger NPT fields, 5.8 Tcm are located on the Yamal Peninsula, and 2.8 Tcm in smaller fields with deep horizons.[11] While there are substantial reserves in the deeper Valenginian horizons of the Urengoy field, these will be more difficult and expensive to develop.[12] Joint ventures with foreign companies – Shell and Wintershall – have been created to produce gas at the Neocomian horizons at Zapolyarnoye and the Achimov horizons at Urengoy respectively. However, progress on these projects appears relatively slow and taken together anticipated gas production would not exceed 25 Bcm/year (see Table 1.6).[13]

New Fields: NPT, Yamal Peninsula, Shtokman

Nadym Pur Taz (NPT). Classifying the fields from the data in Tables 1.4 and 1.5 in terms of those in decline, at plateau and still increasing, shows that of the fields in production in 2005:

– decline has been evident for some years at Urengoy, Yamburg, Medvezhe and Orenburg;
– Komsomoskoye, Yubilyeinoye, Yamsovei and Vynga-Yakhinskoye have already peaked although they are likely to produce at 2004 levels for some years;
– Zapolyarnoye (17.2 Bcm), Yen-Yakhinskoye (1.6 Bcm), Kharvutin-skoye (11.9 Bcm), West Tarkosalinskoye (10.5 Bcm), Pestsovoye (25.8 Bcm) and Yeti-Purovskoye (12.5 Bcm) are expected to increase production up to 2010.

The expected total increase in production from the third group of fields is 79.5 Bcm which, if compared with the average decline in production of the first group of more than 22 Bcm during the period 1999–2004 (and assuming that the second group remains at 2004 levels), suggests that Gazprom's production from the current group of fields can be maintained at 2004 levels and above until 2007–08.

Table 1.6 shows the new fields that Gazprom has announced will be coming into production before 2010, although the timing is not yet certain. At plateau, these fields will provide another 58 Bcm of production per year but, with the exception of Aneryakhinskoye, plateau production levels will not be reached until 2010 by which time, some of the fields that are currently producing at plateau volumes will have begun to decline.

Table 1.6: Gazprom's Current and Future Production Projects

Name of Field	Partner	Estimated Date of Plateau Production	Estimated Plateau Production Bcm/yr
Aneryakhinskoye*	None	2005	10
South Russkoye	None	2010**	25
Zapolyarnoye (Neocomian)	Shell	2010	14.6
Urengoy (Achimovsk)	Wintershall	2010	8.3
TOTAL NPT			57.9

*   section of the Yamburg field;
** may depend on the start date of the North European Pipeline (see chapter 3).

Source: *Loan Notes 2003*, pp. 103–106, and other fragmentary data

All of this points to Gazprom needing to develop major new sources of gas if it is to maintain and/or increase production for delivery to domestic and export customers west of Siberia after 2010.[14] This is one of the most difficult issues facing the company over the next decade. It has studied two other main sources of incremental production – the Yamal Peninsula and the Shtokman field in the Barents Sea – for well over a decade. As shown above in Table 1.1 the Bovanenko and Kharasevey fields on the Yamal Peninsula contain 5.5 Tcm of A+B+C$_1$ reserves, and the Shtokman field 2.5 Tcm. During the 1990s and early 2000s, the Yamal fields and Shtokman were viewed as alternative options for Gazprom's next large-scale source of supply. However, the cost of production and transportation to markets for both these supply sources is substantial, particularly when the future prices which will be paid by consumers in those markets are uncertain. In the 1990s, both Gazprom and the government appeared to see-saw between the Yamal and Shtokman projects in terms of which would be developed first. For example, the 2000 Russian Energy Strategy suggested that Yamal production would begin only after 2015, but, in that document, the Shtokman field was intended to commence production by 2010.[15] There has been a great deal of speculation about the Yamal fields and Shtokman in terms of production volumes, potential transmission routes to markets, and the timing of development. The intention here is not to provide a detailed account of the history of these projects, but rather to give a brief summary of their status and prospects in 2005.

Yamal Peninsula. I have suggested in previous work that it is more appropriate to regard the development of the Yamal Peninsula fields as a concept rather than a project.[16] This is because there are many different permutations which could be adopted by Gazprom in respect of the extent and timing of production and transportation of gas from these fields. A comprehensive study of the options for Yamal development was drawn up by Gazprom's VNIIgaz Institute and formed the basis

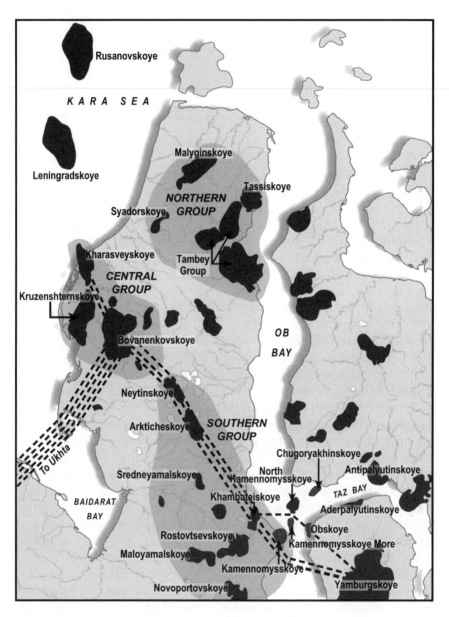

Map 1.2:   Major Gas Fields of the Yamal Peninsula, Ob and Taz Bays

of the framework agreement signed between Gazprom and the Yamal Nenets Autonomous Region Administration in early 2002.[17]

The VNIIgaz study divides the Yamal Peninsula fields into three different groups (Map 1.2):

1. The Central Group: Bovanenko, Kharasevey and Kruzenshtern, which contain 8.2 Tcm or 62% of the gas resources on the Peninsula. Plateau gas production is anticipated to be 211 Bcm/year and 4 mt of unstable condensate, comprising:
    −   Bovanenko 140 Bcm (Cenomanian 115, Neocomian 25)
    −   Kharasevey 38 Bcm (Cenomanian 32, Neocomian 6)
    −   Kruzenshtern 33 Bcm
2. The Northern (or Tambey) Group: South Tambey, North Tambey, West Tambey. Tassiskoye, Maliginskoye, Syadorskoye comprising 3.6 Tcm of gas resources or 27% of Yamal reserves. Plateau production will be 65 Bcm/year and 2.5mt of unstable condensate.
3. The Southern Group: Novoportovskoye, Nuiminskoye, Malo-Yamalskoye, Rostotsevskoye, Arkticheskoye, Sredne-Yamalskoye, Khambateyskoye, Neitinskoye, Kamennomysskoye with 1.4 Tcm of gas resources or 11% of the total. Plateau production will be 30 Bcm/year.

These groups do not include the Kara Sea fields with total resources of 29.8 Tcm, including Leningradskoye and Russanovskoye with reserves exceeding 8 Tcm. They also do not include many of the offshore fields in the Ob and Taz Bays (see below).

The general concept for the Yamal Peninsula fields is that first to be developed will be the Bovanenko and Kharasevey (Central Group) fields, then after 2020, the Tambey Group will be developed and not until after 2030 will the southern group come into production. Table 1.7 shows this scenario for development of Yamal Peninsula production according to the VNIIgaz Institute which in 2002 was envisaging the start of production five years later. Bovanenko production will be the mainstay of Yamal for the period up to 2030 with Kharasevey and Kruzenshtern relatively minor in comparison. By the early 2020s, Kharasevey and Kruzenshtern will be at full production and the Tambey group of fields increasing rapidly.

A slightly strange feature of the projection in Table 1.7 is the expected production from the Kharasevey field which increases relatively slowly to a plateau of 38 Bcm from 2020 onwards. This is a relatively low level of production for a field which − according to international classification (see Table 1.1) − has 1.4 Tcm of reserves.

Table 1.7: Yamal Peninsula Gas Production 2007–2030 (Bcm)

	Bovanenko	Kharasevey	Kruzenshtern	Tambey	TOTAL
		Name of Fields			
2007	10	-	-	-	10
2010	60	-	-	-	60
2012	80	-	-	-	80
2013	90	10	-	-	100
2016	110	25	-	-	135
2017	115	32	-	-	147
2019	125	35	-	-	160
2020	136	38	1	-	175
2021	140	38	20	2	200
2022	140	38	30	17	225
2023	139	38	33	40	250
2025	134	38	33	45	250
2030	122	38	33	57	250

Source: Data from the VNIIgaz Institute cited in *Eastern Bloc Energy*, March 2004, p.7

Equally strange is the timing of the development of the southern group of fields, located in shallow water in the Ob and Taz Bays, discovered in 2000 and said to contain 800 Bcm reserves with estimates for both Bays said to be as much as 7.5 Tcm.[18] In 2000, it was suggested that production from these fields would commence in 2007 and by 2010 they would be producing 50–56 Bcm; an alternative account has a later start date but a higher production of more than 80 Bcm.[19] The VNIIgaz study shows details of the seven fields which have been identified. Of these, the three Kamennomysskoye fields, together with the Obskaya field in the Ob Bay have a potential plateau production of around 35 Bcm/year. In the Taz Bay, the Aderpalyutinskaya, Antipalyutinskaya and Chugoryakhinskaya fields have a potential plateau production of 47 Bcm/year.[20] These fields are of particular importance for two reasons:

– The resource appears large enough to allow these levels of production to be sustained for a decade.
– The fields are in shallow water much nearer to the fields currently in production than the central or northern Yamal Peninsula fields, with much shorter links to the existing transmission system.

This suggests that (at least some of) these fields would be immediately commercially attractive but, as noted above, the VNIIgaz study has them in production only after 2030. In early 2005, there was no suggestion of imminent investment in these fields despite agreement by board level executives that they presented the most economic option for the company.[21]

By the early 2000s, the choice of Yamal production options was relatively well established, but the different transportation options were still being debated. The two original options were either a pipeline taking gas south down the Peninsula, or west across the Gulf of Baidarat connecting with the existing pipeline network at Ukhta. A third option emerged in the 2000s which is to take early gas across the Ob Bay to the Yamburg field allowing Yamal gas to use the processing and transmission facilities of the existing producing fields as their output declines, thereby significantly reducing costs.[22] A fourth option was also suggested for a pipeline via Salehard connecting with the existing pipeline network to Ukhta.[23] In early 2004, Gazprom's VNIIgaz Institute seemed to be focusing on transporting (at least the early development of) Yamal gas through two corridors:[24]

- a three-pipeline, 90 Bcm/year, corridor across the Ob Bay to the Yamburg field;
- a five-pipeline corridor with the eventual potential to carry 160 Bcm/year across the Bay of Baidarat connecting with the existing pipeline network at Ukhta.

In 2005, the three-pipeline corridor across the Bay to Yamburg seemed to have become the most likely early option, especially if it is phased with the decline in NPT production. This would meet the requirement of minimising up-front investment which could be crucial given the competition within Gazprom between domestic and foreign projects for investment resources. However, the regional administration is interested in establishing a single transportation route for evacuation of all the Peninsula's resources.[25]

In the 2000s, Gazprom management has been unclear and non-committal about the timing of Yamal development, suggesting possible differences of opinion within the company. At a March 2004 press conference Alexander Ryazanov (Deputy Chairman) said that the economics of Yamal gas for the domestic market and even for export were 'not very interesting for us'. He suggested that the company would continue to work in 'traditional locations' (i.e. the NPT) and would come to Yamal 'in 5, 6 or 8 years'.[26] The prospectus for the 2004 bond offering explained that funding had been reduced for certain projects within the current investment program:

> These projects include the development of the Kharasevey and Bovanenko fields…Although these projects have not been abandoned, under the current investment program we do not believe they will generate sufficient positive cash flows in the future to recover all costs incurred.[27]

Newspaper reports suggest that there are differences of opinion between Gazprom's senior management as to the attractiveness of investing in Yamal, as opposed to relying on supplies from independent producers and Central Asia.[28] Meanwhile Gazprom's 2005 investment programme, while mentioning the Bovanenko and Kharasevey fields, set no firm date for development or pipeline construction, although the 'first stage of investment planning' was said to have been completed.[29]

Lead times for preparing the Bovanenko field and the first transmission corridor for Yamal gas are not easy to estimate because of the different options for development. The VNIIgaz study suggests (but does not state definitively) a five-year lead time, which would mean that since development has not started in 2005, the earliest date for first Yamal production (assuming 2006 as the start of development) would be 2011.

A widely cited paper by Tarr and Thompson of the World Bank, published in 2003, concluded that undiscounted long-run marginal costs of gas from the Yamal fields delivered to markets in Russia were $35−40/mcm, comprising: development cost $8/mcm, transmission cost $22/mcm, distribution cost $5−10/mcm.[30] These authors reach the conclusion that based on these estimates '…it would be efficient for Russia to raise domestic prices to about $35−40/mcm but not higher'. These prices are consistent with the consensus within Russia for NPT costs, but not for costs from Yamal Peninsula fields. There is no explanation of how these figures have been arrived at (aside from a source citing 'World Bank staff estimates').

Moreover, the problem with citing a single figure for Yamal development and transmission costs is the inability to take into account the multiple permutations of fields and pipeline routes that are available to both Gazprom and other resource holders on the Peninsula. The VNIIgaz study concludes that development of 250 Bcm/year of gas would require a total investment of $25bn in production and $39bn in transmission, with at least three different stages of development each entailing different levels of investment. The study also makes clear the importance of federal and regional taxes in any estimate of Yamal costings, estimating that with the regime in force in 2002, the delivered cost to customers in western Russia would be $80−100/mcm leading to the conclusion that Yamal gas will need a completely different tax regime from other upstream gas (for details of taxes on gas see below).[31]

Shtokmanovskoye (Shtokman) field. The Shtokman field, discovered in 1984, is estimated to have total reserves (A to D in the Russian classification) of 3.2 Tcm (compared with 2.5 Tcm $A+B+C_1$, see Table 1.1) but lies 550 km offshore to the north east of Murmansk at water depths of around 300−330 metres (Map 1.3).[32] Rough sea-bed conditions are compounded by drifting ice and very harsh physical, as well as fragile environmental, conditions. With a total annual production potential of 90 Bcm/year, an important judgement affecting the commercial viability of the original concept of Shtokman development was whether to develop the field by installing 4−5 offshore platforms (each with a production capacity of 20 Bcm/year) sequentially, or to install multiple platforms from the start of the development. In 2004, that concept was shelved in favour of Gazprom cooperation with the Norwegian company Hydro to develop the Shtokman field using subsea completion technology combined with multiphase transportation to shore.[33]

In 1995, a consortium was formed to develop the field comprising Total (France), Conoco (USA), Hydro (Norway) and Fortum (Finland) with 50% of the equity. The other 50% plus one share was held by Rosshelf (a Gazprom subsidiary which held the original licence for the field) giving it a controlling interest in the field, and also potentially the pipeline necessary to transport the gas to Russian and export markets. In 2000, the Russian Duma approved a production sharing agreement for the field but, two years later, the 1995 framework agreement, under which exploratory work had been carried out, expired and the licence for Shtokman (as well as the Prirazlomnoye oil field and three gas fields in the NPT) was transferred to a joint venture Sevmorneftegaz owned 50% by Rosneft Purneftegaz and 50% by Rosshelf.[34] Rosneft Purneftegaz sold its 50% share to Gazprom in 2005 making the latter the sole owner.[35]

From the discovery of the field until the early 2000s, commercialisation of Shtokman gas was conceived in terms of pipeline transportation to markets in north western Russia and Europe. This would involve a 600−650 km offshore line to a landfall at Terebelka; a 1500 km pipeline down the Kola Peninsula with a branch pipeline to the Baltic Sea coast for onward transmission across the Baltic to Germany (with a possible extension as far as the UK). However, as the 2000s progressed it became clear that the Baltic Sea part of the transportation system − the North European Pipeline − would be built independently of Shtokman development. In 2004, it was announced that initial development of the Shtokman field would concentrate on exports of liquefied natural gas (LNG) to the USA.

In 1997, Gazprom and Fortum formed the North Transgas joint

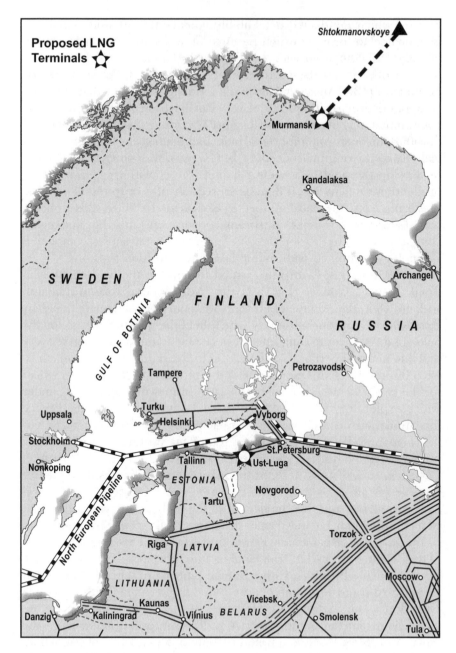

Map 1.3: The Shtokmanovskoye Field and Murmansk Liquefaction Terminal

venture which conducted a feasibility study on the Baltic Sea sector of the pipeline project, which became known as the North European Pipeline (NEP). This project has since attracted interest from a number of potential investors and gas buyers (see Chapter 3). In March 2004, Gazprom's CEO Alexey Miller made a public statement that the NEP would be supplied from the South Russkoye ('Yuzhno-Russkoye' in Russian) field.[36] Later that year, Deputy Chairman Ryazanov confirmed that the pipeline option for Shtokman had been shelved and all efforts were being concentrated on LNG development for export to the United States (we return to this issue in Chapter 3).[37] However, so large are the reserves in the field that it may be more realistic to view LNG supplies as the first phase of development, to be followed by subsequent phases involving pipeline supplies to both domestic and European markets.

Independent Gas Companies

In a Russian context, the term 'independent gas company' is used as shorthand for any organisation that produces or supplies gas not 100% owned by Gazprom. Producers are sometimes referred to as 'independent' when some (perhaps even a majority) of their equity is owned by Gazprom. A somewhat artificial division of the non-Gazprom suppliers can be made between:

1. Companies whose main business is oil, but have significant reserves and interests in gas; this includes all of the well-known oil companies: Lukoil, Surgutneftegaz, TNK/BP.
2. Companies whose main hydrocarbon reserves and business activities are gas-related. In 2004, the two main companies in this group were Itera and Novatek, but including all the companies that comprise the Union of Independent Gas Producers (Soyuzgaz).[38] This group also includes pure gas traders with no production such as Centrrusgaz and Trans Nafta.[39]
3. Companies in which Gazprom has a substantial shareholding, such as Sibur and Purgaz.

The current and future importance of Russian independent gas companies cannot be judged simply in terms of their gas reserves. Many companies have a claim to very significant reserves but, for a variety of reasons – often connected with the location of the fields, complex geology, and lack of investment funds – have little likelihood of commercialising them. To be successful, independents need the right combination of well-located reserves, available capital for development, access to infrastructure – both processing plant and the Gazprom pipeline network – and solvent customers willing to purchase their gas. In 2004, this remained a difficult combination to achieve, even for those companies which were already well-established, and, despite regulatory obligations, depended significantly on Gazprom goodwill in terms of access to networks and processing plant (see Chapter 4).

Vertically Integrated Oil Companies

It comes as some surprise that in the early 2000s, the larger integrated oil companies were relatively modest gas producers. Surgutneftegaz and Rosneft produced more than half of the gas attributable to oil companies (Table 1.11). While most of the major integrated oil companies have ambitious plans for the next two decades, they also have large and competing oil projects which may prove more lucrative, depending on the expected trends in gas and oil prices over the same period. In early 2003, Lukoil agreed to sell gas to Gazprom from the Nakhodinskaya field starting in 2005 and rising to 8 Bcm/year in 2006. The field is located in the Bolshekhetskaya depression, north of Gazprom's major producing fields in Western Siberia. Lukoil has agreed to build a pipeline and deliver the gas to the main compressor station at the Yamburg field where it will be purchased by Gazprom for a minimum price of $22/Tcm (excluding VAT).[40]

Several reasons can be advanced to explain why a company with the financial clout of Lukoil agreed to such an arrangement. First, pessimism about the prospects of arranging cost-effective processing and transportation of the gas with Gazprom; secondly, pessimism about likely increases in regulated gas prices and the company's ability to sell such large amounts of gas at unregulated prices; the company considered it politically advisable not to compete against Gazprom in the gas market; lack of expertise and organisation in gas sales and marketing.

Whatever the reasons, this was not the act of an independent *producer* planning to become an independent *marketing company* in the near future, although little is known about what happens to the agreement post-2006. Lukoil and Gazprom's 'strategic partnership' covers the period up to 2014 and includes not only sales from the Nakhodinskaya field but also cooperation in the Russian sector of the Caspian Sea where they have formed a joint venture TsentrCaspneftegaz with the Kazakh company, Kazmunaigaz.[41] In addition, Lukoil has agreed to sell all the gas that it produces under PSAs in Uzbekistan to Gazprom, even when the latter is not directly involved in the PSA (see Chapter 2).

As far as the other vertically-integrated oil companies are concerned, firm development plans are hard to find. The legal/political crisis that engulfed Yukos starting in 2003 prevented the company from making any significant plans and threatened its survival. Surgutneftegaz is the largest gas producer among the oil companies, with more than 14 Bcm of gas associated with oil production in 2004. However, it joined Gazprom and Rosneft in a consortium with the potential to develop a number of East Siberian fields.[42] Although Surgutneftegaz's ambitions to develop non-associated gas are limited, the company's associated production will continue to increase, particularly if flaring can be significantly reduced from current levels. Whether its production can increase to the 25 Bcm anticipated in Table 1.11, without significant non-associated production, is uncertain. TNK/BP has significant gas reserves, particularly after its purchase of 56% of the equity in Rospan from Yukos in mid-2004 which made it sole owner of up to 950 Bcm of reserves in the Novo-Urengoy and Vostochno-Urengoy condensate deposits.[43] The largest part of the TNK/BP gas resource is in the Kovyktinskoye field in Eastern Siberia and the Far East (see Chapter 3).

Rosneft's gas plans have in the past been strongly linked to its alliance with Gazprom. In October 2001, the two companies agreed a joint development strategy for three fields in the NPT region – Kharampur, Vyngayakhinsk and Yetipurovsk (and the Shtokman field, see above).[44] The decision to allow Rosneft/Yuganskneftegaz to remain an independent company (see Chapter 4) means that the preponderance of oil assets within the company may affect investment available for gas developments. Rosneft has substantial gas production potential in Western Siberia quite aside from its shares in East Siberian and Far East (particularly Sakhalin) fields (see Chapter 3).

In summary, the gas ambitions of the vertically-integrated oil companies seem likely to be limited not by reserves but by investment availability and market attractiveness given that these projects have to compete with oil development. It is significant that the 2002 VNIIgaz study assumed production from these companies would be flat at the 2003 level of 35 Bcm/year until 2020.[45] Lukoil appears to be in the lead but while its production projections of 30 Bcm by 2010 and 80 Bcm by 2020 are realistic as far as reserves are concerned, it remains to be seen whether the company is willing to commit the required investment and has ambitions to develop a gas business beyond the point of production. Lukoil aside, Surgutneftegaz – the largest producer – seems to have little ambition to expand its non-associated gas role beyond production associated with oil, but the latter will continue to grow ensuring the company's future as a leading gas producer. Rosneft's acquisition of Yuganskneftegaz raises doubts as to how quickly the new company will choose to develop gas assets. As far as Sibneft is concerned, both its gas production and ambitions are very modest while the survival of Yukos as a significant player seems unlikely.

Independent Gas Suppliers

Itera, the first major Russian independent gas company, began gas operations in 1994 as a trading company. In the mid to late 1990s, the company rapidly acquired substantial gas properties amounting to nearly 2 Tcm of reserves by participating in auctions, buying into existing joint ventures – including Gazprom joint ventures – holding licences for fields. It also developed a major gas trading business within the CIS, in particular from Turkmenistan – where the management had strong relationships with the President. Itera's gas business developed, at least in part, because gas was one of the only commodities that Turkmenistan could offer to other CIS countries in return for imports of goods and services.

In 2000, Itera produced nearly 18 Bcm of gas, purchased around 30 Bcm of gas on commission from the Yamal-Nenets regional authorities in Siberia, and 35 Bcm from Central Asian countries, mainly Turkmenistan but also Kazakhstan and Uzbekistan. That year, the company sold 85.6 Bcm of gas including more than 40 Bcm within Russia – in particular the Sverdlovsk region where it has a long-term contract to supply the regional administration; and more than 45 Bcm in CIS countries, notably Ukraine (32 Bcm) and Belarus (6 Bcm).[46] The year 2000 proved to be the highpoint in Itera's corporate history thus far, with the company selling record volumes of gas and purchasing substantial equity in both gas and related companies throughout the CIS, including the Baltic countries and trans-Caucasia.[47]

Subsequently, problems began to mount for Itera, of which the first was the order from the Russian Audit Chamber to Gazprom to cease paying taxes to the Yamal Nenets regional authorities in the form of gas supplies. During the period of serious non-payment of bills during the late 1990s, this was a convenient and low-cost means by which Gazprom paid its local taxes. The regional authorities needed to find some way of monetising this gas and Itera provided a highly attractive outlet. Goldman (quoting the *Wall St Journal*) suggests that the Governor of the Yamal Nenets region (who was on Gazprom's Board of Directors) accepted a value for the gas from Gazprom of $2–5/mcm, sold it to Itera for the same price which then sold it to customers for $40–80/mcm. He concludes that '...some of the difference was absorbed by pipeline shipping costs, but this unquestionably was transfer price abuse'.[48] In fact, it is highly improbable that during the period 1998–2000, Itera could have sold the gas for a price in excess of $30/mcm and there is no evidence to support this. While there is no doubt that resale of Yamal-Nenets gas was highly profitable for Itera, what was branded as 'transfer price abuse' might just as easily have been hailed as 'innovative entrepreneurial behaviour' and 'shrewd tax optimisation'.

The loss of gas from the Yamal-Nenets authorities saw Itera's gas deliveries fall from 86 Bcm in 2000 to 70 Bcm the following year. During 2001, the Audit Commission and Gazprom's auditors Price Waterhouse Coopers (PWC) both opened investigations into the relationship between Itera and Gazprom which had become the subject of increasing speculation and widespread, but unproven, allegations of corrupt practices.[49] The investigations centred in particular on:

- the terms on which Itera had acquired gas properties from Gazprom;
- the terms on which Itera's gas was transported by Gazprom;
- ownership relationships between Gazprom's board members and Itera in the light of evidence that, in 1996, a joint venture had been contemplated with a view to Gazprom taking a 20% stake in Itera.[50]

Interestingly, these investigations produced no evidence of any wrongdoing by Gazprom or Itera, an outcome ignored by most subsequent commentary.[51] The Audit Chamber found that transportation tariffs paid by Itera for the use of Gazprom's network were 'within norms'. While Itera had debts to Gazprom in respect of transportation services, there were also reciprocal (but smaller) debts owed by Gazprom. The Audit Chamber suggested that Itera had met in full all of its obligations in relation to the purchase of shares in Purgaz, Rospan International and Tarkosalneftegaz companies with a total gas production of 18.1 Bcm in 2001.[52] These shares were at the heart of the allegations of 'asset-stripping' levelled against the Gazprom management led by Chairman Rem Vyakhirev. Lack of transparency of Itera's ownership and financial operations, and the fact that some members of the Gazprom management had subsequently taken positions at the company, provided easy ammunition for critics.[53] In early 2001, Itera's status as a respectable corporate citizen appeared to strengthen when it signed a contract with the European Commission to supply gas to power plants in Ukraine as part of an EU aid package to compensate Ukraine for the closure of the Chernobyl nuclear power plant.[54] But with the arrival of the new Gazprom management under Alexey Miller in mid-2001 (see Chapter 4), Itera's fortunes steadily worsened both within Russia and in the CIS.

Key to Itera's loss of domestic production – in addition to the loss of the Yamal-Nenets taxation gas – has been the reacquisition of properties acquired under the previous Gazprom management. The PWC report apparently suggested that Gazprom might consider exercising its option to reclaim a 32% stake in Purgaz which had been acquired by Itera. This it subsequently did in April 2002 (bringing Gazprom's share in the company up to 51%) under a repurchase option signed in 1999 when these shares were sold to Itera for a nominal sum. Itera was paid RR33,000 rubles for the shares and Gazprom also paid RR6.6m in recognition of Itera's expenditures in developing the field during the previous three years; the field produced around 13 Bcm of gas in 2003.[55] While many were happy to hail the exercising of the Purgaz option as righting the wrongs of 'asset-stripping' which occurred under the previous management, few recalled that the transaction was sanctioned because Gazprom at the height of the non-payment crisis could not afford to divert financial and personnel resources to the development of minor fields; and it had taken a decision to focus its financial resources on major export projects, such as Yamal-Europe and Blue Stream.[56]

In February 2003, Gazprom acquired Itera's 51% interest in Severneftegazprom for RR102,000 and a nominal sum to reflect development work; this company is important because it holds the licence to develop the South Russkoye field (which was subsequently selected as the production source for the North European Pipeline – see Chapter 3). As part of this transaction, Gazprom sold to Itera a 10% interest in the Sibirsky Oil and Gas Company, and a 7.8% interest in Tarkosalneftegaz.[57]

From 2002 onwards, Itera appeared to be progressively losing sources of supply and markets in what could be construed as a determined effort by the new Gazprom management to reduce its role. Itera proposed a merger with Nofainvest (which subsequently became Novatek, see below) but this was abandoned and subsequently one company's fortunes declined and the other's rose. In late 2002, Gazprom began to restrict Itera's shipments to CIS countries on the grounds that bills for transportation services had not been paid, although Itera denied this.[58] In December 2002, the company was stripped of its position as shipper of Central Asian, particularly Turkmen, gas to both Russia and CIS countries and the task transferred to a new Hungarian-based company Eural Transgas which was unknown in the industry (see Chapter 2). Worse was to come in July 2003, when the Uzbek prime minister informed the company that, due to an increase in Uzbek gas exports, capacity for its exports of Turkmen gas to its CIS customers would be limited in 2003 and non-existent in 2004. The prime minister warned those buying their gas from Itera to 'draw their own conclusions'. [59]

Meanwhile, Gazprom began to progressively eliminate Itera from CIS markets in the Trans-Caucasus. In Azerbaijan and Georgia, Itera was told that there was no capacity to transport their gas to these markets and for this reason they would be taken over by Gazprom. [60] Responding to questions from journalists in early 2004 as to why Gazprom had taken over supplies to Azerbaijan, the General Director of Gazexport said: 'No one is discriminating against Itera. The company is unable to fulfil its contractual obligations since it does not have any gas transmission capacity.' [61]

But perhaps the most serious problem for the company involves the transportation of (its share of) gas from its largest new field, Beregovoye in Western Siberia, with potential production of 12 Bcm/year. Due to its proximity to the Zapolyarnoye field where production increased rapidly in the early 2000s, Gazprom declared there was insufficient capacity to transport Beregovoye gas. [62] There have been suggestions that the capacity problem might be resolved by the joint construction of a new pipeline between Zapolyarnoye and Urengoy but little progress had seemingly been made by mid 2005. This will be extremely important for the company which in late 2004 sold its stakes in both Tarkosalneftegaz and Khancheyneftegaz to Novatek. [63] As a result, aside from its share in Purgaz, Beregovoye is Itera's only remaining significant Russian production asset.

Gazprom's accounts show that 60.9 Bcm of gas was transported for Itera in 2002 and 31.7 Bcm in 2003. Perhaps surprisingly, Itera purchased 8.1 Bcm of gas from Gazprom in 2002 and 15.1 Bcm in 2003 at prices that seemed quite advantageous to Itera. [64] The explanation of these sales was apparently that since Gazprom had exercised its option to take back its stake in Purgaz, Itera, given its problems with transport of Beregovoye gas and its loss of Turkmen gas transit volumes, did not have sufficient gas to fulfil its commitments in the Sverdlovsk region (where it is the major supplier) and was obliged to buy gas to meet them. [65] From 2005, the company will purchase gas from Gazprom and Novatek, the latter on a five-year contract, in order to meet its commitments and shows no sign of leaving the market. [66] Itera remains the second most important independent gas company in terms of sales. In 2005, its future as a producer seemed to have switched to new prospects in Kalmykia (Tatarstan) and Turkmenistan (in the Zarit joint venture), with greater emphasis on oil than gas. [67]

In 2004, *Novatek* became Russia's biggest independent gas producer.

Formed from a pipe manufacturing trust in the 1990s, Novafininvest began as an investor principally in gas and condensate fields, obtaining licences in a number of fields in the Yamal-Nenets region (East Tarkosalinskoye, Yukharovskoye and Khancheiskoye) and then began to acquire properties outside of Siberia. In 2003 it changed its name to Novatek and produced 20.4 Bcm of gas (as well as 2.5 mt of oil and condensate); by 2010, the company expects to be producing more than 50–60 Bcm.[68] The company's wholly owned subsidiary Yukharovneftegaz (producing Valengenian gas from a section of the Urengoy field) will become a very substantial producer in its own right reaching 27–30 Bcm in 2008.[69] In pursuing its independent strategy Novatek has a number of advantages:

- It acquired its properties by auctions and open tenders (its only asset purchase from Gazprom – 8% of the East Tarkosalinskoye field – was transacted with the post-2001 Gazprom management).
- Its cost base provided significant profitability even at 2003 prices.
- It is building processing plants that will increase condensate sales and potentially provide capacity for other independents in western Siberia to process their gas.
- It is public knowledge that its shareholders are Levit 49.23%, Cyprus-registered SWGI Growth Fund 37.54% and Yamal Regional Development fund 7.58%.[70]
- It is making significant progress in terms of governance and transparency with reserves and accounts audited according to IAS.

Novatek has maintained a good relationship with Gazprom by seeking to deliver gas to the Russian domestic market rather than to export. The company has never been the subject of allegations of corruption or insider dealings with Gazprom management. In 2004, Novatek's financial standing took a further significant step forward with the announcement that the international oil company Total intended to purchase a 25% share in the company for a sum reported to be between $850m and $1bn.[71] Around the same time, the company reached a preliminary agreement with the International Finance Corporation for a $120m loan for the development of the Yukharovsk field.[72] The significance of these developments – neither of which had been completed in mid 2005 – is not so much the sums of money involved, but the seal of approval from the international financial community for both the company, and the future financial attractiveness of the Russian domestic gas market.

Nortgaz[73] was formed out of a 1993 joint venture between Gazprom (51%), Bechtel (44%) and Farco (5%) with a licence to develop gas and condensate in the Neocomian horizons of the North Urengoy field.[74] In the mid to late 1990s, equity changes saw the exit of Bechtel, and control of the company passed to Nortgaz, a successor company to Farco. The share of Urengoygazprom (Gazprom's nominee in the original company) was reduced after it failed, according to the Nortgaz management, to fund its share of development expenditure. In 2003, this became the subject of litigation in the Russian courts. Meanwhile the company started production in 2001, intending by the mid-2000s to produce around 5 Bcm (and 1 mt of condensate) per year, a figure which the company believes will rise to 10 Bcm by the end of the decade.[75] One of the best publicised battles between Gazprom and the independent gas producers concerns Nortgaz which since 2003 has experienced increasing problems in gaining access to transportation.[76] Various explanations were advanced ranging from an attack by Gazprom on the entire independent gas sector, to an attempt by Gazprom to coerce the company into resolving the litigation. In April 2005, the Moscow Court of Arbitration annulled Nortgaz's licence to develop the North Urengoy field, although the Ministry of Natural Resources supported an appeal by the independent.[77] Shortly thereafter, the company was reported to have agreed with Gazprom that the latter would purchase a 51% share of its equity which would allow production to continue, albeit under Gazprom control.[78]

Other independent gas companies, such as TransNafta and Centrrusgas are pure traders with no production, and there is little public information about them. Set up in 1999, Centrrusgas acted as a merchant for 7−8 Bcm during the period 2000−2002, buying from independent producers and selling to electricity companies (*energos*) and small customers.[79]

Table 1.8 provides official statistics for Gazprom and total Russian production for the period 1995−2004; production by non-Gazprom companies can be calculated from these as a residual. It shows that non-Gazprom production grew from around 6% of the total in 1995, when more than 70% was associated gas produced by oil companies, to 13% in 2003 by which time only around 45% was associated gas production.

Gas Processing and Production of Liquids

An important part of the Russian gas chain for which regulators have yet to define rules is gas processing. Given how important this function

Table 1.8: Russian Gas Production by Category and Company 1995–2004 (Bcm)

	1995	1996	1997	1998	1999	2000	2001	2002	2003	2004
Russian Federation	595	601	571	591	592	584	581	595	620	634
of which:										
Natural Gas	570	575	544	564	564	555	551	564	581	
Associated Gas	25	26	27	27	28	29	30	31	39	
Gazprom	560	561	534	554	546	523	512	522	540	545
Non-Gazprom	35	40	37	45	46	61	69	73	80	90
% non-Gazprom	6	7	7	8	8	10	12	12	13	14

* provisional

Sources: *Rossiskii Statisticheskii Ezhegodnik 2004*, Rosstat Rosii: Moscow, 2004, Table 14.38, p.379; Table 1.8.

is to both commercialisation of non-Gazprom gas production and reduction of associated gas flaring, it deserves significant attention. Aside from Sibur (see below) and Vostokgazprom (which operates in Eastern Siberia, see Chapter 3), Gazprom has six gas processing plants operated by wholly-owned subsidiaries (Urengoygazprom, Yamburggazodobycha, Surgutgazprom, Severgazprom, Orenburggazprom, Kubangazprom and Astrakhangazprom) with a total annual processing capacity of 52.5 Bcm of gas and 28.6 mt of crude oil and condensate in 2004.[80] From 2003, Gazprom replaced the merchant relationships that had existed previously with tolling arrangements.[81] These plants process only Gazprom's gas, with the exception of gas from the Karachaganak field in Kazakhstan which is processed at the Orenburg plant; negotiations to expand processing capacity via Kazrosgaz (a joint venture between Gazprom and Kazmunaigaz) were on-going in 2004 (see Chapter 2).

Aside from these plants, Gazprom controls processing in Siberia via its subsidiary Sibur (Siberian-Urals Oil and Gas Chemical Company) which owns nine processing plants in Siberia and delivers a range of petrochemical products to Russian customers and export markets. The purchase of a controlling interest in Sibur in 2001 allowed Gazprom to obtain a virtual monopoly of gas processing. But severe problems of governance within Sibur, followed by bankruptcy proceedings initiated by Gazprom, caused a hiatus which was not resolved until 2003. The governance crisis of the early 2000s allowed Lukoil and Surgutneftegaz to acquire a gas processing plant each from Sibur.[82]

During 2003 and 2004, Gazprom acquired additional equity in Sibur increasing its controlling interest to more than 99%.[83] Gazprom/Sibur has a *de facto* monopoly on gas processing in Siberia and any gas producer wishing to obtain transportation rights in Gazprom's network has needed to purchase processing services from that company. Up to the early 2000s, Gazprom/Sibur's dominant position left oil companies with associated gas the highly unattractive alternatives of either flaring the gas or burning it unprocessed in power stations. Up to 2001, the cost of gathering and transporting associated gas exceeded the regulated price that Sibur was required to offer producers; a Gazprom source estimated the cost to producers at RR600/mcm when the regulated price was RR55/mcm. As a result, oil producers boycotted Sibur's plants, preferring to flare huge quantities of associated gas and pay the resulting ecological penalties.[84]

However, other aspects of the problem were the confrontational relationship between the previous management of Sibur and the oil companies, and the lack of reliability of the processing plants. Since

2004 the position – at least according to the Sibur management – is much improved with 80% of the company's raw material coming from non-Gazprom (largely associated gas) feedstock.[85] There are suggestions from both Sibur and oil company managements that gas processed from future oil projects should be arranged as a 51% Sibur/49% oil company joint venture. Sibur is planning to increase processing of associated gas from 12 Bcm in 2005 to 20 Bcm.[86] In 2005, reform of the gas processing sector is underway as part of the general Gazprom reform process (see Chapter 4). In addition, Novatek's condensate extraction plant at Purovsk was commissioned in 2005 and will provide services not simply to that company, but also to third parties on a tolling basis.[87]

An important part of the processing problem is that future Siberian gas production will entail a much greater production of liquids than has previously been the case with the dominance of the large Cenomanian dry gas fields (see Appendix 1.2 for details). As the 2000s progressed, with the development of Valengenian and Neocomian gas, the lack of sufficient condensate pipeline capacity to evacuate liquids from the region became a significant inter-company issue. Around 2000, the Surgut processing plant was running at only 30% of capacity and was soliciting condensate for processing, but with both independents and Gazprom opening up fields with substantial liquids content, the Surgut plant has become over-subscribed.[88] The Deputy Governor of the Yamal-Nenets Autonomous Region revealed that condensate production was growing at 1.5–2 mt per year and that the limit of pipeline capacity had been reached in 2003.[89] In that year, Nortgaz was forced to limit its production of condensate by more than 20% which the company attributed to delays in the expansion of condensate pipeline capacity combined with increased condensate production at Yamburg.[90]

Production Projections: Gazprom and Independents

Table 1.9 shows gas production projections from the 2003 Russian Energy Strategy. It has a base case and an optimistic case for most regions and most years, and for 2010 and 2020 there is also a pessimistic case (*kriticheskii variant*). Despite the fact that the projections for 2005 have already been overtaken by actual production in 2004 it is worth looking at the longer-term projections. The Strategy anticipated slowly increasing production to 635–660 Bcm in 2010 and 680–730 Bcm in 2020. Of these totals, Gazprom's share would increase to 540–570 Bcm in 2010 and 530–590 Bcm in 2020, so that in the worst case Gazprom's production stays flat throughout the period. By contrast, independent

Table 1.9: Russian Gas Production Projections by Region and Company 2005–2020 (Bcm)

	2005*			2010			2015			2020		
	A	*B*	*C*	*A*	*B*	*C*	*A*	*B*	*C*	*A*	*B*	*C*
REGIONS												
West Siberia	559	557		572	564		558	526		541	520	
European Russia	42	41		41	40			48			67	
East Siberia/												
Far East		8		52	31		97	86		106	95	
COMPANIES												
Independents	90	80		115	105		135	120		140	150	
Gazprom	525	530		550	530		570	540		590	530	
TOTAL	615	610		665	635	560	705	660		730	680	610

* the 2005 projections have already been somewhat overtaken by events, with total production having reached 634 Bcm in 2004 comprising Gazprom production of 545 Bcm and independent production of 90 Bcm.

Note: A = optimistic variant, B = base case, C = low case

Source: *Russian Energy Strategy 2003*, Figure 11.

production increases from 80–90 Bcm in 2005 to 105–115 Bcm in 2010 and 140–150 Bcm in 2020.

Government views on the potential importance of independents changed when drawing up the Strategy during 2003. In the draft of the document submitted to the government in May 2003 the production level of the independent companies was quite substantially higher increasing to 115–120 Bcm in 2010, 146–150 Bcm in 2015 and 170–180 Bcm or 25% of the total in 2020.[91]

Over the same period, views on Gazprom's production became more bullish. In 2002, after a year when the company's production had fallen significantly, the talk was of 'stabilising' production at 530 Bcm until 2020. However, by late 2003 company projections had become much more confident suggesting that production could be raised significantly to 580–590 Bcm by 2020 and further to 610–630 by 2030.[92] In early 2004, the Commission of the Gas Industry which focuses on future resource development confirmed the higher ends of these ranges, but warned that these production levels would require annual finding rates of at least 700 Bcm/year during the period up to 2015 and 750–800 Bcm/year during the period 2016–2030.[93] These are very substantially higher figures than the finding rates of the early 2000s which were not high enough to replace current production. In 2004, the company replaced only 390

million tons of standard fuel equivalent − roughly equal to 330 Bcm
of gas in a year when production exceeded 545 Bcm − and liquids will
account for some of that figure.[94]

The motivation for Gazprom to increase its production projections is
uncertain. It could have been caused by pressure from government, or
the promise of increased domestic gas prices, or the reality of increased
export prices in the post 2000 period, or the 'threat' of losing markets
to independent companies.

A key issue arising from this review of resources and supply prospects
concerns the timing of Gazprom's need to make decisions about new
domestic supplies and the options available to it. This is set out in Table
1.10 which looks at the volumes of gas from Gazprom's fields that are
currently in production or have firm development commitments (i.e. ex-

Table 1.10: Gazprom Production Scenario by Field 2003–2020* (Bcm)

	2004	*2010*	*2015*	*2020*
Urengoy	140.6	96	70	52
Yen-Yakhinskoye	3.4**	5	5	5
Yamburg	146.3	104	77	54
Kharvutinskoye	8.1**	20	20	17
Aneryakhinskoye	0.0**	10	10	10
Medvezhe	25.6	15	10	7
Zapolyarnoye***	94.8	112	113	88
Komsomoskoye	30.6	24	14	0
West Tarkosalinskoye	3.5	14	9	5
Yubilyeynoye	21.3	19	10	6
Pestsovoye	2.2	28	29	25
Vyngayakhinskoye	5.8	5	4	3
South Russkoye	0.0	10	25	25
Yeti-Purovskoye	2.5	15	15	9
Urengoy (Achimov)	0.0	4	15	14
Astrakhan	11.4	12	12	12
Orenburg	20.1	12	10	10
Other	32.0	22	12	2
TOTAL****	545.1	527	460	344

* fields currently in production or with firm development timetables
** for 2004 these fields are included in the larger Urengoy and Yamburg totals, for
later years they are not.
*** including production from Neocomian strata.
**** for 2004 this is Gazprom's total actual production, other years are totals of
the columns

Sources: Author's estimates − see text

cluding the Yamal Peninsula and surrounding offshore regions), as they might unfold up to 2020. Table 1.10 is not an attempt to model future production according to the technical characteristics of individual fields. It has been compiled from information interpreted by the author from three sources: new fields anticipated by Gazprom to be brought into production; projections by Gazprom's VNIIgaz Institute on how the major fields are expected to perform in the future;[95] a simple numerical exercise on the evolution of production at some existing fields if current production trends are continued.

The main conclusions from Table 1.10 are that Gazprom's production from fields currently in production and anticipated to be brought into production, will peak in the late 2000s and decline gradually to less than 530 Bcm in 2010.[96] In the 2010s, the decline will accelerate, due to depletion of the three main fields, and production will fall to around 340 Bcm by 2020. This analysis suggests that Gazprom production cannot be maintained at 2004 levels up to 2010, since significant Yamal Peninsula production cannot start prior to 2011. In order to maintain production at around 530 Bcm, let alone at higher figures of 580–590 Bcm, Gazprom will need 70 Bcm of new production capacity by 2015 and 186 Bcm by 2020. The 70 Bcm by 2015 could be provided by the offshore Ob and Taz Bay fields; thereafter only the Yamal Peninsula fields have the capacity to provide such large volumes. These figures are entirely feasible in terms of identified resources and development projections, but lead times for bringing the fields into production and establishing pipelines mean that investments will need to be committed very soon for them to be achieved.

A final issue on Gazprom supply raised by this analysis is that subtracting total projected production for the years 2003–2020 from remaining proven and probable reserves (according to international standards), produces the outcome that more than 1 trillion cubic metres of proven and probable reserves would remain to be produced at Urengoy, and somewhat less at Yamburg.[97] It is not realistic to expect that Gazprom would leave these fields with such volumes of gas in place unless:

- This is a reflection of recovery factors at the fields; the original estimate of reserves at Urengoy was 10 trillion cubic metres which would suggest that ultimate recovery factor will be somewhat less than 90% of proven and probable reserve figures. This may be due to the damage which the fields have suffered in the early years of production when even Soviet geologists admitted that gas was produced at much higher rates than should have been the case.

  – Producing the remaining gas will be very much more expensive than
    the original gas production of the past two decades.

The issue of whether, and at what cost, Gazprom can access the full
extent of remaining proven and probable reserves in Urengoy and
Yamburg given current production decline trends, is crucial for the
future of NPT gas production. It may be that with external assistance,
Gazprom could return to these 'brownfield' developments with the same
impressive results that the vertically-integrated oil companies achieved
in the late 1990s and early 2000s.

    To the extent that Yamal production is delayed, the contribution
of independents (and imports from Central Asia – see Chapter 2) will
become more significant. Indeed, despite the fact that they themselves
have significant reserves on the Yamal Peninsula and therefore would
benefit from the creation of transmission networks to markets, it may
be in the interests of independent producers that Gazprom delays
large-scale Yamal gas development. An estimate of independent gas
production in the period up to 2030 by the Yamal-Nenets authorities
shows production peaking in 2015 at around 170 Bcm.[98] Beyond 2005,
the significant new producers could be Artikgaz (Yukos), Sibneftegaz
(Itera), and Yukharovneftegaz (Novatek) and beyond 2010 Yamalnefte-
gazdobycha.

    Table 1.11 shows production by independent producers in the early
2000s and their production aspirations for the early 2010s. Some of these
aspirations are more realistic than others and although a figure exceeding
200 Bcm is realistic in terms of the reserves held by these companies,
125 Bcm of production in the early 2010s seems more likely, with up
to 150 Bcm as a possibility. A final thought on 'independent producers'
would be to question the notion that these can be thought of as any
kind of cohesive group about which useful generalisations can be made.
The current reality is that five or six companies (Lukoil, Surgutneftegaz,
Rosneft, TNK/BP, Novatek, and perhaps Itera) seem set to dominate
non-Gazprom production and sales over the next decade. The ambitions
and strategies of each of these companies are significantly different from
each other. Lukoil, Surgutneftegaz and Rosneft have thus far seemed to be
producers with little marketing ambition. Itera has declined as a producer
while remaining an important marketer. Novatek is aggressively pursuing
both production and marketing. There are few easy generalisations to
make about the independent gas community.

Table 1.11: Independent Gas Production 2002–2010/15 (Bcm)

	2002	2003	2004*	Expectations 2010–2015
OIL COMPANIES				
Surgutneftegaz	13.3	13.9	14.3	25
Rosneft	6.5	7.0	9.2	45-50
TNK-BP	3.5	5.0	8.0	20**
Lukoil	4.3	4.7	5.0	30 by 2013 (80 by 2020)
Yukos	2.4	3.4	3.4	(survival uncertain)
Sibneft	1.4	2.0	2.0	2
Sidanco	1.8	1.1	***	
TOTAL OIL COMPANIES	34.8	41.4	44.9	122–127
GAS INDEPENDENTS				
Itera	20	14		15
Novatek		13.5	20.5	50
Nortgaz	3.9	4.0	4.7	10 (Gazprom share likely to be 51%)
OTHER, PSAs (including Sakhalin)		3.4		12
TOTAL GAS INDEPENDENTS	36.5	34.9	44.7	77
TOTAL NON-GAZPROM	72.3	76.3	89.6	199–204
TOTAL GAZPROM	523.8	540.2	545.1	530–590

* provisional
** not including Kovykta field in Eastern Siberia
*** included in TNK/BP

Sources: IEA, *World Energy Outlook 2004*, Paris: OECD, 2004, Table 9.5, p.312;
Interfax Oil and Gas Report, December 31, 2004–January 19, 2005, pp.
36–37; company data, author's estimates.

Transmission and Storage

In 2004, the high pressure transmission system – the Unified Gas Supply System (UGSS) – owned and operated by Gazprom comprised 154,000 km of pipeline with diameters up to 1440 mm (56 inches). Seventeen transmission subsidiaries of Gazprom transport gas throughout the country, and some also produce gas (see Chapter 4). Because of the size of the country and the fact that the major producing fields are located in an extremely harsh climatic and territorial environment, thousands of kilometres from the principal centres of consumption, gas transmission has always been a major problem for Russian gas development.

Table 1.12 shows the age of the network at late 2004/early 2005. It can be seen that 58% of pipes are more than twenty years old and only 11% were built during the past decade. This age profile is significant given the problems of harsh environment and terrain mentioned above. The majority of the network was built during the Soviet period at relatively high speed with lower quality corrosion protection than was ideal for the conditions. In addition, Soviet-built compressor stations, while adequate, have relatively low levels of efficiency and reliability.[99]

Table 1.12: Gazprom's High Pressure Gas Transmission Network (UGSS)

Years Since Construction	Length (km)	% of Total
Up to 10 years	17,094	11.1
10–20 years	47,586	30.9
20–33 years	56,518	36.7
Over 33 years	32,802	21.3
TOTAL	154,000	100.0

Source: Pravda Gazovogo Dvizheniya, *Gazprom*, No 1–2, 2005, p.22.

Gazprom's financial problems in the late 1990s gave rise to concerns that insufficient funds were being devoted to maintenance and timely refurbishment of the pipeline network. There is uncertainty as to the 'design life' of the network, but in the conditions encountered in Siberia, it was believed that pipelines would need to be replaced after thirty years. With the recovery of its financial position in the 2000s, Gazprom is paying serious attention to the network with the company reporting in-line inspection of 20,000 km, and electrical inspection of 26,700 km, of pipeline in 2003 alone.[100] It also claims that faults and interruptions in the network are continuously declining. Nevertheless, calculations by VNIIgaz show that in 2002, productivity of the network as a whole was around 9% below its design capacity; of this the greatest loss was located in the central corridor which was more than 12% below capacity.[101]

The main transmission projects in which Gazprom was involved in 2004–05 were:

1. Urengoy field ('SRTO') to the Torzhok compressor station – 2700 km with twelve compressor stations which will deliver gas to north western Russia and through the Yamal-Europe pipeline. The pipeline will be commissioned in stages through 2007.

2. Three 100 km pipelines from the Zapolyarnoye field to Urengoy and the Purtazovskaya compressor station were completed in 2004 raising the capacity of the system to 100 Bcm/year.
3. Pochiniki-Izobilnoye pipeline (1250 km with eight compressor stations) and the North Stavropol underground storage facility. The line will enable NPT gas to be delivered to the Blue Stream pipeline to Turkey instead of gas from Astrakhan and Central Asia which requires substantial processing. Construction is due to be completed in 2005.[102]

The issue of how new pipeline construction should be funded, particularly as independent companies begin to use the network to a greater extent, remains to be decided. Gazprom has suggested that independent companies should be required to contribute funding towards construction costs, but this seems unlikely to be workable for a network that already has regulated third party tariffs (see Chapter 4) and where it is difficult to predict the extent to which companies will use which parts of the network in the future and to what extent. Interestingly, given the government's determined stance that only government companies should be involved in pipeline construction, Lukoil is being required by Gazprom to build a pipeline to deliver its Nakhodinskaya gas to Yamburg; Itera has been involved in pipeline construction in the Sverdlovsk region. This may be a reflection of lack of profitability in the transmission sector due to low end-user prices and third party transmission tariffs. The General Director of Tyumentransgaz confirmed that, at 2003 tariffs, the cost of increasing transmission capacity to accommodate independent gas production was not profitable.[103]

Lack of profitability in the transmission sector is a potentially significant obstacle to timely refurbishment of the network which, as shown in Table 1.12, is becoming an increasingly important problem. Future investment in additional transmission capacity will also require customer tariffs to reflect load factor considerations to a much greater extent, particularly since the most rapidly increasing demand is in the residential/communal sector which pays the lowest prices and has the biggest requirement for daily and seasonal swing.

Gazprom owns all of the gas storage capacity in Russia. The company operates 24 underground storages with a capacity of 60 Bcm. Table 1.3 shows that over the past five years, 50–65 Bcm of gas has been injected into storage each year with similar quantities being withdrawn depending on the severity of winter temperatures.[104] Gazprom is actively developing additional storage with five new storages under construction and a further eight potential sites being studied.[105] This is planned to increase average daily deliverability to 500 mmcm(million cu. m.)/day and maximum deliverability to 613 mmcm/day by the start of the 2007–08 heating season, 6–10% above the capacity in 2004–05.[106]

Nevertheless, Gazprom's storage capacity remains relatively small for a company with such a large market and extreme seasonal demand swings. In addition to its own requirements, Gazprom is also providing storage services for independent gas suppliers for up to 10% of total capacity. Itera and Sibur were the first companies to use Gazprom storages in the early 2000s and there has been no suggestion that independent companies are seeking to build their own storage.[107] Gazprom also has rights to use more than 11 Bcm of storage capacity in Ukraine, Latvia (Chapter 2), Austria and Germany (Chapter 3).

Distribution and Sales

The problems of the 1990s led to fundamental changes in ownership and operation of distribution networks. Emerging from the Soviet era, gas distribution was owned by municipal authorities and Rosgazifikatsiya (an organisation which emerged from the Ministry of Housing and Municipal Affairs) with over 900 branches; Gazprom (and its predecessor the Ministry of the Gas Industry) had no role in distribution.[108] During the non-payment era, distribution companies were in the forefront of those unable (as opposed to unwilling) to pay bills. Many were driven into insolvency or merged with neighbours into regional companies, and Gazprom – to which their substantial debts were owed – exchanged this debt for equity and took over significant numbers of distribution companies, despite such action being directly against the government's economic strategy.[109]

In 1996, Gazprom established Mezhregiongaz as the principal sales organisation for its gas within Russia as a direct consequence of the payments crisis in the country, the rationale being to centralise and coordinate collection of receivables from customers.[110] A Russian Federation Decree of May 2002 then established the principle of regulated prices for gas supply companies.[111] In compliance with that Decree, Mezhregiongaz and regional gas companies began to purchase gas at internal Gazprom prices and sell gas to customers according to regulated prices set by the (Federal Energy Commission which in 2004 became the) Federal Tariff Service. From October 2002, an individual sales margin was established by the regulatory authority for each of the regional gas companies.[112]

In the early 2000s, Gazprom experimented in trying to remove both regional distribution companies and Mezhregiongaz from the sales chain, in order to save both costs and taxes, but this experiment was abandoned. By 2005, 60 regional gas companies had been established, 55 of which are owned or majority controlled by Gazprom.[113] The structure appears to have settled down with Mezhregiongaz coordinating the work of the regional gas companies, and selling directly to the largest industrial and power customers. In May 2004, Mezhregiongaz Holding (Mezhregiongaz 99%, Lentransgaz 1%) was created to manage all of Gazprom's interests in regional transmission and distribution networks. With Gazprom owning or controlling 206 out of 330 regional distribution companies operating 75% (403,000 km) of distribution pipelines, and providing 58% of the total gas consumed to 75% of the country's municipalities, the company's grip on the distribution sector appeared to be increasing.[114] Mezhregiongaz Holding was subsequently re-named Gazpromregiongaz with the same share ownership.[115]

By 2004, all Gazprom's deliveries were sold to customers directly by the regional gas transmission companies with the (low pressure) distribution companies acting only as transporters charging a service payment.[116] Russia is therefore much further advanced than most countries in unbundling gas distribution, although the vast majority of the sector is supplied by the dominant player. But Gazprom is required to work with other shareholders in the distribution companies who may not be happy to have been relegated to transporter status. The Russian anti-monopoly authorities (MAP) have brought actions against Gazprom in respect of gas distribution. By negotiating with regional political authorities, Gazprom is attempting to consolidate large groups of distribution companies within a republic into larger business units, and/or to reach agreements whereby the company pays a single agreed tariff for distribution services throughout a large geographical area served by many companies.[117]

Indeed in late 2004 the General Director of Gazpromregiongaz appeared to be arguing in favour of a single gas distribution organisation, which could be created by the amalgamation of Gazprom's interests with those of the government which owns a controlling stake in 63 companies. Sergei Shilov's argument for the creation of an entity that would control 269 out of the 300 distribution companies is that small distribution companies have been shown to be unable to survive financially and that a unified tariff must be established in each region.[118]

The new distribution arrangements further extended Gazprom's control over the transportation sector, which was not desirable from a competition perspective, at least until legal unbundling with a much greater degree of independent regulation is in place (see Chapter 4). A potentially positive aspect of Gazprom's increasing involvement in distribution is that it is achieving some desperately-needed investment in the low pressure distribution networks. As price increases make distribution customers more valuable to serve, it should become more cost-effective to refurbish distribution networks in order to reduce gas leakage and increase efficiency.[119]

The Domestic Market: Demand, Prices and Payments

The Russian gas market can be considered a difficult subject in general for researchers, but domestic demand and price issues are particularly difficult because of a lack of consistent data which are comparable over time. There has always been a major problem in presenting consistent demand data for regions and end-user groups.[120] This problem is even more difficult as companies other than Gazprom have begun to deliver gas to consumers but do not reveal any details about their customers. Substantial differences in views exist with regard to the interpretation of the pricing and payment policies followed over the past decade. With that as an introduction, this section makes an attempt to steer a path through this minefield of inadequate and problematic data and strongly-held convictions.

Demand

The best description of the domestic gas market is contained in the 2004 OECD Economic Survey of the Russian Federation which describes it as: '…a rationing mechanism with market activity at the fringes'.[121] There is an annual allocation by Gazprom of the quantity of gas that will be supplied to different groups of domestic consumers at regulated prices.[122] Industrial customers are then required to bid for gas which they need during the coming year – quotas may be 'adjusted' quarterly – subject to 'correction' from Gazprom which then informs consumers of their allocation. If industrial customers require more gas, they may be able to purchase it either from Gazprom or from independent companies at higher than regulated prices. There are no long-term contracts and the only allowed off-take profile is flat supply with no make-up/make good provisions, i.e. gas that is not taken during periods of low consumption (summer, weekends and holidays) is forfeited, and additional gas needed during periods of high demand must be paid for at higher prices. According to the OECD:

The administration of this rationing is wholly opaque. Some consumers get what they bid for, while others are allocated far less than their bids and must purchase the rest at higher prices. There are no clearly defined principles of distribution. Even the overall results of the distribution are unknown: the government does not appear to have full data on the actual allocation of regulated-price gas to domestic customers...Some consumers report that their quotas have simply been frozen, so that reliance on other sources grows in line with their demand; this appears to be the case with the power sector.[123]

Table 1.13 attempts to show deliveries of gas to Russian customers by Gazprom and independent companies. The independent figures need to be treated with some caution since they are simply the residual after subtracting Gazprom deliveries from total deliveries. (These figures do not include volumes of gas required to operate the transmission system of 40–50 Bcm, see Table 1.3). The figures for independent producers suggest that for the period 2002–04, less than half of the 73–90 Bcm of gas produced (Table 1.8) was delivered to Russian customers. Internal use of gas by oil companies could account for some of this difference, while gas independents also delivered gas to CIS customers. Nevertheless, the proportion of independent gas actually delivered to customers seems suspiciously low and could fit with Deputy Chairman Ryazanov's assertion that 20% of Russian Federation gas is delivered by independent companies if nearly half those deliveries (44–46 Bcm in 2003–04) were sold to Gazprom.[124]

Table 1.13: Deliveries of Gas to Russian Customers (Bcm)

	1999	2000	2001	2002	2003	2004
Gazprom Customers	268.2	267.2	282.1	283.5	291.0	289.7
Independent Producer Customers	31.6	41.2	35.4	35.6	36.0	43.8
Total Deliveries	299.8	308.4	317.5	319.1	327.0	333.5

Sources: Russian customers see Table 1.3, Gazprom customers, *Gazprom Annual Report 2003*, p.70; *Results of the meeting with leaders of the Russian Federation's regional administrations*, Gazprom Press Release, March 10, 2005.

Whatever the actual figures, there is no doubt that substantial volumes of gas are being sold by independent companies direct to consumers. In 2003, Itera supplied all of the gas to Sverdlovsk Oblast, and according to Mezhregiongaz, the percentage of independent supply to the following regions was: Tyumen Oblast 82.4%, Kurgan Oblast 69.7%, Komi Republic 28.2%, Bashkortostan Republic 26% and Astrakhan Oblast 21.9%.[125]

The CEO of Novatek confirmed that in 2004 the company was supplying gas to twenty oblasts but not beyond the Po-Volga region because of the transportation costs. He also revealed that 10% of the company's sales were at regulated prices (which may have been to Gazprom).[126]

Table 1.13 shows that total Russian gas demand (not including volumes used by the transportation system) increased by more than 11% over the period 1999–2004, while Gazprom deliveries increased by the same percentage up to 2003 but appeared to decline in 2004.[127] Table 1.14 is a very partial attempt to track demand by customer class over the period 1993–2003. The data are highly problematic because the 2003 figures are not compatible with those of previous years as can be seen by comparing these data with those in Table 1.13. The total figures for 1993–2000 almost certainly include pipeline fuel while the 2003 figure does not, but the difference is not consistent with the data in Table 1.3.

Table 1.14: Russian Gas Demand by Sector 1993–2003 (Bcm)

	1993	*1994*	*1995*	*1996*	*1997*	*1998*	*1999*	*2000*	*2003**
Power	165.4	147.2	138.9	139.3	135.8	132.0	134.8	135.6	103.4
Oil Industry	9.8	9.3	9.3	8.1	9.0	8.4	8.0	8.1	
Metallurgy	34.2	30.9	30.9	28.8	27.5	26.5	27.0	27.5	28.8
Chemicals	17.6	16.3	16.0	15.2	15.2	13.6	16.4	17.5	19.3
Cement	6.4	5.1	5.0	3.9	3.9	3.9	4.2	4.8	5.7
Petrochemicals	7.6	6.5	6.8	6.2	6.0	5.5	5.5	4.8	
Agriculture	23.5	20.7	18.5	17.9	16.7	15.9	15.1	14.8	
Communal/ District Heat	21.5	21.7	20.9	22.8	23.7	24.4	24.1	25.3	32.1
of which: Communal/ residential gas/heat	15.6	15.6	15.2	16.1	16.3	16.5	13.2	13.4	
Network heat	5.9	6.1	5.7	6.7	7.4	7.9	10.9	11.9	
Population	22.9	26.7	30.1	33.6	36.9	37.2	38.3	39.5	44.9
Other industry	57.6	50.7	47.3	45.6	45.1	44.5	49.5	49.7	46.7
									280.9
TOTAL	382.9	350.6	339.4	337.3	335.6	331.2	338.3	348.7	327.0

*   Gazprom deliveries only; 2003 data are not comparable with previous years

Source: Gazprom

Despite the shortcomings of Table 1.14, it clearly demonstrates that power and industry account for more than 70% of Russian gas demand with only around 20% delivered to households; the figure is difficult to determine accurately because there are no data on the proportion of the communal/district heating sector devoted to residential users.

Deliveries from independent producers are almost entirely concentrated in the power and industrial sector and are not delivered to residential customers or even to distribution companies. In a speech to the representatives of Russian regional authorities in April 2004, Deputy Chairman Alexander Ryazanov revealed Gazprom's priorities in respect of demand by different groups of end-users:

> Sometimes Gazprom is forced to forward the consumers asking for additional gas volumes to independent gas producers since we're occasionally unable to provide the required gas amount. But I want to stress it once again, Gazprom guarantees 100% full-amount payment to the residential and housing sectors. The same policy is implemented towards gas exports: we never impose limits on those...we unfortunately can't reduce deliveries to the power sector. Practically the whole Russian power generation sector is gas-fired. We consider it to be threatening for the country...'[128]

The reform of the power sector – currently planned for end-2006 – has significant consequences for both the gas sector and Gazprom (see Chapter 4).

Prices and Costs

Comparing even Gazprom's 2003 sales of 291 Bcm with consumption of 425 Bcm for twenty European countries in the same year shows the relative size of Russian gas demand.[129] But this figure becomes even more dramatic when it is realised that during the period 1999–2003 virtually all of these volumes were delivered at a loss to Gazprom. The company calculates the losses made on the domestic market during this period at $25bn (see Figure 1.1).

Gazprom's assertions about its losses in the domestic market should not be accepted uncritically and raise very complex issues of pricing of gas to customers relative to costs of delivery. Given that Russia is a very large country and that the majority of the gas is produced in Siberia, transportation costs mean that gas prices should vary substantially between locations close to, and far from, the producing fields. In 1997, regulated prices were established for seven geographic zones – depending on their distance from the NPT region in Siberia (Table 1.15). The intention is for the price differences between zones to be cost-reflective of the (very considerable) distance that the gas has to be transported. In 2004, transmission accounted for 44% of the differential between industrial prices in Zones 0 and 6 which is relatively low for a transportation distance of more than 3000 km. Outside Siberia, this differential dropped sharply and was only 21% between Zones 2

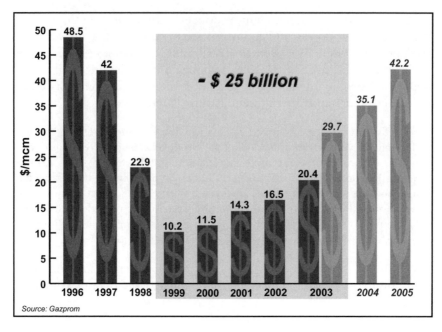

Figure 1.1: Russian Industrial Gas Prices, 1996–2005

and 6. It needs to be stressed that these are regulated prices at which Gazprom is required to sell; independent producers are not subject to these prices.

If pricing to industrial customers is not easy, the problems of residential gas pricing are much more complex and difficult. The residential prices in Table 1.15 are not final prices; to these figures distribution and marketing charges need to be added. In addition, these figures do not reflect further regulated discounts for elderly citizens and war veterans. Residential differentials are even less cost reflective than for industrial prices – there is only a 24% difference between the 2004 prices in Zones 0 and 6. The residential prices in Table 1.15 are not strictly comparable to industrial prices (since they do not include distribution and customer charges) but it is clear that in the period 2000–2005 progress towards raising wholesale residential prices relative to industrial prices was slow: from 64% in 2000 to 73% in 2005.

At the beginning of 2004, industrial gas prices in Zone 5 (around Moscow) were raised to 912 Rubles (around $30.4) per thousand cubic metres (mcm) from RR760 ($25.3)/mcm in 2003.[130] Gazprom Deputy Chairman Ryazanov reported that: '...the domestic market has unfortunately been unprofitable for Gazprom until now...in 2004

Table 1.15: Russian Domestic Gas Prices by Zone, 1997–2004 (rubles per thousand cubic metres)

DATE	10/97	4/98	7/98	3/99	2/00	3/01	2/02	1/03	1/04
RESIDENTIAL									
Z 0					157	226	271	387	464
Z 1			132	157	165	238	286	410	492
Z 2			144	172	181	260	312	447	536
Z 3			156	185	194	279	335	480	576
Z 4			159	189	198	285	342	490	588
Z 5			162	193	203	291	349	500	600
Z 6			165	196	206	296	355	508	610
CONCESSIONS*									
Z 0									
Z 1				132	132				
Z 2				144	144				
Z 3				156	156				
Z 4				159	159				
Z 5				162	162				
Z 6				165					
INDUSTRY									
Z 0					224	264	317	438	526
Z 1	224	224	224	224	258	319	383	528	634
Z 2	245	245	245	245	283	372	446	616	739
Z 3	264	264	264	264	305	417	500	690	828
Z 4	270	270	270	270	312	438	526	726	871
Z 5	275	275	275	275	317	458	550	760	912
Z 6	280	280	280	280	323	472	566	781	937
ELECTRICITY									
Z 0									
Z 1	193	188	168	168	219				
Z 2	211	204	183	183	239				
Z 3	227	220	197	197	257				
Z 4	236	229	205	205	262				
Z 5	236	229	205	205	267				
Z 6	241	233	209	209	273				

Zone 0: Yamal-Nenets Autonomous Okrug
Zone 1: Khanti-Mansi Autonomous Okrug
Zone 2: Komi Republic, Nenets Autonomous Okrug, Astrakhan Oblast, Orenburg Oblast, Tyumen Oblast
Zone 3: Republics of: Bashkortostan, Kalmykia, Udmurt. Oblasts of: Arkhangelsk, Kirov, Kurgan, Novosibiirsk, Omsk, Perm, Sverdlovsk, Tomsk, Chelyabinsk
Zone 4: Republics of: Marii-el, Mordovia, Tatarstan, Chuvash. Oblasts of: Vladimir, Vologodsk, Ivanovsk, Kastroma, Nizhgorod, Pensensk, Samara, Saratov, Ulyanovsk, Yaroslavl'.

Table 1.15: Continued

Zone 5: Cities of Moscow and St Petersburg, Republic of Karelia, Altai region. Oblasts of: Leningrad, Belgorod, Briansk, Voronezh, Kaluzh, Kemerova, Kursk, Lipetsk, Novgorod, Orlov, Pskov, Ryazan, Smolensk, Tversk, Tula, Tambov.

Zone 6: Republics of: Adegey, Daghestan, Ingushetia, Kabardino-Balkarsk, Karachaevo-Cherkasssk, Chechnya. Regions of Krasnodar and Stavropol; Oblasts of Kaliningrad and Rostov.

* elderly and war veterans

Source: Renaissance Capital citing: Gazprom, Federal Energy Commission and Ministry of Energy.

the company plans to avoid losses while carrying on gas business on the internal market not to mention any profits'.[131] But the meaning of 'profitability' and how it is calculated is unclear and most parties were in agreement that a price of $30/mcm (excluding VAT) in Zone 5 would not cover long-run marginal costs of Gazprom production even in the NPT region, let alone the cost of producing gas from the Yamal fields, which should probably be regarded as Gazprom's true long-run marginal costs.[132]

The question of whether this level of prices covered operating (short-run marginal) cost is more difficult to determine given the lack of cost transparency. The relatively small allowance for transmission costs in the final price significantly decreases profitability the further away from the production source that customers are located. While it may be that at $30/mcm Zone 5 customers were barely profitable, Zone 1 customers (located less than 1000 km from the gas fields) were significantly profitable at the January 2004 price of $21.1/mcm, and may have been profitable prior to that. Gazprom has said that it expected to 'break even' on domestic sales *as a whole* at 2004 prices.[133] Therefore prices did not necessarily need to be raised uniformly throughout the country if tariffs were adjusted to take transmission and other costs more accurately into account. While there needed to be some increase in order for long-run marginal costs to be reflected, 'rebalancing' tariffs to take account of location and customer class was an important priority.

This began in January 2005, when the number of price zones was expanded from 7 to 12 – a configuration that is expected to remain in place until 2010. The first set of prices for this new zonal configuration is shown in Table 1.16 from which it is clear that price increases were greater for zones further from the fields and less for those located closer to Siberia – 18% for industrial prices in Zone 1 (Zone 0 under the

Table 1.16: Russian Gas Prices by Zone, 2005 (rubles per thousand cubic metres)

Region of Russia	Wholesale Price for Gas (not including VAT)	
	Industrial*	Residential**
ZONE 1 Yamal-Nenets Autonomous Okrug	619	619
ZONE 2 Khanti-Mansi Autonomous Okrug	745	660
ZONE 3 Tyumen Oblast	879	720
ZONE 4 Oblasts of Udmurt, Kurgan and Perm'	985	773
ZONE 4A Republic of Komi; Oblasts of Astrakhan and Orenburg	923	730
ZONE 5 Republic of Bashkortostan; Oblasts of Arkhangelsk, Sverdlovsk and Tomsk	1005	778
ZONE 6 Republics of Kalmykia, Oblasts of Marii-El, Tatarstan and Chuvash; Kirov, Omsk and Chelyabinsk	1033	783
ZONE 7 Republic of Mordovia; Oblasts of Volgograd, Nizhegorodosk, Novosibiirsk, Penzensk, Samarsk, Ulyanovsk, Yarolavl'.	1040	792
ZONE 8 Republic of Karelia; Oblasts of Vladimir, Ivanovo, Kostroma, Leningrad, Lipetsk, Novgorod, Saratov, Tambov, Tversk; City of St Petersburg	1088	802
ZONE 9 Altai Krai; Oblasts of Belgorod, Bryansk, Volgagrad, Voronezh, Kaluzh, Kemerova, Kursk, Moscow, Orlov, Pskov, Ryazan, Smolensk, Tula; City of Moscow	1119	810
ZONE 10 Oblasts of Kaliningrad and Rostov	1154	822
ZONE 11 Republics of Adegey, Daghestan, Ingushetia, Kabardino-Balkarsk, Karachaevo-Cherkasssk, North Ossetia- Alania, Chechnya.	1160	810
Krasnodar and Stavropol Krai	1160	826

* January 2005 ** April 2005

Source: *Na Saite Opublikovan Prikaz "Ob Optovikh Tsenakh na Gaz Dobivaemim OAO Gazprom i ievo Affilirovannimi Litsami Realiziruemi Potrebitelyam"*, Federal Tariff Service Press Release December 20, 2004, http://www.fstrf.ru/press/releases/23

previous structure) and 24% for Zone 11 (Zone 6 under the previous structure). The Head of the Oil and Gas Department at the Federal Tariff Service has suggested that although the zones will not be changed until 2010, relative prices will continue to be adjusted.[134] Transmission costs are not adequately reflected in the difference between the January 2005 prices in Zone 1 and Zone 11 of RR541/mcm, or around $0.54/mmbtu, but the position is much improved compared with the past. The same can be said of industrial gas prices in the Moscow region which reached $40/mcm in 2005 when, back in 2000, this seemed an impossible dream.[135]

If industrial gas sales have, until the mid-2000s, been unprofitable for Gazprom, it is clear from Table 1.15 that wholesale prices to residential customers were significantly less profitable. As noted above, regulated residential gas prices were 30–40% below industrial prices, and this was the full regulated wholesale residential price before discounts for elderly people and war veterans are applied. The prospects for residential prices are a rarely heard subject in the debate over price reform in Russia. This may be in part because the sector is a relatively small proportion of total demand (at least compared with many OECD countries) but mainly because the issue is so political that not even the government is willing to be specific about a reform timetable. In general, it seems that residential prices will continue to be raised at a slightly higher rate than those for industrial customers. In order to reflect costs of delivery, the price premium of residential over industrial sales in OECD countries is around 250%, compared with a price discount of 40–60% in Russia between 1997 and 2000.[136] Most recent developments show the change that has taken place with April 2005 residential prices ranging from parity with industrial prices in Zone 1 to 70% in Zone 11. With the majority of residential customers unable to control the amount of gas (or in most cases heat) they use due to lack of meters and temperature controls, more substantial price increases may have to await changes in the housing stock.[137]

Another part of the gas price problem has been the low price of gas in comparison to other fuels. During the 1990s and early 2000s, the price of gas was held below the prices of fuel oil and even coal. These price advantages led to substantial customer switching into gas. In 2004, the regulated price of gas was approximately 88% of the price of coal for power generation, and less than half the price of fuel oil.[138] It is intended that gas prices will rise above coal prices in 2006 (in European Russia and prior to that in Siberia), and are intended to reach parity with fuel oil prices by 2010 (although this will depend on levels of domestic and international oil prices at that time).[139]

Payments

The mid to late 1990s saw the worst of the non-payment nightmare in the Russian gas industry. Non-payment of bills was a phenomenon that gripped a large part of the Russian economy during the 1990s. The principal causes were: general economic crisis and dislocation, rapid increases in gas prices during the early/mid 1990s, inability/refusal of the Russian government to impose hard budget constraints, and problems in the banking system. During the 1990s, non-cash instruments such as barter, promissory notes and debt offsets predominated. Large-scale non-payment began in 1992 and steadily increased as prices were raised massively towards 'market levels'. In 1996, Gazprom's Accounts published for the first time according to international accounting standards (IAS) stated that 57% of accounts receivable settled during the calendar year were in the form of barter trade or inter-enterprise transfers.[140] The 1997 IAS Accounts suggested only 26.6% of gas delivered was paid for, but cash payments by the end of the year accounted for 15% – a considerable increase from the 7% figure at the beginning of the year. However, 58% of gas payments were made in the form of 'mutual cancellations' (that is inter-company debt offsets) and barter, of which the latter appears to have accounted for 11–20%, leaving around 30% for which no payment at all was received in the calendar year in which the gas was delivered.[141]

At the same time, Gazprom was constrained by the government against using disconnection in order to control non-payment. Various orders and regulations prevented the company from cutting gas supplies to household utilities – such as water and electricity suppliers, hospitals, military and state telecommunications organisations and other consumers whose activities were held to be vital to national security and environmental safety.[142] In fact there is evidence that around 1998, Gazprom began to use disconnection more widely as a means of debt control. During 1997, only 50 customers were disconnected; but during the first half of 1998, the number was 2,230. This does not mean that those customers necessarily remained disconnected from the system over a long period, but the change in policy regarding disconnections signalled a turnaround for payment even if, as shown in Table 1.15, this coincided with a four-year standstill in industrial prices and a decline in prices to power generators. In that situation, it would be logical for Gazprom to have total discretion as to whether it chose to continue to deliver gas to non-paying customers. However, non-payment is a highly political issue, given that unemployment and social unrest could result from payment enforcement. Large-scale disconnections would therefore constitute a major political issue, as they would involve substantial bankruptcies and unemployment. In the post-1993 period, successive governments tolerated non-payment of utilities as a way of reducing direct government subsidies to the industrial and manufacturing sector. A different interpretation of the non-payment crisis sees it as a function of poor governance (see Appendix 4.1 in Chapter 4).

Table 1.17: Domestic Payments for Gas 1997–2003

	1997	*1998*	*1999*	*2000*	*2001*	*2002*	*2003**
% Payment	29.0	59.1	96.4	114.8	118.6	101.3	99.3
% Cash	12.0	24.3	39.1	84.6	96.2	85.3	92.5

*   nine months only

Source: A.A. Petrov, *Liberalisation of Russian Gas Market: New Forms of Trade in Gas*, IEA 2003.

Table 1.17 shows Mezhregiongaz data on payment progress during the period 1997–2003. From a low in 1997 where the company was paid less than 30% of receivables in the calendar year they were due, and only 12% of these in cash, the position progressively improved to such an extent that Gazprom has received more than 100% of its receivables (i.e. customers have been paying off arrears from previous years) and cash payment was around 95% in 2003. Alternative data, also provided by Gazprom suggest a less healthy picture in that, although non-cash settlements continue to decrease, in 2004 20% of domestic sales were still settled by non-cash instruments – predominantly short-term promissory notes (*veksels*) which are freely traded between Russian companies. By end 2003, consumer debt had fallen to R38bn. While still in excess of $1bn, it had become much more manageable – although there was evidence that total 'accounts receivable' increased again in 2004.[143] The most serious payment problems are concentrated in regions such as Chechnya and the North Caucasus.[144]

The Future of Russian Gas Demand: The Potential Impact of Pricing, Conservation and Efficiency and Industrial Restructuring

A previous study published by this author in 1995 suggested that Russian gas demand would be in the range of 300–340 Bcm in 2000, and 350–400 Bcm in 2010, compared with a figure of 360 Bcm for

1994 and over 400 Bcm for 1990.[145] At the time, such projections were somewhat controversial because Gazprom was projecting an increase in demand to more than 400 Bcm in 2000. In fact, demand in 2000 was just below 310 Bcm, increasing by 2004 to 334 Bcm (Table 1.3). The reasonable accuracy of the 1995 projections would be some cause for confidence for future projections, were it not for the fact that they were based on the premises of higher prices and payment enforcement giving rise to substantial conservation and efficiency, and significant industrial restructuring away from energy-intensive industries towards light industry and services. As we now know, few of these trends were in evidence prior to 2000 and most were in the opposite direction:

- Real prices fell during the mid to late 1990s, although they did begin to increase again by 2000.
- Payments worsened dramatically over the same period although again they were improving by 2000.
- No conservation and efficiency improvements were discernible during that period;
- Some industrial restructuring was visible but this was hardly a major trend.

So the most likely explanations for the fall in demand during the period 1994–99 are (i) that heavy industrial sectors contracted with the decline in GDP during that period;[146] and (ii) the increase in real gas prices in the mid-1990s had a significant impact – despite rising levels of non-payment – which reversed after the 1998 economic crisis when prices fell to relatively low levels.

Demand is difficult to project even using conventional measures of economic growth since so much depends on sectoral and regional developments. This is particularly true as regards demand in power generation, especially whether and how quickly old gas turbine plant will be replaced by new and much more efficient, combined cycle plant; and demand in industry, in particular in the metallurgical and chemical sectors where plant replacement could see very substantial savings.

But the biggest problem is to know how quickly regulated industrial prices will be raised and what will be the demand response to increased prices. It is for this reason that the future development of regulated industrial prices will be so important. Assuming that the prices agreed between the EU WTO negotiators and the Russian government in May 2004 will be implemented (expressed in real 2004 dollars at the 2004 dollar/ruble exchange rate), it would mean that by 2006, prices will be 20–35% higher than in 2004 and by 2010, prices will be 58–84% higher than in 2004.[147]

Russian literature rarely makes any connection between demand and price but Deputy Minister of Economic Development Andrei Sharonov has noted the importance of price elasticity of demand for gas: 'with a price of over $50/mcm we might not have sufficient demand for gas.'[148] In 2004, there was evidence that Gazprom itself was becoming interested in the relationship between gas demand and price, quoting work by the Academy of Sciences showing that the substantial price increases of the early 2000s had not produced any evidence of energy saving in the cement and fertiliser industries. It was clear from these studies that only 8–14% of enterprises showed any inclination to invest in more energy-efficient plant. This was perhaps not surprising given that the figures quoted for the impact of a 23% increase in regulated gas prices on the costs of industry as a whole was 1.1%, with the impact on enterprises in individual sectors as follows: food 0.2%, machine tools 0.5%, ferrous metallurgy 0.5%, chemicals and petrochemicals 2.1%, building materials 2.2%, power 2.7%.[149]

This only seems to confirm that Russian industry has yet to be given incentives to save energy and/or invest in energy saving plant and technology. It is difficult to predict when such incentives will be applied on a large scale and whether this is simply dependent on continued price increases backed by payment enforcement. Perhaps one important trend is that, having taken over a considerable proportion of the distribution infrastructure, thereby bringing itself much closer to end-users, Gazprom has a greater interest and potential influence on 'rational

Table 1.18: Russian Energy and Gas Demand Projections 1990–2020[1] Mtsfe*

	1990	1995	2000	2005	2010	2015	2020
Gas Demand	531	469	450	466–480	497–531	511–558	525–580
Gas Demand**	446	394	378	392–403	418–446	429–469	441–487
Energy Demand	1268	939	904	945–975	1020–1095	1090–1180	1145–1270
% Gas	42	50	50	48–50	45–49	43–51	41–51

1 The figure of 378 Bcm for 2000 is substantially higher than the figures in Table 1.3 which even if 'own use and losses' and 'pipeline expansion' are included, only amounts to 360 Bcm. This illustrates the difficulty of working with Russian gas demand figures but does not substantially affect the arguments being advanced here.
* million tons of standard fuel equivalent
** in billion cubic metres (1Bcm = 1.19mtsfe)

Source: *Russian Energy Strategy 2003, Figure 7, p.49*

use of energy' than previously.[150] An important first step would be the abolition of the current system whereby Gazprom continues to allocate the majority of gas to the domestic market on unknown criteria, and its replacement by a more market-oriented mechanism.

The 2003 Russian Energy Strategy identified the growing dominance of natural gas as a 'negative tendency' and projected that gas's share of primary energy demand would fall from 50% to 48% in 2010 and 45–46% in 2020.[151] But in fact, as Table 1.18 shows, the projections range more widely, showing that although the share of gas demand could fall as low as 41% of total energy demand by 2020, it could also retain its current share of 50% of energy demand.

Table 1.18 shows gas demand increasing throughout the period although it does not regain its 1990 level until 2010 at the earliest and, at the lower end of the projections, not even by 2020. Using the mid-point of the 2020 range, gas demand increases at around 1% per annum between 2000 and 2020 compared with an increase in energy demand of 1.5% per annum over the same period.

On a sectoral basis the Strategy projects that residential gas demand will increase, as will demand for non-fuel sectors such as fertilisers. Regionally, demand in Eastern Siberia and the Russian Far East is projected to grow strongly. In power generation, the Strategy foresees a switch from gas-fired to coal-fired (and also nuclear power) generation; backing this up will be an increase in regulated gas prices such that by 2006 these will be above coal prices (which will be set by the interaction of supply and demand), rather than the position for much of the 1990s when gas prices have been substantially lower than those of coal (or oil).[152] In comparison to its coverage on supply, the Strategy has relatively little to say about detailed development of energy demand.

The 'reference scenario' of the International Energy Agency's World Energy Outlook mirrors these projections with gas demand increasing at 1.5–1.7% per annum during the period 2002–2030, with a 1.0–1.3% per annum increase in the power sector and a much faster 1.8–2.7% per annum increase in other sectors, reflecting the more rapid increase in residential gas demand during the late 1990s and early 2000s.[153] The Outlook's 'alternative scenario' has a significantly lower demand horizon with gas demand growth of only 0.7% per annum up to 2030, with very slow growth in the power sector (0.1% per annum) and 1.5% per annum in the other sectors.[154] In absolute terms, in the reference scenario gas demand increases by 194 Bcm during the period 2002–2030 (127 Bcm up to 2020), and in the alternative scenario by 83 Bcm (63 Bcm by 2020). The IEA's alternative scenario for demand is close to the Russian Energy Strategy projections in Table 1.18.

The 2003 Energy Strategy and the IEA's 'alternative scenario' see modest but steady growth in demand of less than 1% per annum during the period 2000–2020. However, during the period 1999–2003, demand appeared to increase by more than 2%/annum (Table 1.13) which, even allowing for the problems inherent in the data (including lack of temperature correction), is a substantially faster growth rate. An important question for projections of gas demand over the next two decades is the extent to which substantially higher prices will exert downward pressure on gas demand. This is likely to be a more important determinant than any switch away from gas to coal and nuclear power which – at least for this author – is profoundly unlikely for financial and logistical reasons, almost irrespective of relative fuel prices over the period.[155] Much more likely – and necessary – is the replacement of old gas-fired power stations with more efficient plant burning less gas.

Possibly the most important issue for the fuel that comprises 50% of primary energy demand is the future of the Russian economy over the next two decades in terms of (1) general economic and market reforms which in turn will determine the speed with which market signals will dictate conservation and efficiency measures, particularly replacement of very old Soviet-era plant; (2) industrial restructuring away from heavy industry and substantial plant replacement in the remaining sectors.

While rapid and radical economic reform during President Putin's second term of office appeared unlikely in 2005, the sheer scale of the Russian energy and gas sector and the degree of inefficiency and scope for low-cost savings give some cause for optimism. The IEA calculated that Russian energy intensity per unit of GDP increased during the 1990s – an extraordinary development considering the huge inefficiencies of the Soviet economy. Russian energy intensity in 2000 was around 2.8 times higher than the average OECD level and more than twice the level of Canada – a country of a similar geographic size and climate.[156] This is a simple indication of the potential for energy efficiency at the macro-level – a commitment which is reflected in government targets. Further supporting the optimistic case for demand reduction was tangible evidence of a move towards higher prices, foreseen both in the Russian Energy Strategy and Russia's WTO commitments to the EU. This trend will be further supported by independent gas producers selling increasing volumes at unregulated prices with the possibility that the entire non-residential gas market could be open to competition at some stage in the 2010s (see Chapter 4).

However, there is also a pessimistic view on gas demand which is held by Russian analysts who suggest that there is no pressing reason for large gas users to save, partly because gas is still cheap relative to plant refurbishment or replacement, and partly because of the inertia in industrial decision-making. According to this view, it is more profitable for owners of large Soviet-era energy-intensive plant to continue to maintain it at low cost, than to make major investment in new plant. Some of this reluctance of owners of industrial plant to make major investments is connected with uncertainty over their property rights. But there is also significant inertia in radically changing a production process which has been established for several decades. According to this argument, the longer a plant can continue functioning with Soviet-era equipment the more profit for the owners of that plant despite rising gas prices.

These entirely valid differences in views as to how Russian gas demand may evolve, hampered by a lack of detailed historical data compiled on a consistent and temperature-corrected basis, are strong barriers to any confident projections. With those caveats, Table 1.19 shows some scenarios from different sources including two simple scenarios constructed by the author:

- a 'business as usual' projection of 1% increase per annum up to 2020;
- a 'market and price reform' projection which produces the same outcome up to 2010 but thereafter demand declines by 1% per annum.

The results amount to a difference in demand of 70 Bcm in 2020, and a change in demand ranging from minus 10 Bcm to plus 61 Bcm

Table 1.19: Russian Gas Demand* Scenarios 2000–2020 (Bcm)

	2003 (actual)	Author's Scenario**		Russia Energy Strategy		IEA WEO 2004***	
		2010	2020	2010	2020	2010	2020
'Business as Usual'	327	351	388	418–446	441–487	406	474
Market and Price Reform	327	351	317				415

* Gas demand is defined as delivered to consumers, it does not include pipeline fuel and losses.
** demand in Western Siberia and western Russia only and therefore not strictly comparable with the Russian Energy Strategy which certainly includes eastern Russia and the IEA which probably does.
*** the figures in the first row are the Agency's 'reference scenario'; in the second row is the 'alternative scenario'.

Sources: Table 1.18; IEA 2004, pp. 423 and 474.

compared with 2003. Given the potential pressure on Russian supply in the late 2010s, demand in this range would remove some of the urgency to make such substantial investments in high-cost production and allow for the possibility of taking increasing risks with imported supplies.

These scenarios also bear some similarity to the Energy Strategy figures in Table 1.18 which − despite the absolute numbers being substantially higher than these projections (largely because of the inclusion of pipeline fuel and losses) − project that 2020 demand will be 50−85 Bcm higher than in 2003. The IEA projections are similar to the Russian Energy Strategy except for the 'alternative scenario', but even this envisages substantial demand growth to 2020.

Taxation

Together with non-payment, one of the most difficult problems for Gazprom in the 1990s was dealing with governments desperate to raise receipts from taxation. In 2003, the company represented 5% of GDP, 5−8% of industrial production and around 15% of foreign currency earnings, which presented a huge target for government. At mid-1998, Gazprom's payments to the State Tax Service represented one-quarter of Federal tax receipts, a figure which had fallen to 20% in 2003.[157]

In July 1998, a crisis was created when the Russian government − desperate for immediate cash and forced to meet IMF conditions on tax collection so that further substantial loans would be granted − ordered the Federal Tax Service to confiscate property at Gazprom's subsidiaries who owed significant amounts of tax. However, when the detail of indebtedness was revealed, it turned out that government organisations owed more to Gazprom in unpaid gas bills than Gazprom owed to the government in taxes.[158] Following that episode, both sides avoided subsequent eruptions by carrying out a monthly mutual cancellation procedure between the company's tax bill and the government's gas debt.[159]

During the non-payment crisis Gazprom was under severe political pressure (particularly from regional political authorities) not to disconnect customers (particularly industrial customers) who did not pay bills.[160] At the same time, the position of the government was that if Gazprom delivered gas to a customer it was liable for tax on those deliveries irrespective of whether payment had been received in cash, in kind, or indeed at all. The requirement to pay taxes irrespective of receivables deepened the losses that Gazprom was making in the domestic market and, when the government proposed taxing Gazprom's European exports – the only sales on which the company was making a profit – new tensions

arose.[161] In the 2000s, the focus moved from non-payment to the level
of gas prices. Gas prices and subsidies to Russian industrial customers
became a controversial issue in negotiations between Russia and the EU
over accession to the World Trade Organisation (WTO), and we return
to this issue in Chapter 3.

In the period up to 2004, all other taxes were dwarfed by excise taxes
on gas which started at a level of 30%, and in 1999 were reduced to
15% for domestic sales and exports to Belarus but remained at 30% for
sales to the rest of the CIS and Europe.[162] In 2000, an export tax of 5%
was introduced on sales of gas to Europe, and this proved to be a pointer
to future trends in the taxation of gas. January 2004 saw a complete
overhaul of the taxation of the gas industry:[163]

- Excise tax was abolished.
- Mineral extraction tax was increased from 16.5% to a flat rate of
  RR107/mcm; in January 2005 this increased again to RR135/
  mcm.
- Export tax was increased from 5% to 30%.
- VAT was reduced from 20% to 18%; in January 2005, VAT was
  abolished for exports to CIS Customs Union countries.

Exactly how these changes affected the tax burden on different companies depended on complex calculations of depreciation allowances and
amendments to the Tax Code, but it seemed likely that the reasoning
behind the changes were the huge increases in European export prices
in the 2000s (arising from very high oil prices), combined with significantly increased, but still relatively low, domestic prices.

The change from excise tax to mineral extraction tax was fiercely at-
tacked by independent producers claiming that this was a plot to put them
out of business, despite statements by the government that they were to
become an increasingly important element in the Russian gas balance. But
the fact that the level of mineral extraction tax was originally proposed
at RR197/mcm and was reduced to RR107/mcm by fierce lobbying
from the independents, reveals government aspirations in respect of
future tax policy for the sector. It also demonstrates the ability of the
government to restrict producer profitability despite increasing prices
in the domestic market.

Summary and Conclusions

The future of Russian gas supply and demand in the twenty-first century will be substantially different from the past – not just the Soviet

past but also the early post-Soviet period. On the supply side more than 90% of Gazprom's production has been sustained by six fields − three supergiant Cenomanian fields in Western Siberia (Urengoy, Yamburg and Medvezhe) and three smaller fields (one of which is in Siberia). In the early 2000s, declines at existing fields have been compensated by a new supergiant Siberian field (Zapolyarnoye) and in 2004 Gazprom's production returned to 1999 levels after a period of decline. During the same period, production from non-Gazprom sources became much more important with the appearance of gas-producing companies, as opposed to oil companies producing gas in association with oil.

The future of Russian gas production will be substantially more complex than in the past and presents the company with difficult choices. On the one hand, its resource endowment is huge, easily adequate for much higher production levels. On the other hand, the company needs to bring on a larger number of smaller fields in the Nadym Pur Taz (NPT) region of Western Siberia simply to offset the decline of 22 Bcm/year at existing fields. These smaller fields involve production of liquids and therefore more complex processing and transportation of different hydrocarbon products than the previous dry gas fields. Gazprom's key strategic production decisions are:

(1)   Whether to develop lower cost offshore Ob/Taz Bay fields first (but with lower production volumes) and if so...

(2)   ...when to move to the supergiant fields of the Yamal Peninsula which can − for the period 2015−2040 (and probably beyond) − play a role in the Russian gas industry similar to that of the NPT over the past quarter century.

However, Gazprom is uncertain about the commercial viability of the Yamal fields because of the tens of billions of dollars of investment needed for their development. Delays in Yamal development increase the medium-term importance of independent gas suppliers which are the obvious domestic bridge between Gazprom's declining 'Soviet gas dowry' and its future production potential. But, in another sharp break with the past, future development of fields by both Gazprom and independents depends on perceptions of the profitability of markets for gas. Only five or six other companies will make a significant difference to Russian gas production over the next decade: the oil companies Lukoil, Surgutneftegaz, Rosneft and TNK/BP; and the independent gas companies Novatek and Itera. Of these, Lukoil and Novatek will have the fastest growth in production. As foreseen in the Russian Energy Strategy 2003 the independent sector is capable of producing 120−135 Bcm in 2015, perhaps up to 150 Bcm. By contrast, Gazprom does not seem likely to be able to maintain production of 530 Bcm beyond the late 2000s – let alone the higher figures from the Russian Energy Strategy in Table 1.9 – until and unless it brings fields on and around the Yamal Peninsula into production and this is not possible until the early 2010s at the earliest. In that situation, non-Gazprom production would be around 20% of total Russian production in the early 2010s.

As for production, the Russian gas market in the mid-2000s presents a sharp break with the past when Gazprom was required to deliver gas to customers with, at best, a considerable subsidy, and, at worst, no payment at all. Although it is always possible that the Russian gas market will fall back into subsidy/payment problems, the 2000s have seen considerable advances towards price levels for industrial customers which, in 2005, ensured profitability of NPT fields currently in production and under development. There is still far to go in developing cost-related prices for customers in different regions of Russia and different categories of customer. Even more time will be needed before the same cost disciplines can be applied to residential customers where the building infrastructure means that there are no metering and temperature controls for individual apartments, and it is politically impossible to cut off customers who, in the winter months, will die without heating.

Probably the greatest unknown factor in the Russian gas market is the point at which price increases and other structural reforms will produce a demand response in a sector where conservation and efficiency have been entirely lacking thus far. The key judgements appear to be whether price increases will in themselves provide sufficient market signals to cause demand reduction – and if so what level of prices this would require – or whether large-scale plant replacement requires more fundamental legal and structural reforms than are currently anticipated. Replacement of Soviet-era plant will embody huge energy savings, but the timing of that replacement remains uncertain and subject to very different interpretations of incentives likely to be brought to bear on owners of that plant.

In the 2000s, the Russian gas market is therefore coming to resemble a 'market' at least in the sense that the majority of gas delivered to customers is paid for at prices that enable the gas to be delivered at a profit to the producer, and that if customers fail to pay their bills they can expect to be disconnected. While this may seem a rather unambitious definition of market development, it represents a quantum leap forward towards commercialisation in respect of the past, and lays the foundation for future competition between producers.

Appendix 1.1: Russian and International Classifications of Reserves[164]

Russian Reserves

The estimation of reserves of natural gas, gas condensate and crude oil can be broken down into two components: (i) geological reserves, or the quantities of natural gas, gas condensate and crude oil contained in the subsoil and (ii) extractable reserves, or the portion of geological reserves whose extraction from the subsoil as of the date the reserves are calculated is economically efficient given market conditions and rational use of modern extraction equipment and technologies and taking into account compliance with the requirements of subsoil and environmental protection. The Russian reserves system is based solely on an analysis of the geological attributes of reserves. Explored reserves are represented by categories A, B, and C_1; preliminary estimated reserves are represented by category C_2; potential resources are represented by category C_3; and forecasted resources are represented by the categories D_1 and D_2. Natural gas reserves in categories A, B and C_1 are considered to be fully extractable. For reserves of oil and gas condensate, a predicted coefficient of extraction is calculated based on geological and technical factors. This appendix provides information only about explored reserves, or reserves in categories A, B and C_1.

Category A reserves are calculated on the part of a deposit drilled in accordance with an approved development project for the oil or natural gas field. They represent reserves that have been analysed in sufficient detail to define comprehensively the type, shape and size of the deposit; the level of hydrocarbon saturation, the reservoir type, the nature of changes in the reservoir characteristics, the hydrocarbon saturation of the productive strata of the deposit, the content and characteristics of the hydrocarbons, and the major features of the deposit that determine the conditions of its development (mode of operations, well productivity, strata pressure, natural gas, gas condensate and oil balance, hydro and piezo-conductivity and other features).

Category B represents the reserves of a deposit (or portion thereof), the oil or gas content of which has been determined on the basis of commercial flows of oil or gas obtained in wells at various hypsometric depths. The type, shape and size of the deposit, the effective oil and gas saturation depth and type of the reservoir, the nature of changes in the reservoir characteristics, the oil and gas saturation of the productive strata of the deposit, the composition and characteristics of oil, gas and gas condensate under in-situ and standard conditions and other parameters, and the major features of the deposit that determine the conditions of its development have been studied in sufficient detail to draw up a project to develop the deposit. Category B reserves are computed for a deposit (or a portion thereof) that has been drilled in accordance with either a trial industrial development project in the case of a natural gas field or an approved technological development scheme in the case of an oil field.

Category C_1 represents the reserves of a deposit (or of a portion thereof), the oil or gas content of which has been determined on the basis of commercial flows of oil or gas obtained in wells (with some of the wells having been probed by a formation tester) and positive results of geological and geophysical exploration of non-probed wells. The type, shape and size of the deposit and the formation structure of the oil- and gas-bearing reservoirs have been determined from the results of drilling exploration and production wells and by those geological and geophysical exploration techniques that have been field-tested for the applicable area. The lithological content, reservoir type and characteristics, oil and gas saturation, oil displacement ratio and effective oil and gas saturation depth of the productive strata have been studied based on drill cores and geological and geophysical exploration techniques. The composition and characteristics of oil, gas and gas condensate under in-situ and standard conditions have been studied on the basis of well-testing data. In the case of an oil and gas deposit, the commercial potential of its oil-bearing fringe has been determined. Well productivity, hydro- and piezo-conductivity of the stratum, stratum pressures and oil, gas and gas condensate temperatures and yields have been studied on the basis of well testing and well exploration results. The hydro-geological and geocryological conditions have been determined on the basis of well drilling results and comparisons with neighbouring explored fields. Category C_1 reserves are computed on the basis of results of geological exploration work and production drilling and must have been studied in sufficient detail to yield data from which to draw up either a trial industrial development project in the case of a natural gas field or a technological development scheme in the case of an oil field.

Society of Petroleum Engineers (SPE) International Standards

While the Russian reserves system focuses on the actual physical presence of hydrocarbons in geological formations, and reserves are estimated based on the probability of such physical presence, SPE International Standards take into account not only the probability that hydrocarbons are physically present in a given geological formation but also the economic viability of recovering the reserves (including such factors as exploration and drilling costs, ongoing production costs, transportation costs, taxes, prevailing prices for the products, and other factors that influence the economic viability of a given deposit). Under SPE International Standards, reserves are classified as 'proved,' 'probable' and 'possible,' based on both geological and commercial factors.

Proved reserves include reserves that are confirmed with a high degree of certainty through an analysis of the development history and/or volume method analysis of the relevant geological and engineering data. Proved reserves are those that, based on the available evidence and taking into account technical and economic factors, have a better than 90% chance of being produced.

Probable reserves are those reserves in which hydrocarbons have been located within the geological structure with a lesser degree of certainty because fewer wells have been drilled and/or certain operational tests have not been conducted. Probable reserves are those reserves that, on the available evidence and taking into account technical and economic factors, have a better than 50% chance of being produced. An evaluation of proved and probable natural gas reserves naturally involves multiple uncertainties. The accuracy of any reserves evaluation depends on the quality of available information and engineering and geological interpretation. Based on the results of drilling, testing and production after the audit date, reserves may be significantly restated upwards or downwards. Changes in the price of natural gas, gas condensate or oil may also affect proved and probable reserves estimates, as well as estimates of future net revenues and present worth, because the reserves are evaluated, and the future net revenues and present worth are estimated, based on prices and costs as of the audit date.

Differences between SPE International Standards and Securities and Exchange Commission (SEC) Standards

DeGolyer and MacNaughton has conducted evaluations of Gazprom's fields using SPE International Standards, which differ in certain material respects from SEC Standards. The principal differences include certainty of existence and duration of licence.

Certainty of Existence. Under SPE International Standards, reserves in undeveloped drilling sites that are located more than one well location from a commercial producing well may be classified as proved reserves if there is 'reasonable certainty' that they exist. Under SEC Standards, it must be 'demonstrated with certainty' that reserves exist before they may be classified as proved reserves. In their evaluations of proved reserves, DeGolyer and MacNaughton has applied the stricter SEC Standards with respect to certainty of existence.

Duration of Licence. Under SPE International Standards, proved reserves are projected to the economic production life of the evaluated fields. Under SEC Standards, oil and gas deposits may not be classified as proved reserves if they will be recovered after the expiration of a current licence period unless the licence holder has the right to renew the licence and there is a demonstrated history of licence renewal. Gazprom prepares and submits for government approval development plans for its fields based on the economic life of the field, even where this life exceeds the primary term of the associated licence. The company believes that it is in material compliance with the licence agreements, and intends to request extending them to the full economic lives of the associated fields upon the expiration of their primary terms.

Appendix 1.2: The Geology of Gas Basins in Western Siberia

Geological time periods

The Cretaceous geological period is divided into two parts, Upper and Lower (if referring to rock) or Late and Early (if referring to time). In European geology, the lower (earlier) half of the Lower Cretaceous is collectively called the Neocomian Epoch. The Neocomian Epoch extended between (roughly) 125 to 145 million years ago. It, in turn, is divided into four (three by the count of some) ages: Berriasian, Valanginian, Hauterivian and Berremian, each about 5 million years long. These are divisions of the geologic time scale that are recognised all over the world. There are Valanginian age rocks that produce oil and gas in Australia.

Most of the oil/gas/condensate reservoirs in the northern part of West Siberia are in the Neocomian, some even a little older (and deeper) in the very upper part of the Upper Jurassic (right above the Bazhenov shale). The deepest significant oil/gas/condensate reservoirs are in the Achimov Formation, which was deposited at the very end of the Late

Jurassic through the Berriasian. Above it are the Megion, then Vartov formations; these are Berriasian, through Valanginian and Hauterivian in age, so they were deposited over about a 15 million-year time period. The Cenomanian age were deposited about 30–40 million years later and are at 1,000 to about 1,400 m.

Cenomanian gas

The gas fields of northern West Siberia are 'two-storied.' At approximately 1,100 metres below the surface are the principal reservoirs. These contain roughly two-thirds of the region's gas. The reservoirs are sandstones of Late Cretaceous (Cenomanian) age, which have very good production characteristics; wells can produce in excess of a million cubic metres per day. Gas in the shallow reservoirs is 'dry,' i.e. it contains no associated oil or natural gas liquids. The gas is dry because it is biogenic methane generated in the same way as 'swamp gas', by the bacterial degradation of the remains of plant matter accumulated across a vast lowland swamp that prevailed over northern West Siberia in Late Cretaceous time. As a result of the shallow depth, good reservoir quality and absence of liquids, Soviet and then Russian engineers have produced nearly all West Siberian gas from the Cenomanian reservoirs at a small number of fields.

Neocomian gas

Approximately 1,300 metres deeper, at the same gigantic fields, is a second set of reservoirs, containing about one-third of West Siberia's gas. They are in rocks of Early Cretaceous (Neocomian) age, deposited 40 million years before the shallow reservoirs. These accumulations are, however, heavily laden with hydrocarbon liquids – both crude oil and lighter liquids. Very substantial volumes of hydrocarbon liquids are present in the deep reservoirs of the gas fields. However, the deeper gas and liquid resources in West Siberia have been little exploited due to greater depth (and hence higher drilling cost), much more complex geology and a more challenging producing environment. The liquids and gas in the Neocomian reservoirs are thermogenic, or formed from the thermal cracking of marine organic matter in the same Late Jurassic (Bazhenov) shale that source the massive oil fields in central West Siberia to the south.

All of the reservoirs in the Neocomian package of rock (usually from about 2000–3000 m deep), and there are hundreds of them (several dozen at Urengoy field alone), are saturated with hydrocarbon liquids, as well as gas. The liquids often include crude oil, but almost universally, lighter natural gas liquids. These liquids were generated in the underlying Bazhenov shale. The Bazhenov shale (of latest Jurassic age, right under the Achimov), is what generated the major oil fields to the south. In the north, because of the regional dip of beds in West Siberia, they were buried more deeply than in the south. This exposed the organic matter in the Bazhenov (and the shaley parts of the Achimov, Megion and Vartov) to enough extra heat and pressure to crack beyond crude oil (found in the south) to a mixture of crude oil, natural gas liquids and gas-phase natural gas. There is also a chemical change in the organic matter, going north, that favours lighter hydrocarbon liquids.

Source: drawn from material provided by Dr John Grace, Earth Science Associates, Long Beach, California.

CHAPTER 2

CIS GAS TRADE AND TRANSIT

Trade and Transit in the 1990s and Early 2000s

Following the break-up of the Soviet Union in 1991, geoeconomics and geopolitics moved to the top of the agenda in terms of trade and transit of former Soviet gas. As far as the former Soviet states were concerned, formal commercial relationships needed to be created, where none had existed, in a climate of unrealistic commercial expectations and resentments which had been barely submerged in opaque Soviet politics. For the Russian Federation, two distinct markets for gas exports evolved: the 'near abroad' CIS countries or former Soviet republics; and the 'far abroad' countries of Europe.

The creation of commercial relationships between newly emerging sovereign states, which, with one significant exception, had previously treated gas trade as an internal transfer of energy without financial significance, has been a protracted and painful process. Two sets of interrelated issues – sales (imports and exports) and transit – have concentrated the minds of companies and politicians in the search for bilateral solutions between Russia and the former republics. This chapter focuses principally on the bilateral relationships between Russia and other former republics, it does not deal in any detail with other bilateral CIS gas trade relationships (excepting the Turkmen-Ukraine trade), notably those between the Central Asian republics.

Transit of gas is a key issue in both inter-republic trade, and trade with Europe. There are two essential aspects to this transit: (1) All pipelines taking Central Asian gas exports outside the region pass through Russia,[1] putting Gazprom in complete control of those supplies. (2) In the past, virtually all Russian gas exports to Europe needed to transit through Ukraine, and around 15% also passed through Moldova. With the opening of the Yamal pipeline in the late 1990s (see Chapter 3), Belarus became an increasingly important transit country (Map 2.1).

The break-up of the USSR caused immediate and continuing problems in gas trade between all the republics. The essence of these problems was a demand for gas and transit tariffs to be paid for at prices and in currencies that (with the possible exception of Russia) none of the recipients could afford. Refusal and/or inability to pay resulted in the amassing of huge debts to suppliers (principally Russia and Turkmenistan) and periodic cutbacks in supply because of non-payment. When Gazprom reduced deliveries because of non-payment, this action caused not only hardship but, in cases where gas has been in transit to European markets, the diversion of supply intended for those markets. For European observers, the most visible manifestation of these problems has been in Ukraine and Belarus, but similar events have been common in trade between Central Asian and Caucasus countries.[2] These transit problems account for Gazprom's repeated attempts to gain ownership and control of the pipeline networks through which its gas travels to Europe.

This chapter divides the former republics into three groups:

1. Central Asian exporting countries – Turkmenistan, Kazakhstan and Uzbekistan – which are becoming increasingly important sources of gas supply for CIS countries, including Russia. Kazakhstan and Uzbekistan are also transit countries, as of course is Russia itself.
2. Importing countries in the Caucasus – Azerbaijan, Armenia and Georgia – which are small-scale importers of Russian and Central Asian gas and have opportunities to both produce gas and import from other sources over the next decade.
3. Importing countries that are also transit countries for Russian exports to Europe: Ukraine, Belarus and Moldova, which receive the majority of Russian and Central Asian deliveries to the CIS, command the transit routes for the majority of Russian gas exports to Europe.

This division is not entirely satisfactory as some of the 'importers' also export gas and vice versa. Nor does it include the Baltic countries – former Soviet republics which became members of the European Union in 2004 – which are more appropriate to include in a discussion of European exports, despite the fact that logistically, they remain very much part of the former Soviet gas system. For this reason they feature in this historical overview of trade between former Soviet republics (and again in Chapter 3).

Aside from bilateral trade between countries, there is also the important issue of the companies that are conducting the trade and transit of gas within the CIS. Up to 1994, Russian trade with CIS countries was handled exclusively by Gazprom; after that date, fragmentation of suppliers presented increased statistical challenges. As far as Gazprom's trade relationships are concerned, all business with CIS countries is subject to long-term intergovernmental agreements signed by presidents and/or prime ministers.[3] These agreements (which may then be supplemented by additional protocols) provide a framework for sales, transit, prices and tariffs, and sometimes other issues such as storage and the formation of joint ventures. While year-to-year commercial details are negotiated by the commercial parties, the intergovernmental agreements provide a framework to which those parties can always refer and appeal to their political leaders to enforce. For this reason, politics are never very far away from the negotiating table in CIS gas trade.

Tables 2.1 and 2.2 present data on deliveries of Russian and Central Asian gas to CIS countries from the break-up of the Soviet Union to 2004.[4] Table 2.1 shows a sharp fall in deliveries after 1992 most of which was accounted for by the reduction in Gazprom's exports to Ukraine. Itera commenced exports in 1994 although data are not available until 1996. Given that by 1996 Itera was delivering 17.5 Bcm to Ukraine, the company may have compensated substantially for the shortfall of Gazprom deliveries during 1994−95.

Table 2.1: Gazprom Exports to Former Soviet Republics, 1991–95 (Bcm)

	1991	1992	1993	1994	1995
Ukraine	60.7	77.3	54.9	57.0	52.9
Belarus	14.3	17.6	16.4	14.3	12.9
Moldova	2.5	3.4	3.2	3.0	3.0
Georgia				0.4	
Lithuania	6.0	3.2	1.9	2.1	2.5
Latvia	3.2	1.6	1.0	1.1	1.2
Estonia	1.9	0.9	0.4	0.6	0.7
Kazakhstan		1.7	1.1	0.4	
TOTAL*	90.0	106.4	78.6	78.8	73.2

*   totals do not add

Source: Gazprom statistics for respective years

A comparison of Tables 2.1 and 2.2 shows that during the period 1993−97 Gazprom deliveries to the former republics declined from 79 Bcm to 72 Bcm. A turning point was reached in 1998, a year when Russian economic crisis coincided with the virtual cessation of Turkmen gas exports. Gazprom deliveries fell to just over 50 Bcm and, up to 2002, did not exceed that figure, falling to less than 40 Bcm in 2001 when Itera's deliveries exceeded those of Gazprom by a wide margin. Indeed by 2001, aside from Gazprom's deliveries to Ukraine, Belarus

Table 2.2: Gazprom and Itera Gas Deliveries to Former Soviet Republics (excluding Russia), 1996–2004 (Bcm)

	1996			1997			1998		
	Gazprom	*Itera*	*Total*	*Gazprom*	*Itera*	*Total*	*Gazprom*	*Itera*	*Total*
Ukraine	51.0	17.48	68.48	49.2	13.55	62.75	30.5	22.88	53.38
Belarus	13.7	-	15.2	15.2	0.48	15.50	14.7	1.11	15.81
Moldova	3.2	0.29	3.49	3.2	0.40	3.60	2.9	0.43	3.33
Georgia		0.89	0.89	0.1	0.87	0.97	0	0.92	0.92
Armenia		1.12	1.12		1.44	1.44	0	1.51	1.51
Azerbaijan		-					0	0	0
Lithuania	2.6	0.05	2.65	2.2	0.32	2.52	2.2	0	2.2
Latvia	1.1	-	1.1	1.1	0.30	1.40	1.3	0.30	1.60
Estonia	0.8	-	0.8	0.8	-	0.8	0.8	0	0.8
Kazakhstan		3.05	3.05	0.1	1.89	1.99	0	1.95	1.95
Uzbekistan		2.32	2.32		0.61	0.61	0	0	0
TOTAL	73.0	23.20	96.20	72.1	19.84	91.94	52.4	29.1	81.5

	1999			2000			2001		
	Gazprom	*Itera*	*Total*	*Gazprom*	*Itera*	*Total*	*Gazprom*	*Itera*	*Total*
Ukraine*	29.6	31.1	60.7	27.2	32.41	59.61	21.9	34.8	47.6
Belarus	12.2	4.3	16.5	10.8	5.78	16.58	11.6	5.10	17.8
Moldova	2.1	0.7	2.8	1.8	0.62	2.42	2.1	0.6	2.0
Georgia		1.1	1.1		1.00	1		1.0	1.5
Armenia		1.3	1.3		1.40	1.4		1.4	1.4
Azerbaijan					0.26			3.1	
Lithuania	1.8	0.6	2.4	2.0	0.57	2.57	2.2	0.5	2.8
Latvia	1.0	0.3	1.3	1.0	0.36	1.36	1.1	0.4	1.7
Estonia	0.5	0.2	0.7	0.6	0.19	0.79	0.7	0.2	1.3
Kazakhstan		1.7	1.7		2.66	2.66		2.9	3.5
Uzbekistan					0.22				
TOTAL	47.2	41.3	88.5	43.4	44.99	88.87	39.6	50.0	89.6

	2002			2003			2004 (preliminary data)		
	Gazprom	*Itera*	*Total*	*Gazprom***	*Itera*	*Total*	*Gazprom***	*Others*	*Total*
Ukraine*	25.9	30.4	56.3	26	0.3	26.3	34.34		
Belarus	10.2	5.9	16.1***	10.2	6.2	16.4	10.21	8	18.21
Moldova	2.1	0.2	2.3	2.4	0.26	2.66			
Georgia		0.8	0.8	0.2	0.75	1.05			
Armenia		1.1	1.1	0.3	0.91	1.21			
Azerbaijan		3.9	3.9		4.1	4.1			
Lithuania	2.4	0.3	2.7	2.9		2.9	2.93		
Latvia	1.1	0.3	1.4	1.2	0.65	1.85	1.5		
Estonia	0.6	Negl	0.6	0.9		0.9	0.92		
Kazakhstan		2	2		0.91	0.91	0.82		
TOTAL	42.3	44.9	87.2	44.1	14.08	58.27	52.47	8	60.47

Table 2.2: Continued

*   Itera figures for Ukraine do not distinguish between sales of gas and shipments of Turkmen gas. What appears to be a very sharp reduction in Russian gas supplies in 2003 in fact reflects only the removal of Itera as shipper of Turkmen gas in that year. The sharp reduction of Russian supplies occurred after 1998 when Itera began to deliver Turkmen gas first as supplier and then as shipper.

**   not including Central Asian gas supplied under contract with Gazexport (see Table 2.7)

***   independent companies supplied at least 0.6 Bcm in addition to this figure

Sources: Gazprom and Itera data.

Table 2.3: Imports of Natural Gas by CIS Countries from CIS Countries 2000–2003* (Bcm)

	2000	*2001*	*2002*	*2003*
Azerbaijan	0.05	3.34	3.94	4.08
Armenia	1.38	0.99	1.07	1.21
Belarus	17.11	17.27	17.58	18.11
Georgia	0.92	0.96	0.81	1.01
Kazakhstan	4.22	4.23	8.18	8.67
Kyrgyzstan	0.65	0.67	0.86	0.70
Moldova	1.04	1.15	1.15	1.24
Russia*	12.49	3.75	6.85	8.33
Tajikistan	0.73	0.57	0.49	0.53
Ukraine	59.22	56.94	56.23	55.27
TOTAL	97.81	89.87	97.16	99.15

*   in all countries other than Russia, imports were exclusively from CIS countries, the figures here are Russian imports only from CIS countries; total Russian imports were up to 0.5 Bcm higher each year

Source: *Statistika SNG*, Statitisticheskii Bulleten' 7 (334), Mezhgosudarstvennaya Statisticheskii Komitet Sodruzhestvo Nezavisimikh Gosudarstv, April 2004, Table 2.1.7, pp. 49–50; and Statitisticheskii Bulleten' 9 (336), May 2004, Tables 2.1.27 and 2.1.28, pp. 79-80.

and Moldova – a large part of which were in exchange for transit services – Gazprom appeared to have almost withdrawn from CIS gas trade. It will be seen below that this trend decisively reversed in the post-2001 period. There was also a substantial fall in deliveries to the Baltic countries (see Chapter 3 for more details).

Table 2.4: Exports of Natural Gas by CIS Countries 2000–2003* (Bcm)

	2000	*2001*	*2002*	*2003*
Kazakhstan				
total exports	5.21	5.54	10.44	11.01
exports to CIS	5.21	5.54	10.10	9.38
Russia				
total exports	193.86	181.16	185.53	189.38
exports to CIS	60.05	49.23	51.29	47.33
Turkmenistan				
total exports		37.34	39.30	43.40
exports to CIS		32.81	32.01	30.72
Ukraine				
total exports	2.87	1.02	1.59	5.33
exports to CIS	0.13	Negl	Negl	Negl

* in neither this table nor Table 2.3 does this source give figures for Uzbekistan

Source: *Statistika SNG*, Statitisticheskii Bulleten' 7 (334), Mezhgosudarstvennaya Statisticheskii Komitet Sodruzhestvo Nezavisimikh Gosudarstv, April 2004, Table 2.1.7, pp. 49-50.

Table 2.5: Inter-Republic Natural Gas Trade Between CIS Countries, 2003 (Bcm)

	Kazakhstan	*Russia*	*Turkmenistan*	*Uzbekistan*	*TOTAL*
Azerbaijan	0.72		3.36		4.08
Armenia		1.21			1.21
Belarus		18.11			18.11
Georgia		1.01			1.01
Kazakhstan		6.08	1.29	1.30	8.67
Kyrgyzstan				0.70	0.70
Moldova	0.50	0.73			1.24
Russia	7.06			1.27	8.33
Tajikistan				0.53	0.53
Ukraine		26.43	26.47	2.38	55.27
TOTAL	8.28	53.57	31.12	6.18	99.15

Source: *Statistika SNG*, Statitisticheskii Bulleten' 9 (336), Mezhgosudarstvennaya Statisticheskii Komitet Sodruzhestvo Nezavisimikh Gosudarstv, May 2004, Table 2.1.27, p.79.

Tables 2.3 and 2.4 show imports and exports of gas by CIS countries for the period 2000–03; Table 2.5 gives details of trade between all the republics for 2003. Inter-republic gas trade in the 2000s reached a level of 90–100 Bcm/year. During the 2000s Ukraine accounted for well over half – and Ukraine and Belarus for more than three-quarters – of total CIS gas imports. The 2003 'snapshot' in Table 2.5 shows that Russia and Turkmenistan accounted for more than 85% of total exports; of the remainder, Uzbek exports focused exclusively on Central Asia and the majority of Kazakh exports were to Russia.[5] For some inexplicable reason (given that the source is the main CIS statistical office) Uzbek data are not available for Tables 2.3 and 2.4.[6] Russian deliveries to Ukraine and Belarus, and Turkmen deliveries to Ukraine are the three largest bilateral trading relationships and accounted for 72% of inter-republic trade in 2003.

Central Asian Exporting Countries: Turkmenistan, Kazakhstan and Uzbekistan

Turkmenistan

During the Soviet era, Russia and other republics received significant quantities of gas from Turkmenistan. This was the only intra-Soviet gas trade to which significant monetary value could be attributed. In return for supplying volumes of around 90 Bcm to other Soviet republics, including Russia, Turkmenistan received a hard currency 'quota' for gas it was deemed to have exported to Europe. During the period 1990−93 for which data are available, this quota varied between 15 and 25% of the volumes supplied to former Republics.[7] How these volumes were determined and translated into revenues and in what currency they were paid for, is not known. However, the arrangement began to break down almost immediately following the break-up of the Union, and had ceased by 1994.

After the break-up, Turkmenistan demanded payment for its gas from all former republics, including Russia, in hard currency at 'world prices'. There followed a catalogue of disputes over non-payment and non-delivery of gas between Turkmenistan and all its former Soviet customers, of which the problems with the Ukraine were the most serious since volumes of up to 25 Bcm/year were involved.[8]

A variety of methods were attempted to find a new basis for regularising Turkmen deliveries to Ukraine and other former republics. Notable among these was the formation in November 1995 of Turkmenrosgaz – a joint venture between Gazprom (45%), Turkmenneftegaz (51%) and Itera (4%) – which was given the right to handle all sales of Turkmen gas.[9] As payment became an increasing problem in the former republics and commerce retreated to the barter basis reminiscent of Soviet times, Gazprom increasingly allowed the trading company Itera

Table 2.6: Turkmen Gas Production 1991–2004 (Bcm)

Year	Production
1991	84.3
1992	60.1
1993	65.3
1994	35.7
1995	32.3
1996	35.2
1997	17.3
1998	13.3
1999	22.9
2000	46.5
2001	51.4
2002	53.5
2003	59.1
2004	58.6

Sources: 1991–1999 from: Turkmenistan, *Vozrozhdeniya Geniem Velikovo Turkmenbashi*, Ashkhabat: 2002, p.23; 2000–2003 from David Cameron Wilson, *CIS and East European Energy Databook*, 2004, Eastern Bloc Research, Table 3, p.97; 2004 from *Central Asia Energy Monthly*, January 2005, p.2.

to take over Russian trade with the former republics. During the mid to late 1990s, Itera's view of the viability of trade at different prices was the key factor determining the level of exports.

Turkmen gas exports outside the Central Asian region were stopped in March 1997 and the Turkmen government unilaterally dissolved Turkmenrosgaz due to debts which had not been paid by Itera with respect to deliveries of gas to Ukraine.[10] A meeting in August 1997 between the Russian prime minister, the Turkmen president and Gazprom's chairman failed to agree a commercial basis for a resumption of Turkmen gas exports to former Soviet republics (principally the Ukraine) signifying that these markets would henceforth need to be supplied with Russian gas; although there were reports that Uzbekistan began to export gas to Ukraine in 1998 using Itera as the shipper.[11] A further meeting between the parties in January 1998 failed because of the same disagreements on price.[12] Table 2.6 shows that, deprived of export markets, Turkmen production fell to very low levels in 1997–98.[13] Meanwhile Turkmenistan commenced exports to Iran, and signed a framework agreement with the Turkish company Botas to deliver 30 Bcm/yr to Turkey via a pipeline across the Caspian Sea and Azerbaijan (the Trans-Caspian pipeline) with Shell and Bechtel as co-sponsors.[14] Gazprom viewed the prospect of the Trans-Caspian pipeline as direct competition for its Blue Stream pipeline to Turkey and, in response, accelerated the development of the latter project (see Chapter 3).[15]

In January 1999, after a stoppage of nearly two years, Turkmen deliveries to Ukraine recommenced with an agreement for 20 Bcm/year, at a price of $36/mcm at the Turkmen border paid 40% cash and 60% barter. Itera was appointed as the shipper of this gas through Kazakhstan, Uzbekistan and Russia to Ukraine, and was paid for its services in gas.[16] But deliveries were halted in April when Ukrainian importers, already $100m in debt, were unable to pay for any more gas.

In December 1999, Gazprom Chief Executive Rem Vyakhirev officially apologised to the President of Turkmenistan and the Turkmen people for 'anti-Turkmen sentiments' which had been attributed to him in the Russian press over the previous two years.[17] The transcript of the meeting strongly suggested that Vyakhirev had few corporate motivations for the meeting (which reached the same deadlock over pricing) but had been under severe pressure from the Russian government – headed by prime minister (soon to be President) Vladimir Putin – to mend fences with the Turkmen President, not least because the latter was forging a close relationship with the American government and companies over the Trans-Caspian pipeline.

The Gazprom CEO eventually signed an agreement with Turkmenistan for the sale of 20 Bcm/yr to Russia, which press reports suggested was priced at $36/mcm (although it later transpired there had been no agreement on prices).[18] The Gazprom CEO gave two reasons for signing the agreement: non-payment in the domestic market and unauthorised diversions of gas by Ukraine.[19] By spring 2000, a bilateral commission comprising Gazprom, Itera and the Turkmen Deputy Prime Minister was formed to draft a long-term, large-scale gas agreement between Russia and Turkmenistan – up to 50 Bcm/year for 30 years, with Turkmenistan's president Niyazov expressing a willingness to export up to 100 Bcm/year.[20] This was further reinforced at a meeting in May between the presidents of the two countries when it was announced that Russia would import 30 Bcm of Turkmen gas in 2001, 40 Bcm in 2002 and 50–60 Bcm thereafter. However, again there was no sign of any agreement on prices, with the Russian president remarking that prices 'are an issue for commercial talks' (strongly suggesting that what had taken place was purely political).[21]

Perhaps not coincidentally, these offers of substantially increased deliveries to Russia emerged as Turkmenistan's Trans-Caspian pipeline project began to face major problems. With that pipeline needing to run through Azerbaijan – and the Azeris having established their own major resource of Shah Deniz gas to be developed jointly by an international consortium headed by BP and Statoil – it was natural that a substantial part of the Trans-Caspian capacity should be reserved for Azeri gas.[22] However, this proposal did not please the Turkmen president who suggested that Turkmen gas could reach Turkey by a number of routes, of which the Trans-Caspian was only one (Russia and Iran being the others). But Azerbaijan held all the key negotiating cards given that its own gas reserves are nearer to the Turkish (and European) market, that Turkmen gas needed to transit through its country, and that it was supported politically by the United States.[23] By mid-2000, the international partners in the Trans-Caspian Pipeline quietly pulled out of the project and nothing more was heard of it.[24]

In the summer of 2000, a preliminary agreement was initialled by Turkmen and Ukrainian Deputy Prime Ministers for 20 Bcm to be imported in the second half of that year, followed by imports of 50 Bcm/year for the period 2001–2010. The price was \$42/mcm at the Turkmen border, although the 50:50 cash/barter provision in the price significantly reduced the cash element. This was immediately criticised by Ukraine's President Kuchma for being far too expensive and the two presidents committed themselves to work towards a mutually agreeable price, including a settlement of Ukraine's gas debt to Turkmenistan.[25]

An agreement was signed by the two presidents in October 2000 for 5 Bcm to be delivered before the end of that year, and 30 Bcm in 2001, at a price of \$40/mcm (50% cash/50% barter). As a result of past non-payment, the agreement included provision for a \$7 million insurance fund and weekly advance payments.[26] This new Ukrainian contract caused Turkmen supplies to Itera to be halted in January 2001 – when only 6 Bcm out of the 10 Bcm agreed between the parties in the August 2000 contract had been delivered. The Turkmen side was demanding that the Russian company match the payment terms agreed with Ukraine (a significant increase compared with the \$38/mcm 60% Barter/40% cash that Itera was paying) and this was agreed in February 2002.[27] Although this contract was referred to in the press as 'exports to Russia', Itera probably sold the gas to CIS countries – Ukraine, Belarus and the Caucasus countries. In May 2001, the two presidents signed a bilateral contract covering the period 2002–06 for a total delivery of 250 Bcm with an expectation of 40 Bcm being delivered in 2002, 50 Bcm in 2003 and increasing thereafter. The price had been increased to \$42/mcm with 50% cash and the remainder to be paid by projects connected with the Turkmen gas industry.[28] The date at which the agreement concludes, 2006, is significant, as we shall see below.

Remarkably, given the history of the trade during the 1990s, the Turkmen-Ukraine contract successfully delivered 30 Bcm in 2001 and, with up to 40 Bcm/year of deliveries agreed up to 2006, discussions recommenced regarding the elusive long-term contract between Turkmenistan and Russia.[29] These continued sporadically and inconclusively throughout 2002, along with discussions about the modernisation of the Central Asia-Centre pipeline system (Map 2.1) which carries (mainly)

Map 2.1: Major Gas Fields and Pipelines of Central Asia and the Caspian Region

Turkmen and Uzbek gas in Russia and thence to Ukraine and Caucasus countries, built to carry 100 Bcm/year during the Soviet era but reduced to less than half of that capacity by the early 2000s due to lack of maintenance and refurbishment. In October, a meeting between the Ukrainian and Turkmen presidents announced a contract for 2003 for 36 Bcm and a price increase to $44/mcm (50% cash/50% barter) with the renewal of Itera's 10 Bcm/year contract on the same terms.[30] But at the end of 2002, Itera was replaced as the shipper of Turkmen gas by Eural Transgas (see below), an event which did not seem to cause any problems in the conduct of exports.

In April 2003, presidents Putin and Niyazov finally signed the long-term gas agreement that had been conceived at the December 1999 meeting between Chairman Vyakhirev and the Turkmenbashi. Covering a period of 25 years (2003–2028) the agreement contained two main time scales:[31]

– 2004–2006 when Gazprom would purchase 4–10 Bcm at a price of $44/mcm, 50% cash/50% barter. Specific volumes were 4–6 Bcm in 2004, 6–7 Bcm in 2005, and 10 Bcm in 2006.
– Post-2006 when volumes would increase to 60–70 Bcm in 2007, 63–73 Bcm in 2008, and 70–80 Bcm in 2009 and thereafter. According to Gazprom CEO Alexey Miller: 'Russia and Turkmenistan would change over to payment for gas at world prices using a payment formula that is used in contracts with western partners, which is tied to the oil product basket'; this commercial development would be of great significance if it was to happen.

Given how difficult it had been to reach this agreement, it is significant that the 2004, relatively small, volumes were traded using the price formula initially agreed with Ukraine in 2000; no pricing arrangements were agreed post-2006. The increase in volumes between the two time scales – up to 10 Bcm/year scheduled for 2006 and 60–80 Bcm/year thereafter – was significant because the contract between Ukraine and Turkmenistan finishes at the end of 2006. Thus the long-term Gazprom-Turkmen contract envisaged that Gazprom would take over the supply of Turkmen gas to Ukraine when the current bilateral contract between the countries expired. These arrangements were intended to bring to an end the period of seven years during which independent companies – first Itera and then Eural Transgas – played a major role in the purchase, sale and/or shipping of 30–40 Bcm of Turkmen gas through Central Asian and Gazprom pipelines to Ukraine.[32]

In early December 2004, the Turkmen authorities requested their

Russian and Ukrainian counterparts to raise the price of gas to $60/ mcm for 2005.[33] On December 31, flows in the pipeline were abruptly halted. This precipitated a rapid negotiation between Ukraine and Turkmenistan allowing flows to restart to Ukraine on January 3, 2005 at a price of $58/mcm (50:50 cash/barter).[34] Deliveries to Russia did not resume until May 2005 after negotiations between Turkmen President Niyazov and Gazprom Chairman Miller established that the price of $44/mcm would remain for 2005−06 but would be 100% cash rather than 50/50 cash/barter. Prices for the larger volumes due to start in 2007 are due to be negotiated by mid-2006.[35] Deliveries to Russia remained suspended through April 2005 with press reports that deliveries for 2005 and 2006 would be 4 Bcm and 7 Bcm respectively, significantly less than envisaged in the April 2003 agreement.[36]

The change in the Turkmen export price to $44/mcm on a cash-only basis at the Turkmen border caused Turkmen gas to become uncompetitive in the Russian market. When transit charges through Kazakhstan and Uzbekistan − variously estimated at $17−21/mcm in 2004 − are added, the price at the Russian border rises to $61−65/mcm. It might be acceptable on a temporary basis (i.e. for 2005/06) for Gazprom to purchase volumes of 4−7 Bcm on these terms, but it would be commercial suicide for the company to contemplate long-term imports of 60−80 Bcm/year unless it could be confident that this gas would be sold in Russia at least at a breakeven price. Referring back to the discussion of Russian domestic pricing in Chapter 1, it is clear that even at the much higher regulated prices of 2005, Turkmen gas can only be sold at a considerable loss in Russia, and this may account for the fact that Gazprom Deputy Chairman Ryazanov's view in 2003 was that $25−27/mcm was a 'fair price'.[37] Even assuming that Turkmen import prices, and Kazakh and Uzbek transit fees, remain roughly constant, for Gazprom to break even on Turkmen gas purchases, domestic Russian prices will need to increase to levels that are not anticipated to be reached until 2010.

The January−April 2005 supply interruption and price renegotiation was a very important episode for Turkmen-Russian gas relations, and may play a significant part in shaping Gazprom's view of the reliability and longer-term competitiveness of Turkmen gas in CIS markets. Turkmen arguments that the value of the dollar had fallen 35% over the previous year, the price of steel products delivered in exchange for gas had risen, and that the existing price was low by international standards, were all respectable reasons for seeking a price renegotiation. Less respectable was the act of cutting off supplies at short notice in the middle of winter, in the knowledge that Ukrainian dependence on

Turkmen gas was substantial and there were no alternative supplies available at short notice. A supplier willing to act in this way is likely to create substantial incentives among customers to seek alternative sources of supply.

In reaction to fears that Turkmen trade with CIS countries may fail to develop, there have been a number of proposals floated over the past decade to take Turkmen gas to Pakistan and India (across Afghanistan).[38] These have failed to make progress due to a combination of political, commercial and financing problems and the fact that, thus far at least, they promise lower profitability than Russian and CIS alternatives. One commentator has suggested that the 2003 Gazprom-Turkmen agreement was concluded because of Russian fears that the Turkmens would conclude a contract to sell gas to Pakistan and India via the Turkmenistan-Afghanistan-Pakistan (TAP) Pipeline. While this is not credible (at least to this author) in terms of the commercial viability and financing of such a pipeline, it shows that, in the region at least, such prospects are taken seriously.[39]

Kazakhstan

Russian gas trade with Kazakhstan, even during the Soviet period, never involved large volumes, although the exchanges between the countries were logistically useful because of the location of Kazakh gas fields far from centres of population. For the same reasons as in the Turkmen case, the break-up of the Union quickly saw the trade reduced to negligible levels, although some Kazakh gas continued to be sold to the Ukraine. However, the inclusion of Gazprom in a joint venture to develop the Karachaganak gas field (with significant condensate and very large gas reserves) in northern Kazakhstan was a potentially significant development.

In early 1995 Gazprom signed a production sharing principles agreement with partners including British Gas and AGIP (part of the Italian ENI group), to restore production capacity at the field to relatively small Soviet-era levels in anticipation of paving the way for a major export project through Russian pipelines potentially to Europe.[40] Barely a year later, Gazprom withdrew from the joint venture, selling its stake to Lukoil, on the grounds that the non-Russian partners were unwilling to recognise the financial contribution that the company had made to the development of the field in the Soviet era, and that it was unwilling to contribute additional finance to the venture unless that contribution was recognised.[41]

This signalled a decisive withdrawal by Gazprom from the country,

following a very firm announcement by its chairman that neither Kazakhstan nor Turkmenistan would be allowed to export gas to European
markets using the company's pipeline system.[42] By 1998, other foreign
partners had joined the project and oil production and export (via
the CPC system) were under development. Meanwhile in 1997, the
Kazakh government awarded the Belgian company Tractebel a 15-year
concession to operate the country's gas transmission network.[43] After
a number of serious problems involving non-payment and disputes
with the government, which led to the freezing of its bank accounts,
Tractebel eventually withdrew from the country in 2000 having sold
its equity to Kaztransgaz, a newly created state-owned transmission
company.[44]

In May 2000, Gazprom created a new joint venture with Kaztransgaz to transport and sell gas, taking the place of Tractebel.[45] While
there were few concrete developments over the next two years, it was
clear that relations between the two sides were improving both at a
governmental and a commercial level with the processing of Karachaganak gas at the Orenburg plant.[46] In June 2002, at a meeting of
the presidents of both countries, Gazprom and Kazmunaigaz set up
the joint venture Kazrosgaz to market Kazakh gas.[47] Although not
launched with much fanfare, president Putin said: 'At the initial stage
we are talking about 3.5 Bcm of gas annually and in the future it will
be possible to reach 30–50 Bcm annually'; while the Kazakh president
suggested that the joint venture's production could reach 80 Bcm annually within 8–10 years.[48] The president of Kazmunaigaz suggested
that the joint venture's principal sales market would be in Europe with
exports of 29–34 Bcm by 2015, but Gazprom's view of the venture
seemed more firmly rooted in CIS markets.[49] Nevertheless, Table 2.4
shows that of the 10 Bcm exported in 2002, around 0.3 Bcm was sold
outside the CIS, a figure that rose to more than 1.6 Bcm in 2003. In a
meeting with Azeri journalists in early 2004, the General Director of
Gazexport made clear that the new Russian contract with Azerbaijan
for 4 Bcm/year (see below) would be delivered by Kazrosgaz.[50]

In 2004, another major breakthrough appeared to have been made
in gas relations between the two countries with a 15–20 year agreement
between Gazprom, Orenburggazprom and the Karachaganak partners
to process 7–8.5 Bcm of Karachaganak gas per year at the Orenburg
plant. In 2004 the CEO of Gazprom and the Kazakh energy minister
agreed that future gas development would require the modernisation
and expansion of the capacity of the Orenburg plant to 15 Bcm/year.[51]
In March 2005, Gazprom and Kazmunaigaz created a joint venture to
implement that capacity expansion and signed a long-term transporta-

tion and transit contract for Central Asian gas through the Kazakh network.[52]

Future Kazakh gas exports depend significantly on the volumes of gas available at three big hydrocarbon developments: Tenghiz, Karachaganak and Kashagan. There is little information about the availability of gas in any given time frame. Tenghiz gas is associated with oil production and therefore relatively low cost. Karachaganak is also – the way the field has been developed – associated with the development of liquids, although the gas resource is by far the largest part of the field. As was made clear above, the potential is in the range of 30–100 Bcm/year, but much depends on the pace at which the liquids in the fields are developed and the consequences of that development for gas availability. The Kashagan partners have yet to reveal the size of their gas resource base and how they intend to produce it, but it is understood that they may decide on processing and transportation arrangements separate from the other fields, depending on the size and timing of production.

While this discussion has assumed that Russia and CIS countries will be the main markets for Kazakh gas, sporadic enthusiasm has been expressed for a pipeline to China.[53] Whether the Chinese market will be able to offer an attractive netback to Kazakh sellers – given the distance required for the gas to travel to markets – remains to be seen.

Uzbekistan

With gas production of around 57 Bcm in 2003, Uzbekistan was, after Russia, by far the largest gas producer in the CIS during the 1990s after Turkmen production began to decline (Table 2.6). Uzbekistan is unusual within the CIS in having a very substantial gas market but a relative lack of trade. It exported around 3 Bcm in 2002 and this more than doubled to 6.2 Bcm the following year, most of which remained within the Central Asian region, delivered to Kyrgyzstan, Tajikistan and Kazakhstan (Table 2.5).[54] Along with its resource potential, Uzbekistan is in a strategic position with respect to transit of Central Asian gas to CIS and other markets. In the 2000s Uzbekistan has become much more engaged outside Central Asia, albeit with Gazprom as its principal partner. But as early as 1998, Uzbekneftegaz began to deliver small volumes to the Ukraine (with Itera as the shipper) following the breakdown of Turkmen-Ukraine trade.[55]

In 2002, Gazprom signed a long-term agreement with Uzbekneftegaz covering the period 2003–2012 with volumes starting around 5 Bcm/year in 2003, 7 Bcm in 2004 and set to reach 10 Bcm/year from 2005.[56] Shortly thereafter, Gazprom became the operator for both Kazakh and Uzbek gas in transit through Uzbekistan en route to Russia.[57] This increase in export volumes was the main reason given by the Uzbek prime minister for the enforced phase-out of the transit of Turkmen gas purchased by Itera in 2004 (see Chapter 1). In addition, Gazprom has signed one production sharing contract in Uzbekistan and expressed an intention to sign another agreement which should yield up to 5 Bcm/year over the next decade.[58] Lukoil will sell its share of the gas from its joint venture with Uzbekneftegaz (which will produce around 9 Bcm/year) to Gazprom.[59] If all of these developments proceed as anticipated, some 25 Bcm/year of Uzbek gas could be delivered to Russia (and beyond) after 2010. However, as with Kazakhstan, Gazprom had yet to achieve a long-term transportation and transit agreement which would provide contractual security for these deliveries.

Kyrgyzstan and Tajikistan

In 2003, Gazprom signed long-term (25-year) cooperation agreements with the prime ministers of Kyrgyzstan and Tajikistan.[60] Neither country is a major producer or consumer of gas and demand in both countries is significantly less than 1 Bcm/year, which is mostly imported from Uzbekistan. Both agreements envisage joint development of exploration and production, upgrading and expansion of facilities and, although expressed in very general language, the possibility of Gazprom selling gas in both countries from its Uzbek developments.[61] At the end of 2004, Gazprom was said to be negotiating a joint venture with Tajikgaz which would develop a part of the reserves of 200 Bcm in the south of the country.[62]

Table 2.7 shows how volumes of Central Asian gas, sold by Gazexport, additional to Gazprom's contracts under intergovernmental agreements, have been growing in the 2000s. At more than 8 Bcm in 2004, this is becoming a useful additional source of supply, albeit one which may not be entirely reliable from year to year.

The Caucasus Republics: Azerbaijan, Georgia and Armenia

The Caucasus ceased to be an important gas-producing region in the Soviet Union in the 1970s and the southern republics of the Union needed increasingly to be supplied with gas from further afield, principally Turkmenistan. As Table 2.2 shows, in the post-Soviet period it was Itera which took on the Soviet-era role of supplier and shipper of

Table 2.7: Deliveries of Central Asian Gas to CIS Countries Under Contract with Gazexport, 2003–04 (Bcm)

	2003	*2004*
Azerbaijan	0.0	4.93
Armenia	0.29	1.33
Georgia	0.26	1.23
Moldova		0.93
Estonia	0.106	
TOTAL	1.56	8.42

Sources: *Razvitie sotrudnichestvo v gazovoy svere co stranani bivshevo SSSR*, Gazprom Presentation, Spravka I Brifingi, June 7, 2005. www.gazprom.ru

Central Asian, largely Turkmen, gas to the Caucasus republics. Georgia and Armenia were among its earliest customers, while Azerbaijan did not start to import gas until 2000. Although Gazprom delivered very small volumes to Georgia in 1997 and possibly also Armenia in 2001, it was not until 2003 when Gazexport took over negotiations, that volumes delivered to the two countries became significant.

In 2004, Gazexport became the sole commercial negotiator for sales to Azerbaijan (replacing Itera) with 4.5 Bcm/year contracted, and the possibility that volumes could reach 5.5 Bcm, at a price of $52/mcm. During 2004, volumes were affected by accidents and disruptions on the main pipeline transporting gas via North Ossetia and Georgia, some of which were said to be the consequence of Chechen insurgency.[63] The gas is being delivered by Kazrozgas – the Gazprom-Kazmun-aigaz joint venture – and at a press conference in Baku the general director of Gazexport made a point of stressing the relevance of CIS cooperation:

> I would like to emphasise once again that Kazrosgaz...is unique in the CIS market since, by starting natural gas trading business it is already moving to the next stage of development. Therefore Kazrosgaz has become an instrument of Russia-Azerbaijan cooperation. If you look at the situation in broader terms, you realise this is an example of trilateral cooperation since the parties involved include our colleagues from Ukraine and Turkmenistan, and gas supplies to Ukraine are also part of the process.[64]

In 2003, Gazprom also began to take over the Georgian market, which it had hardly supplied since the break-up of the Union, from Itera. Itera had managed to make a profitable business out of the Georgian market by operating a tough payment policy and converting debt into assets – in particular a 90% share in the Azot nitrogen plant, the biggest gas user in the country.[65] But Gazprom's retaking of the market was assisted by the purchase (from the American company AES) of both the Georgian electricity network and a number of power plants by Russia's UES.[66] In late 2003, Itera's Chairman was asked in a press interview whether the company was being squeezed out of Georgia by Gazprom and answered that despite Gazprom's presence, Itera would continue to supply 0.8 Bcm as before.[67] However, following a meeting between the Gazprom Chairman and Georgia's International Gas Corporation in early 2004, Gazprom made it clear that it was taking over supply to the Georgian gas market including supply to Itera's subsidiaries.[68]

In May 2004, a meeting between the Chairman of Gazprom and the Prime Minister of Georgia agreed a range of issues from settling debts to future supplies and it was stated that the republic would receive all of its 1 Bcm/year supplies from Gazexport.[69] Yet at the same time this agreement was being signed, Gazexport had been forced to cut back supplies to gas distribution company Tbilgaz by half, due to non-payment which had caused debts to rise to $10m.[70] This was why Itera had agreed to supply Tbilgaz only under a condition of 100% prepayment.[71] In September 2004, the new government of President Sakashvili brought the 'Moscow Georgians' into government in Tbilisi, and in particular Minister of Economic Development Kakha Bendukidze. This has significantly helped Gazprom's cause in Georgia with suggestions that it may take over Itera's stake in Azot.[72] In 2005, Gazprom has shown interest in bidding for the Georgian gas network if and when it is privatised, despite significant opposition from the US Adminstration.[73]

The gas supply to both Azerbaijan and Georgia will experience substantial change when large-scale Azeri gas supplies from the Shah Deniz field, plus associated gas from oil fields, begin to flow in large volumes, starting in 2006.[74] Not only does the Azeri Fuel and Energy Ministry see the possibility of phasing out imports from 2007, but Georgia will also benefit from payments in gas for transit to Turkey which could increase to as much as 0.5 Bcm/year depending on how much gas is transited through the country.[75] Given the size of Azerbaijan's gas reserves, combined with the proximity of the Georgian market and the presence of a pipeline that may have some spare capacity in the early years of development, it is difficult to see these countries needing to import additional gas. Nevertheless, this will depend on the security situation in the region, and the relative attractiveness of the different supplies. For this reason, ownership of the major gas users in Georgia, such as the power and fertiliser plants, and ownership of the pipeline network, is very important. On the one hand, given the size of the Azeri resource base and limited opportunities for local marketing of the gas, all regional countries, including Russia, could become importers of Azeri gas in the future. On the other hand, Russian ownership of key consuming enterprises could mean priority being given to Russian gas for as long as Gazprom wishes to supply them.

As Table 2.3 shows, over the past decade Armenia's gas imports have ranged from 0.99–1.5 Bcm per year. But the problems of arranging and maintaining these deliveries have been out of all proportion to their small size. The early 1990s were years of crisis for Armenian energy supplies with disruptions arising from problems in relationships between other CIS states in which Armenia was not directly involved.[76] The ArmRosgazprom joint venture, created in 1997 and owned 45% by Gazprom, 45% by the Armenian Energy Ministry and 10% by Itera, included plans to both deliver gas and build pipelines and underground storage facilities.[77] Little had been heard of the activities of ArmRosgazprom since its creation until, just as it did in Georgia, Gazprom began to supply the country again in 2003 and became the sole supplier in 2004.[78] Yet the joint venture is important because it is one of only two examples where Gazprom has substantial equity in the pipeline network of a CIS country.

The disruptions of the early 1990s, caused both by natural disasters and by terrorist actions around the Georgian/Armenian/Azeri border, left Armenia extremely exposed and desperate to develop alternative sources of gas supply.[79] These events brought forth a proposal to build a gas pipeline from Iran to Armenia dating from at least 1993; in the late 1990s Gazprom expressed a willingness to fund the 140-km line designed to carry up to 3 Bcm.[80] But it was only in 2004 that a 20-year contract was signed for deliveries of Iranian gas to start in 2007, increasing from 1.1 Bcm/year to 2.3 Bcm/year with payment being in electricity exported to Iran.[81] After more than a decade of discussions on this relatively short pipeline costing a total of $220 million ($120m for Iran and $100m for Armenia), construction finally started in late 2004.

The Iran-Armenia pipeline became an extremely complex project with its own Presidential Decree involving both gas and electricity, and Gazprom and (Russian electricity giant) UES.[82] Armenia will pay Gazprom for its role in construction with a share of the gas supply which will be sold to the Razdan power station (owned by UES), which will then market the electricity and pay Gazprom from that revenue.[83] Georgia, despite its imminent anticipation of deliveries of Azeri gas, has shown interest in taking Iranian gas through Armenia.[84] Iran will also supply the enclave of Nakhichevan with 0.35 Bcm/year by means of a swap arrangement that will see a corresponding volume of Shakh Deniz gas delivered from Azerbaijan to Iran (though a pipeline which, during the 1970s, carried up to 10 Bcm/year of Iranian gas to the USSR).[85]

Ukraine, Belarus and Moldova

It was noted above that imports of gas by Ukraine and Belarus account for nearly three-quarters of all CIS gas trade. It was also noted that a very large proportion of Russian gas to Europe needs to transit through these three countries. Not all of the gas transit volumes in Table 2.8 are destined for Europe; likewise not all exports to Europe transit through these countries (the exceptions are deliveries to Finland and the portion of Turkish exports delivered via Blue Stream). Nevertheless, the significance of Russia's, and specifically Gazprom's, transit dependence on these countries is clear. The countries depend on Gazprom for gas supplies and transit from Central Asian countries, and Gazprom depends on them for transit of gas to Europe. The management of these relationships has been one of the most challenging tasks for Gazprom in the post-Soviet period. The volumes of gas and the sums of money involved in trade with, and transit through these countries are such that on both sides presidents and prime ministers have been involved in every major decision.

Table 2.8: Transit of Russian Gas Across CIS Countries 2001–04 (Bcm)

	2001	*2002*	*2003*	*2004*
Belarus	24.1	27.4	33.1	35.3
Moldova	18.5	21.0	22.1	20.4
Ukraine	122.7	119.7	122.0	126.3

Source: *Razvitie sotrudnichestvo v gazovoy svere co stranani bivshevo SSSR*, Gazprom Presentation, Spravochnyi Materiali, June 7, 2005. www.gazprom.ru

Ukraine

Ukraine holds the pivotal geographical position in the trade and transit of Russian gas. In terms of volume, the export of gas from Canada to the United States is the only other bilateral gas trade worldwide that exceeds Russian exports to Ukraine. Ukrainian transit flows (Table 2.8)

are by far the largest in international gas trade and although much of Gazprom's export strategy since the break-up of the Soviet Union has been oriented towards reducing (or at least not increasing) transit through the Ukraine, it is probably the case that in 2004, around 80% of gas exports to Europe were delivered via that route.

During the 1990s, the Ukrainian/Russian gas relationship was characterised by:

- Ukrainian inability to pay for the huge volumes it contracted, leading to very high levels of debt and unpaid bills which in turn led to...
- ...reduction of Russian gas supplies to Ukraine for short periods of time, aimed at restoring payment discipline which in turn led to...
- ...unauthorised diversions of the volumes in transit to European countries.

During this period, details of the levels of debt, the delivery reductions which took place and whether they were justified, as well as the diversion of gas by Ukrainian parties, became hotly contested issues.[86] Gas became connected with national security issues in 1993 when the Russian government reportedly proposed that gas debt would be cancelled if Ukraine returned control of the Black Sea Fleet to Russia and returned all remaining nuclear warheads.[87]

Ukrainian political sensitivity towards Russian influence has been a considerable obstacle to finding any commercial solution that involves Gazprom taking some degree of ownership in Ukrainian gas transmission and storage assets. A large part of the Ukraine's 35 Bcm of storage capacity was built for the specific purpose of ensuring security of Soviet and now Russian exports to Europe. Successive Ukrainian governments and/or the Ukrainian parliament have refused to countenance significant Gazprom equity shares in Ukrainian gas enterprises. During the debt crises there had been numerous proposals that, in exchange for writing off debt, Gazprom should take equity in the Ukrainian transmission system (and storages) carrying Russian gas to Europe. All were rejected by the Ukrainian parliament on the grounds that there should be no foreign ownership in the network. A proposal by Shell that a joint European/Russian/Ukrainian consortium might jointly be responsible for refurbishing and operating the Ukrainian network also came to nothing.[88]

The February 1994 Inter-Governmental agreement setting out a framework for the terms of sales and transit for a ten-year period, failed to provide a sound basis for the trade, principally because of the general economic and energy crisis conditions in Ukraine. As the 1990s progressed, tensions in the Gazprom-Ukraine gas relationship seemed to moderate as both sides recognised the need to make progress towards a workable medium-term contractual framework. The 1998 agreement appeared to be a significant step in this direction but lacked a comprehensive solution for dealing with the debt which Gazprom claimed various Ukrainian organisations, both state-owned and private, had accrued for gas deliveries since 1991. Under the 1998 agreement, the Ukraine was supposed to receive 52 Bcm of gas priced at $50 per thousand cubic metres ($/mcm); a considerable price reduction from the 1997 price of $80/mcm. This was to be achieved by means of a similar reduction in the transit tariffs charged by Ukrgazprom from $1.75/mcm per 100 km to $1.01–1.09/mcm/100 km. It was intended that around 30 Bcm out of the 52 Bcm of total deliveries would be delivered in exchange for transit (the actual figure would depend on the volume of gas transited to Europe), and the remaining 22 Bcm would be priced at $50/mcm.[89]

We now know that the 1998 agreement did not remotely reflect the next several years in terms of Gazprom deliveries which were almost immediately restricted to the volumes made in payment for transit. As shown in Table 2.2, Gazprom's deliveries were 25–30 Bcm during the period 1999–2003, with the balance (up to 2002) being provided by Itera mainly from Turkmenistan (see above). However, the 1998 agreement proved to be durable in the important respect that it established a relationship between the price of gas supplied to Ukraine, and the tariffs charged for transit by Ukraine; this has since been applied by Ukraine and other CIS transit countries. We also know that the 1998 agreement was the calm before the storm in the gas relationship between the countries.

The period between late 1998 and 2000 must count as one of the most acrimonious in Russian-Ukrainian gas relations. Undoubtedly much of the problem was caused by the Russian economic crisis of 1998, the consequences of which were felt throughout the CIS. In addition, the mid-1990s to early 2000s saw political scandal and corruption allegations connected with the gas industry at the highest levels in the Ukraine, involving former Prime Minister Pavel Lazarenko (subsequently put on trial in the United States) and Deputy Prime Minister Yulia Timoshenko.[90] At the same time a combination of the huge non-payment problem in the Russian domestic market (see Chapter 1), and record low oil prices in the international market reduced Gazprom's foreign exchange earnings to very low levels and placed huge additional pressure on the company to collect the maximum possible revenues from export markets.

By the end of 1998, Gazprom claimed that huge volumes were being illegally diverted by Ukrainian organisations each month – 2.5 Bcm in December 1998 alone – from the transit pipelines, and that debt in respect of gas deliveries had reached $1.6bn.[91] Gazprom's Chairman responded to government pressure to increase its domestic taxation by saying that the Ministry had done little about the continued theft by Ukrainian companies from export pipelines which was causing losses of $3–5 million per day.[92] The Russian Energy Minister did temporarily halt exports of oil and electricity to Ukraine in response to the theft of nearly 4 Bcm of gas in November 1999.[93] Recognising that it had no control over transit volumes, but determined not to allow Ukrainian profiteering without extracting further recompense, Gazprom declared that any gas taken illicitly from the transit pipelines would be charged at $83/mcm and added to the existing debt mountain which, according to Gazprom, had already reached $2.8bn.[94]

In mid-2000, with claims that 9 (and perhaps as much as 15) Bcm had already been taken from the transit pipelines during the current year, Gazprom proposed the construction of a bypass pipeline to allow 30 (and in some accounts up to 60) Bcm of gas to move directly from Belarus into Poland and south to Slovakia, bypassing 25% (and possibly up to 50%) of Ukrainian transit capacity. The 600 km pipeline was costed at $1bn and would have provided no net increase in Russian export capacity to Europe.[95] Gazprom's reasoning was that, since around $1bn worth of gas had been taken from the transit pipelines each year for the previous two years, the pipeline would pay for itself very quickly. However, two factors conspired to delay any progress on the project:

1. Gazprom was clearly looking to its European customers to provide funding for the bypass, but it was difficult for the European companies to see how such a line would pay for itself unless they were allowed to own a proportion of the capacity – and this had been traditionally opposed by Gazprom.[96]
2. The Polish government was opposed to participating in such a project, given that the Ukrainians would undoubtedly construe such participation as a hostile act, jeopardising Polish-Ukrainian relations.[97]

Despite the lack of progress, the bypass proposal brought some frank admissions from the Ukrainian side in terms of capacity to pay for gas. The president publicly stated: 'Neftegaz Ukraine is not capable of paying for gas...what structure will take on responsibility of paying for gas?' He also reminded his audience that gas debts were owed to Itera as well as Gazprom.[98]

The events of mid-2000, and the bypass proposal, proved to be a watershed for Russian-Ukrainian gas relations. Both sides agree that

June 2000 was the last incident of unauthorised removal of gas from the transit pipelines and although this left the issue of future supplies and past debts to be settled, it nevertheless represented a necessary and welcome break with the past.[99] The eventual agreements on supply and transit for 2001 were extremely complicated and formalised a new position on Ukrainian supplies (which has continued through 2004): the only gas that Ukraine would receive from Gazprom would be 26–28 Bcm as payment for transiting gas to Europe. The country's other supplies would be approximately 30 Bcm from Turkmenistan – sold and/or shipped by Itera – and 18 Bcm from its own production. A meeting between the presidents and prime ministers of the countries also established a restructuring of the existing debt, the exact proportions of which had yet to be decided.[100] Other major elements of the 2001 agreement were: [101]

- If problems arose in the delivery of Turkmen gas, Gazprom would be obliged to provide a reserve volume of not more than 5 Bcm.
- Gas in excess of the transit volumes would be purchased at $80/mcm of which half would be paid in dollars and in cash, and half by means of a credit arrangement whereby debt would be converted into Eurobonds and transferred to Russian ownership.
- Ukraine would guarantee 124.6 Bcm of transit of Russian gas in 2001.
- Gazprom would allow a technical credit of 1 Bcm/month for two months in winter; any gas taken in excess of that authorised from transit pipelines would incur a debt at an agreed rate of interest.
- Ukraine would introduce an export duty of $140/mcm on gas in order to prevent re-exports of Russian gas.

Under this agreement, Gazprom (and the Russian government) sought to regularise supplies to, and payments from, Ukraine. It was a carefully structured attempt to break with a lawless past which recognised that Ukraine could not be prevented from taking additional supply, but that such supply would be recorded and paid for at agreed prices with agreed debt arrangements. In October 2001, the two prime ministers agreed the gas debt of Naftogaz Ukraine to Gazprom at $1.4bn (a significantly lower amount than Gazprom had been claiming previously) which would be converted into Eurobonds.[102]

The terms for 2002 supply and transit were set as follows: 124.5 Bcm to be transited in total, of which 106.8 Bcm to Europe; transit charges for the first half of the year to be $1.094/mcm per hundred km, rising to $1.46/mcm/00km for the second half of the year; Gazprom guaranteed a minimum of 26 Bcm based on transit charges with additional supply to be paid in cash; Gazprom agreed to transit up to 34 Bcm of gas to Ukraine from Central Asia charging $1.094/mcm/00km (i.e. the same transit charge as Gazprom paid to Ukraine for transit to Europe). [103]

By mid-2002, a ten-year agreement on transit and storage formalised most of these terms and included a provision for Ukrainian storage of 5 Bcm of Russian gas during 2003.[104] This was a very significant development since Gazprom is highly dependent on being able to store gas relatively close to the European market so as to maintain deliveries during the winter peak demand season. The agreement for 2005 was similarly structured: 112 Bcm is to be transited to Europe; transit tariff $1.09/mcm/00km (equivalent to a gas purchase cost of $50/mcm); 23 Bcm to be paid in gas and the remainder in cash; a Gazprom guarantee that 37 Bcm of Central Asian gas would be transited to Ukraine, and that it would increase deliveries in the event that such volumes are not available; a gas export duty of $100/mcm but – following a change in 2004 – 6 Bcm of gas to be exempt from this duty of which 5 Bcm could be supplied to European countries through Gazprom's intermediaries (i.e. Gazexport). [105]

As relations began to normalise and a new Gazprom management (see Chapter 4) took over the running of the company in 2001, the Poland-Slovakia bypass pipeline was quietly shelved although in early 2002 Chairman Miller was still saying that a formal decision would be taken later that year.[106] The bypass line was replaced in June 2002 by the far more consensual notion of an 'international consortium' agreed between the Russian and Ukrainian presidents with the aim of operating and refurbishing the transit pipelines in the Ukraine. The day after that agreement, German Chancellor Schroeder signed a trilateral agreement with the two countries hailing the project as a key step in ensuring 'economic stability'. The finance originally envisaged was $2.5bn for refurbishment followed by $15bn over the following decade for further development of the network.[107] With Ruhrgas firmly established as the German corporate representative in the consortium, the Ukrainian government announced that Italy and France had also expressed interest in joining.[108]

Despite expressions of optimism and encouragement, few concrete advances were made following the signing of the founding documents by Naftokhaz Ukrainy and Gazprom in November 2002.[109] By 2004, the focus of attention had shifted to the expansion of the Ukrainian network with the building of a new Bogorodchany-Uzhgorod line (part of the Novopskov-Uzhgorod line) to bring additional Central

Asian gas to Ukraine and thence to Europe; this project appeared to be accelerated following the February 2004 hiatus in the relationship with Belarus (see below). Despite periodic expressions of interest from European governments and companies, there was no concrete indication that any parties other than Gazprom and Naftokhaz would participate in the consortium or how its activities – other than the new Bogorodchany-Uzhgorod line – would be funded. In addition, it seemed likely that extra Ukrainian legislation would be needed for the creation of a consortium with powers to refurbish and allocate capacity in the existing transit network.[110]

In the summer of 2004, the crucially important issues of arrangements for transit of Central Asian gas to Ukraine and settlement of debts were agreed. The two issues, which the Gazprom announcement made clear should be regarded as a single package, assigned the full $1.62bn of gas debt for the period 1997–2000 to Vnesheconombank which settled these obligations with Gazprom. Contrary to previous plans, Gazprom refused to accept the 2001 settlement of a transfer of Naftokhaz bonds worth $1.437bn (reportedly because of the tax implications) and insisted on a package of measures to resolve all its concerns, and serve as final closure on the unfortunate events of the 1997–2000 period.[111]

Aside from the financial arrangements, the agreement included a number of other provisions designed to establish more predictability in the relationship over the next five years. The most interesting element of this is described as:

a single advance payment [by Gazprom] of $1.25bn to Naftokhaz of the Ukraine as payment for the transit of 19.2 Bcm of gas via the Ukraine over 2005–2009. Said advance payment will make it possible to fix $1.09/mcm/00km as a gas transmission tariff between 2005 and 2009.[112]

Gazprom will pay off the advance by reducing the annual payments for transit via Ukraine from 26 Bcm to 21 Bcm for the period 2005–09, and more gas from Turkmenistan will be delivered to compensate for this.[113] It is difficult to interpret this one-off payment as anything other than a Gazprom loan to Naftokhaz enabling it to pay past debts, and to provide an agreed foundation for at least five years of deliveries of Turkmen gas and transit of Russian gas to Europe. While Gazprom was forced to give up a portion of the past debts owed by Ukraine and provide an interest-free loan on the rest of the debt, it probably regarded this as worthwhile in order to create a new status quo for sales and shipping of Turkmen gas.[114]

The other part of the agreement concerned transit of Turkmen gas to Ukraine. The creation of a new joint venture (RosUkrEnergo) to ship mainly Turkmen gas to Ukraine, starting in January 2005, requires some additional historical background. It was shown above that in the mid to late 1990s, Itera acquired a key role in the supply and shipping of Central Asian – particularly Turkmen – gas to Ukraine and other CIS countries. Table 2.2 shows that, during the period 1998–2002, Itera was a significantly larger supplier of gas to Ukraine than Gazprom and acted as the shipper for all supplies (including those negotiated bilaterally between the Ukraine and Turkmenistan). However, as we also saw in Chapter 1, allegations concerning the legitimacy of Itera's operations began to be increasingly heard and the company's business started to suffer following the arrival of the new Gazprom management in mid-2001. It was still a considerable surprise however, when in December 2002 – less than two weeks before the New Year – it was announced that Gazprom itself would take over the shipping of Turkmen gas to Ukraine from Itera, as from January 2003.[115]

Although it later transpired that a new intermediary had been appointed as shipper in December, it was not until March 2003 that Gazprom and Naftokhaz Ukraine released minimal details that Eural Transgas (a previously unknown company) had taken over Itera's role of shipping Central Asian gas to Ukraine under a three-year contract 2003-06.[116] The creation and appointment of Eural Transgas (ETG) gave rise to a wave of allegations of corrupt practices and links with organised crime comprehensively set out in an anonymous document circulated widely among OECD governments in 2004.[117]

ETG was contracted by Gazprom and Naftokhaz Ukraine to ship up to 36 Bcm of Turkmen gas, purchased by Naftokhaz Ukraine at the Turkmen-Uzbek border, to the Russian-Ukrainian border. In addition, ETG signed a ten-year contract with the Ukrainian company in 2003 for the transit of 10 Bcm/year and for underground storage of 5 Bcm/year.[118] The latter was extremely important for it allowed ETG to market the 13.5 Bcm of gas received as payment for shipping 35.4 Bcm of (mostly Turkmen) gas in 2003, of which 31.3 Bcm was sold and 4.1 Bcm was stored in Ukraine.[119] The company marketed this gas directly in the Ukraine and Poland; around 2 Bcm of gas was sold to Germany and other European countries via Gazprom subsidiaries. These activities resulted in a 2003 turnover of $2bn with a gross profit of $180m; a significant achievement for a newly created company.[120] In 2004, the company's activities expanded considerably with more than 42 Bcm of gas due to be shipped from Central Asia and direct sales to Polish and Hungarian customers, increasing the company's European sales to an anticipated 8 Bcm.[121]

At the appointment of ETG – a company based in Hungary for tax reasons – it was assumed that joint ownership of the company by Gazprom and Naftokhaz Ukraine would follow, and that it had not been established only because of the speed with which these commercial arrangements had been put in place. In the event neither company took equity in ETG which – when its restructuring was announced in 2004 – was owned by JKX Gas 30%, Atlantic Caspian Resources 44.67% and DEG Handels 25.33%; a former CEO of British Gas became the (non-executive) chairman of the company.[122]

The abrupt ending of ETG's contract as a shipper of Turkmen gas – two years before it was due to expire – and its replacement by Ros-UkrEnergo, raises fascinating questions: why was ETG invited/created to carry out this task, and why was it dismissed as from January 2005 having done a creditable job at very short notice? The answers may be important for an understanding of the future of Central Asian gas supplies to Ukraine and Europe. As far as Gazprom is concerned, in mid-2004 the General Director of Gazexport spelled out for journalists the Gazprom version of this episode:

> ETG is the nominated agent for the transit of Turkmen gas to Ukraine, it was nominated not by Naftokhaz Ukraine but by the Ukrainian government; the reasons why the Ukrainian government selected ETG are beyond our competence as is the system of mutual payments between these parties.[123]

This response, when added to a very terse announcement on the Gazprom website and a press comment in response to criticism from the financial markets, strongly suggests that ETG's appointment was at the behest of the Ukrainian government which wished to remove Itera from its position as shipper.[124] Two years later, the then chairman of Naftokhaz Ukraine explained that the company had replaced Itera because:

> it used Ukraine's market as a means of earning money only, investing no money in it. It appeared on the Russian-Ukrainian border, sold gas to grey dealers...using loopholes in the legislation as [these companies] took away the most solvent [customers] from Naftokhaz Ukrainy...and Naftokhaz Ukrainy had to settle disputes between municipal heat suppliers and households [whose payment rates are low].[125]

By contrast, ETG sold gas to Naftokhaz at the border, thus eliminating this source of competition. Its senior management were known to both Naftokhaz Ukraine and Gazprom from previous business contacts – energy and non-energy – and from this arose a number of allegations of corruption and poor governance none of which were ever substantiated.[126] In addition, the failure of either Gazprom or Naftokhaz to take equity in ETG combined with the company becoming a highly profitable and increasingly important gas supplier began to cause alarm in both Moscow and Kiev.

From the Russian side, an important reason for the replacement of ETG was Gazprom's determination to bring CIS trade back under its sole or joint control. Apparently this had not been foreseen in June 2004, less than two months before the RosUkrEnergo announcement, when Gazprom management confirmed ETG's transit contract up to 2006.[127] In what may be a key sentence (not included in the Gazprom press release), the press report from Kiev stated that: 'Before settling the gas debts, Russia and Ukraine agreed to drop mediators in gas trade in Europe.'[128] This may suggest that elimination of third parties was a key condition for settling the debt which – as noted above – included the provision of a $1.25bn loan by Gazprom.

The new shipping joint venture RosUkrEnergo was registered in Switzerland by Gazprombank and (Austrian) Raiffeisenbank and will be jointly managed by a consortium of Gazprom, Naftokhaz Ukraine, Gazprombank and Raiffeisenbank.[129] Over time, Raiffeisenbank is expected to sell its share in the joint venture to other investors.[130] RosUkrEnergo has a contract to ship gas until 2028 with volumes anticipated to increase to 44 Bcm in 2005 and 60 Bcm thereafter. It did not seem a coincidence that shortly after the issues of supply and transit had been settled, an intergovernmental agreement was signed for the expansion of the Bogorodchany-Uzhgorod pipeline anticipating an additional 5 Bcm of transit in 2005 increasing to 19 Bcm in 2010 and possible further increases depending on market developments.[131] There is nevertheless some confusion remaining because the relevant Gazprom press release mentions only a 50 km section of the pipeline and the need to raise the capital of the consortium to $34m.[132]

A second reason why Gazprom sought to replace ETG was that the company – seemingly unnoticed by the international community including EU WTO negotiators who actively (and unsuccessfully) campaigned for it (Chapter 3) – had broken Gazprom's monopoly on Russian gas exports to Europe and was threatening to substantially expand its commercial presence. Exports to Poland began in late 2003 augmented by Hungarian (and possibly also Romanian) sales in 2004. Despite the fact that Gazprom treated such exports as being within the framework of allowable Ukrainian exports, it was a matter of time before the opening of markets in other European countries allowed the company to gain access elsewhere.[133]

In December 2004, dramatic political events in Kiev saw the election of President Yushchenko and his government headed by Prime Minister Timoshenko who promised to give Ukraine a greater political orientation towards Europe, with the eventual possibility of European Union membership. For natural gas trade, the most immediate consequence may be a revival of the idea of European participation in the pipeline consortium, and therefore a return to the original idea of refurbishment as the most urgent and important task.[134] Refurbishment of the Ukrainian pipeline network to modern specifications would remove one of the most serious threats to technical breakdown of Russian gas supplies to Europe. In early 2005, loans of up to Euro 2bn from international banks were being discussed although it was not clear what proportion of these funds would be devoted to gas pipeline refurbishment.[135]

A potentially dramatic early initiative from the Yushchenko administration was the suggestion that gas transit tariffs should be moved to 'European' levels and paid in dollars.[136] This proposal was enthusiastically received by Gazprom and although subsequently heavily qualified by the Ukrainian side, it raised the possibility that the latter would consider paying European market prices for Russian gas. At the same, time the new administration in Kiev raised objections to the participation of Raiffeisenbank in RosUkrEnergo, asking for a 50:50 partnership – and a split of the profits from this venture – with Gazprom.[137]

In the aftermath of the December 2004 Turkmen price increase for Ukrainian, and the April 2005 increase for Russian, exports, it was announced that Turkmenneftegaz had signed a new contract with Naftokhaz Ukraine for 50–60 Bcm/year for the period 2006–26, with the Ukrainian side deciding on the shipper of the gas.[138] This would appear to violate the terms of the 2003 Turkmen-Gazprom agreement, in which the volumes of up to 90 Bcm/year envisaged that Gazprom would supply the Ukraine with the totality of its Turkmen requirements. It would also violate the terms of the August 2004 Russian-Ukrainian agreement by which RosUkrEnergo was defined as the sole shipper of Turkmen gas to Ukraine. Where this development leaves the trilateral issue of Turkmen-Russian-Ukrainian gas supply and transit is therefore uncertain.

Belarus

Compared with the Ukraine, Russia's other bilateral gas trades pale into insignificance in volume terms; although deliveries of 15–19 Bcm per year to Belarus are by no means negligible. The country traditionally provided transit for up to 7 Bcm per year to Poland, but the importance of Belarus as a transit route grew significantly as Gazprom's desire to diversify away from transit dependence on the Ukraine and to establish a second export corridor, gave rise to the building of the Yamal pipeline (see Chapter 3).

Russian-Belarusian relations in the post-Soviet period centred on a proposal to unify the two countries economically and politically made in the early 1990s during the Yeltsin presidency.[139] The monetary union proposals contained within them a Belarusian demand for continued deliveries of Russian fuels at subsidised prices.[140] The Russian gas relationship with Belarus is underpinned by 1993 and 1995 intergovernmental agreements setting out the sale and transit relationships between the countries over a 20-year period. Under these agreements the assets of Beltransgaz, the gas transmission company, were to be transferred to Gazprom under a 99-year lease.[141] In return, Russia was said to have agreed to double its deliveries to Belarus by 2010, although it was never clear how the country would use such large quantities of gas. These arrangements began to take shape when Beltransgaz was converted into a joint stock company in 1996, but were not approved by the Belarusian parliament.

Starting in 1997, Beltransgaz purchased small quantities of gas from Itera (Table 2.2) and these purchases increased to a position where, in the 2000s, Itera provided well over a third of the country's gas supplies, with other independent companies known to have supplied around 0.6 Bcm in 2002.[142] Regarding payments for gas, Gazprom's relations with Belarus in the late 1990s and early 2000s mirrored its relationship with Ukraine, with the exception that unauthorised diversion of transit volumes were not an option for Belarus until gas began to flow through the Yamal pipeline in 1999. By late 1998, Belarusian gas debts were $0.25−0.5bn and failure to agree on prices caused gas to be delivered without a contract in the first few months of 1999.[143]

The Intergovernmental agreement of April 2002 set out the terms for future Russian sales to Belarus and the development of the Beltransgaz joint venture for the management of the gas network in the country. As described by Gazprom, the agreement stated that Belarus would pay for up to 10.3 Bcm of gas at the regulated price paid in the 5th zone in Russia (for details of Russian internal pricing see Chapter 1).[144] This resulted in gas being supplied by Gazprom at $24/mcm in 2002 while Itera's price was $38/mcm and other independents charged around $42/mcm.[145] However, apart from approval by the Belarus House of Representatives, little progress was made towards creating the Beltransgaz joint venture and increasing debts gave rise to Gazprom warnings of suspension of deliveries.[146] By July 2003, when a Gazprom delegation visited Belarus, patience was clearly wearing thin on the Russian side, with the Belarusians claiming that the value of the network was $5bn (meaning that Gazprom would need to contribute $2.5bn in order to purchase half of any joint venture) and that $1.73bn needed to be spent on refurbishment.[147] By September 2003, the Gazprom Chairman reported that negotiations between the two sides had been broken off and the 'deadline' of July 2003 for setting up the joint venture had passed. 'So, all in all, we are calling it a day. We are putting a full stop under this agreement. We have parted ways, because we have different ideas.'[148] President Putin's comment, following discussions with his Belarusian counterpart was significantly more commercial. Having noted that it was almost impossible to agree on a figure for debts in respect of past gas supplies, he said: 'We have decided that Russia and Belarus should switch to market relations in this industry without ceasing negotiations to create a single transportation company.'[149]

With hindsight, these developments should have provided ample warning that a crisis was imminent. The 2003 supply agreement expired at the end of the year and, with no basis on which to renew the agreement, Gazprom ceased supplying its own gas to Belarus. In the early part of 2004, Russian gas was supplied to Belarus on short-term contracts by independent suppliers, in particular Itera, and Russian intentions were reinforced in January when Prime Minister Kasyanov signed a decree approving the construction of the North European Gas Pipeline through the Baltic Sea (see Chapter 3). Despite the cessation of Gazprom supplies, a meeting between its chairman and the general director of Beltransgaz in late January yielded no results.[150] On February 12, Gazprom briefly cut all supplies to Belarus – aside from exports in transit through the Yamal pipeline – but these were restored when Beltransgaz signed a contract with the trading company Transnafta covering 5–6 days of supply.[151]

On February 18, when that short-term contract expired, Gazprom again cut off all supplies to Belarus but accounts of the exact chain of events and the reasons behind them are conflicting. The only facts that can be independently verified are that Gazprom cut off supplies – including supplies destined for European customers – at 18.00 Moscow time on February 18, and restored supplies before midnight on February 19. Thus the stoppage – from cut-off to restoration – lasted for not more than 30 hours although the Gazprom spokesman announcing this said that it would take 'several hours' to restore full-scale transit shipments to foreign customers.[152]

As to why supplies were cut off, Reuters reported the Gazprom press spokesman as saying: 'They [the Belarusians] failed to sign new contracts and started siphoning gas from transit pipelines...'[153]

With respect to the lack of new contracts, the General Director of TransNafta confirmed that his company had offered a new contract (to replace the one which expired on February 18):

> ...to supply gas at $26.58/mcm, the price charged in 2003. The contract to this effect, signed by TransNafta, has already been submitted to Beltransgaz. However, it has not been signed by Beltransgaz yet. As soon as it is signed, gas deliveries will be resumed. [154]

With respect to the illegal siphoning of gas, the position is less clear. It is certainly possible that, lacking any other gas, Belarusian customers may have decided to take the gas in transit to third countries. But such action had not been mentioned by Gazprom previously and, if the siphoning only began after the TransNafta supply contract was terminated on February 18, Gazprom must have detected such behaviour within a few hours and made the instant decision to cut all supplies. Several months later, Gazprom Chairman Miller repeated the reasons for the action and confirmed that it had been approved by the Russian government:

> ...we...coordinated gas supply limitations with the RF government. And as for the termination of gas deliveries to Belarus in February, I'll repeat it once again that the situation we had stemmed from the absence of a gas marketing contract and non-sanctioned withdrawals by Belarus of Russian gas transited via its territory...and moreover it is the end-use customers located in other countries that suffered most of all. We simply had no other solution to this. I hope that this situation won't ever repeat again. [155]

Supplies were restored when the contract with TransNafta (referred to above) was signed, but cutting off gas supplies in the middle of winter to a range of third countries including Poland, Latvia and Lithuania as well as the Russian enclave of Kaliningrad caused a wave of anxiety and protest. The European Commission expressed concern, and significant political problems arose in Poland as a result of the incident. The Gazprom version of events was that Poland suffered a shortfall of Russian gas amounting to 35% on February 18 and 50% on February 19, and that there was 'no catastrophic situation' because Poland received some gas via Ukraine.[156] Naturally the Polish version was quite different, with claims from Polish Oil and Gas Company (PGNiG) that it was not forewarned, or kept informed, about the Belarus incident and intended to claim compensation for losses suffered as a result of the shortfalls. During the following two weeks there were heated debates in the Polish parliament about the wisdom of over-reliance on Russian gas supplies, and this gave rise to immediate negotiations on emergency measures for both expanding storage within Poland and creating additional interconnections and supply routes for gas to reach the country.[157] The consequences of the Belarus incident for Latvia were not serious as the country has such substantial stored gas that it was able to meet its own requirements plus those of Lithuania.[158] The least fortunate customers were those in Kaliningrad who were forced to switch to fuel oil and hot water supplies were cut off in order to maintain heating.[159]

As far as Belarus was concerned, President Lukashenko accused Russia of:

> An act of terrorism at the highest level. When temperatures have plunged to minus 20, they are cutting off gas to a country and its people – not foreign people, but people half of whom have Russian blood in their veins...If Putin wants us to pay this money, let us take it from the Chernobyl victims who need treatment, from those who were rotting in trenches during World War II.[160]

The aftermath of the February 18–19 incident continued to unfold throughout the first half of 2004. Negotiations continued between the two sides and a great many options for prices and transit charges were rehearsed by Gazprom.[161] In the meantime, Belarus continued to be supplied by independent companies, specifically Transnafta and Sibur.[162] In June 2004, with another cessation of supplies to Belarus seemingly only days away, the two sides agreed a supply and transit contract for 2004 where the main provisions were:

- Gazprom would supply 10.2 Bcm to Belarus at $46.68/mcm (similar to the price that some independents had been charging and substantially above the Russian price in the 5th zone of around $30/mcm which Belarus had paid in 2003);
- A transmission tariff of $0.75/mcm for delivering gas through Beltransgaz-owned networks;
- A transit tariff of $0.46/mcm for gas flowing through the Yamal pipeline to Europe;
- Negotiations on the creation of a Beltransgaz joint venture would continue;
- 32 Bcm of gas would be transited via Belarus including 23 Bcm through the Yamal pipeline.[163]

In late August 2004 at a meeting of the two presidents in Sochi, the main conditions for the 2005 contract were established with 19.1 Bcm due to be delivered at the 2004 price of $48.68/mcm, the main difference being that Gazprom intends to deliver all of the gas rather than relying on independents.[164] President Putin was clearly soft-pedalling on the joint venture but remaining firm on the trade-off between its creation and gas prices: 'There is still an opportunity to reorganise the Beltransgaz company into a Russian-Belarusian joint venture. If Gazprom and Beltransgaz agree to set up a joint venture, we will keep our promise to deliver gas at Russian domestic prices.' [165]

Gazprom and the Russian government are attempting to establish a new status quo under which Gazprom will take over the supply of Russian gas to the country; payment will be slightly below the 'going rate' of $50–52/mcm for gas deliveries to CIS; rights to transport and transit through networks owned by Beltransgaz and the Yamal pipeline (owned by Gazprom) will be maximised; the option of creating a joint Gazprom/Beltransgaz joint venture remains on the table and the next move is to await an independent valuation of the assets.

On December 27, 2004, the two sides confirmed the August agreement for the 2005 contract with the gas price and transit tariffs remaining the same. The only addition was that Gazprom agreed to supply 19.1 Bcm and an additional 1.4 Bcm 'if it was technically possible'.[166] The fact that the agreement was signed so close to the end of the year suggests considerable resistance from the Belarusian side to the terms being offered. However, by April 2005, the parties stated that the terms would remain the same for 2006 as long as the construction and property registration of the remaining compressor stations for the Yamal Pipeline (see Chapter 3) went ahead as planned.[167]

Moldova

With an annual requirement of only 2–3 Bcm, it is easy to overlook Russian sales to Moldova. However, the country is also an important transit route along which all gas to south-eastern Europe (Romania, Bulgaria and western Turkey) – amounting to more than 22 Bcm in 2003 – must pass. During the 1990s, Moldova's relations with Gazprom followed the familiar CIS pattern of periodic debt crises. This was temporarily resolved in October 1998 by which time the debt had risen to $600m (of which $400m was owed by the TransDnestr region) when Moldova Gas was created, owned 50% by Gazprom, 35.3% by Moldova, 13.44% by the TransDnestr region and 1.23% by individual shareholders (mostly employees).[168]

Very severe problems of indebtedness continued through the late 1990s and early 2000s with periodic reductions in supply and even complete cut-offs by Gazprom. Moldova was charged a high price for its gas, $80/mcm, although the October 2001 agreement between the countries allowed for an immediate payment of $60/mcm with $20/mcm accumulating as a debt to be paid after 2004. This high price was counterbalanced by a very high transit tariff of $2.50/mcm/00km.[169] Throughout the late 1990s and early 2000s, Gazprom remained the dominant gas supplier, although during the period 1999−2001 Itera delivered 0.6−0.7 Bcm, more than a quarter of the country's supplies, and purchased a controlling stake in Moldova's main metallurgical works. The price charged by Itera in 2002 was said to be $46.7/mcm, substantially below the Gazprom price, and this led to allegations that senior government officials had pocketed the difference between the two prices.[170]

By 2004, the obligations of Moldova and TransDnestr Republic had been separated out by Gazprom with both entities having difficulty in collecting payments from consumers; Moldova's collection rate was just above 85% while TransDnestr's was substantially lower at 67%. By April 2004, debts (including interest penalties) had mounted to $308m for Moldova and $960m for TransDnestr with renewed threats to cut off the latter's supply in the absence of satisfactory payment guarantees, but there were problems of implementing such threats because of the Republic's transit role.[171]

Renewal of the 2005 transit contract by Moldova for 21.8 Bcm at the end of 2004 at $2.50/mcm/00km, half to be paid in money and half in deliveries of around 0.3 Bcm of gas, seemed a positive step. More complicated was the relationship with the TransDnestr region which − due to deteriorating relations between Kishinev and Tiraspol akin to a 'war of economic sanctions' − had, according to Gazexport, raised the possibility that the region would withdraw from Moldova Gas.[172] This appeared to be strongly connected with heavy Russian backing for the TransDnestr leadership against the Moldovan (Communist) leadership in the March 2005 elections.[173] With election victory leading to a more pro-European stance from the government in Chisinau, it remained to be seen how far Gazprom's tolerance of non-payment would continue.

The Broader Political and Geopolitical Context

Natural gas fits into Russian relations with CIS countries in a much broader political and geopolitical context which can only be discussed briefly here. This chapter has repeatedly illustrated the importance of bilateral political relationships at the highest level. It is no accident that all gas trade takes place under the umbrella of intergovernmental agreements, or that all commercial gas agreements are approved and signed by presidents and prime ministers. Among the most visible, but by no means the only, manifestations of the broader bilateral and regional political context of CIS gas relationships are the following:

1. The (unsuccessful) attempt to trade Russian gas debt off against Ukrainian nuclear weapons and the Black Sea fleet;
2. the crisis over the creation of the Beltransgas joint venture with 50% Gazprom participation at the same time as ongoing negotiations between the Russian and Belarusian presidents on unification of the countries;
3. the building of the Blue Stream pipeline to Turkey in order to counter the strong American support for both the Trans-Caspian pipeline from Turkmenistan, and Azeri gas deliveries from the Shah Deniz field to Turkey and further west.

Post-Soviet relations between the former Union republics have spawned a variety of multilateral institutions, some of which appear to be loose groupings of countries with dubious institutional relevance or cohesiveness. Indeed the relevance of the Commonwealth of Independent States (CIS) – to which the title of this chapter refers – has become increasingly questionable beyond its usefulness as a collective label for the former Soviet republics (minus the Baltic States).[174] Russian-inspired groupings such as the Eurasian Economic Community of five CIS states created in 2000 have had little practical impact.[175] The 2003 agreement between Russia, Ukraine, Belarus and Kazakhstan to create a Common Economic Space – akin to the European Union – has also seemingly made little progress and its status appeared further diminished with the arrival of the Yushchenko administration in Ukraine.

   The politics of the gas relationships between Russia and Central Asian countries are very important to both the Putin administration and other national governments. President Putin's suggestion in early 2002 at a meeting with a delegation headed by the Turkmen president, to create an 'alliance' of Eurasian gas producers was detailed only to the extent of mentioning the need to 'bring an element of stability to long term transportation of gas'.[176] Prime Minister Kasyanov's urging of the Eurasian Economic Community in early 2003 to set up a gas alliance 'that can later be joined by other CIS countries', may have been the result of a predictable lack of keenness from the Turkmenbashi about the concept.[177] Nevertheless, some attribute the Turkmen-Russian gas rapprochement to regional political changes in the post-9/11 world including President Niyazov's concerns about the fate of those who might be regarded as the same type of dictator as Saddam Hussein.[178] Given the overall judgement that '[t]here is little evidence that Putin's Administration has developed (and it has certainly not published) a regional strategy for Central Asia that would integrate Russian security, political, energy and economic interests', natural gas strategy seems to have been particularly well and efficiently carried out by Gazprom.[179]

On a broader geopolitical level, the arrival of US troops in Uzbekistan post-September 11, 2001 both sharpened Russian interest in reasserting strategic interests and emboldened Uzbekistan in its new status as US strategic partner in the region, to become what one author has called the 'regional hegemon'.[180] The impact of future security tensions between the Central Asian states – and particularly between Uzbekistan and its neighbours – on gas trade should not be underestimated, particularly with all Turkmen exports needing to transit through that country.[181] Regional security concerns about the potential influence of Uzbekistan may have been a contributory factor in helping Russia and Gazprom to re-establish itself in Central Asian gas commerce, particularly in Tajikistan and Kyrgyzstan, but also in Turkmenistan.

In the mid 2000s, political change in the CIS appeared to be accelerating with the replacement of Soviet-era regimes in Georgia, Ukraine and Kyrgyzstan by leaderships who, at least in their early months, showed a desire to engage with the institutions of the European Union and NATO. It is too early to be sure that such developments will lead to any decisive and long-lasting weakening of Russian influence over these countries, but not too early to discern an increasing concern in Moscow about such a prospect. With natural gas being a key energy resource for the majority of CIS countries, and with many of those countries being unable – for reasons of geography and finance – to obtain supplies from sources other than Russia or Central Asia (requiring transit through Russia), gas will remain a very important element in economic and political relationships between Russia and its former Soviet neighbours.

It is often said that Gazprom acts as an agent of Russian foreign policy, and the company's actions would certainly feature in any study of Russian relations with CIS countries. However, purely political commentaries tend to neglect how serious natural gas has become in terms of finance and business in Gazprom's (and hence Russia's) external relationships. As we have seen in a range of examples, notably Belarus in 2004 and Turkmenistan in 2005, even when it is Russia's foreign policy interest to be conciliatory, the amount of money involved in paying higher prices for gas makes such political gestures very expensive, and consequently there is a tendency for them to be short term.

Summary and Conclusions

The general trend in Russian gas trade with CIS countries during the post-Soviet period has been one of disengagement in the mid to late 1990s, followed by strong re-engagement in the 2000s and in particular post-2002. Part of the explanation for these trends is economic and commercial – the problems of Russian and CIS economies in the 1990s led to mounting debts and frequent confrontations, with deliveries being restricted and interrupted. During this period, Gazprom's domestic problems seemed so overwhelming that the inability of CIS countries to sign any commercial agreements that they could honour – principally because of their own problems of revenue collection – allowed for an argument that handing the business over to intermediaries was not necessarily a bad strategy.

As the principal intermediary up to 2002, Itera did not suffer from the political restrictions of Gazprom in terms of its relationships with the Russian government, or vulnerability to diversions of gas in transit to Europe. In the late 1990s, Itera demonstrated – both in Russia and other CIS countries – that it was possible to enforce payment (even if not in cash) in all countries and thereby operate a profitable gas business within and between CIS countries. In so doing, Itera both reintegrated Central Asian gas into CIS trade (following the hiatus of 1998) and was the commercial lynch-pin of this trade from 1998 to 2002.

As the 2000s progressed, several important developments saw Gazprom largely take CIS gas trade back under its control. These were first, arrival of the Putin administration and the change of Gazprom management in 2001 which much more closely aligned the company with government policy (see Chapter 4). Secondly, a change of Gazprom's supply position led to Central Asian gas becoming a much more important potential component of its future supply portfolio. Thirdly, the recovery of CIS economies meant that it became much easier to operate gas trade as a profitable business.

In the period 2001–04 Gazprom succeeded in establishing con-tractual relationships throughout the CIS. A series of interlocking agreements for the supply and shipping of Central Asian gas to Rus-sia and Ukraine has been accompanied by the company's apparent determination to re-establish itself as the sole supplier of gas to the Caucasus countries and Belarus. The pattern of trade established by Gazprom in the 2000s is consistent in each of the three groups of countries: Central Asia, the Caucasus, Ukraine/Belarus/Moldova. The strategy is clearly to create long-term contractual relationships between Gazprom and the national companies in order to:

- eliminate intermediaries or limit their activity to a peripheral role;
- achieve commercial closure on the years of non-payment, debt and upheaval of the 1990s and early 2000s;
- establish a commercial basis for trade that does not depend on subsidised prices unless there is a quid pro quo in terms of Gazprom ownership of assets;
- reinforce foreign policy initiatives of the Russian government in these countries.

Since 2003, Gazprom has acted very determinedly to take over CIS trade eliminating other Russian suppliers and shippers. It is not certain that such action will be completely successful or that Gazprom may not yet relent in some circumstances – as in the first half of 2004 when it was encouraging independent producers to supply gas to Belarus. Most of the outstanding CIS debts to Gazprom had been settled by late 2004 – with the exception of Moldova and the TransDnestr republic – but given past history there must be some uncertainty that the arrangements with Ukraine will work out as planned, and the Belarus situation remained unresolved and therefore potentially unstable.

In contrast to its successes, Gazprom has not succeeded in gaining control of many CIS network assets. Only in Armenia (45% of Armrosgazprom) and Moldova (50% of Moldovagaz) has Gazprom been able to form a joint venture that gives it some control of the network.[182] Despite having strenuously sought asset ownership in both Ukraine and Belarus since the break-up of the Union, it made very limited progress. The Ukraine Consortium – in reality Gazprom and Naftokhaz Ukraine – transferred its attention to building new capacity rather than the more urgent task of refurbishing the existing network, and the arrival of the Yushchenko administration in 2005 did not seem likely to change that situation substantially. Gazprom's participation in a Beltransgaz joint venture was stalled and seemed unlikely to be quickly resolved.

For Gazprom, future relations with CIS countries raise four interrelated questions. First, can Central Asian countries be relied upon for secure supplies of gas? Secondly, can Ukraine, Belarus and Moldova be transformed into profitable markets? Thirdly, can those same countries provide secure transit for gas supplies to Europe at reasonable cost? Fourthly, will Caucasus countries remain linked to the rest of the CIS, or become increasingly detached with respect to gas supply.

The security aspects of increasingly heavy dependence on Central Asian gas is a risk that will need to be carefully evaluated by Gazprom if these supplies are to be used as a substitute for new domestic gas development. 'Security' in this context has two important aspects

– affordability and reliability; events such as the Turkmen demand for higher prices followed by cutting off exports to both Ukraine and Russia at the end of 2004, jeopardised the company's carefully constructed CIS gas strategy. Gazprom has strong economic power over Central Asian gas suppliers given that it controls their transit routes to markets in both the CIS and beyond. But Ukrainian dependence on Turkmen gas, and potential Russian dependence anticipated by the 2003 long-term gas agreement, substantially complicate Gazprom's bargaining position. In the longer term (beyond 2010), additional problems for the company would arise should east and south Asian markets present themselves as credible commercial alternatives to those of Russia and the CIS, which would be welcomed by Central Asian sellers anxious to improve their bargaining power.

If supply and price dependence on Central Asian gas looms as a possible future problem for Gazprom, its ongoing achilles heel is its transit dependence on Ukraine, Belarus and Moldova because of the ability of those countries to interrupt gas deliveries to Europe. Transit has introduced substantial commercial and political complexity into Gazprom's relationships with the three countries because of the lack of available finance to fully monetise these relationships. The company cannot afford to cut off gas to these countries because of the hardship caused to their citizens, their ability to take gas destined for European customers, and the alarm that such action causes in Europe (see Chapter 3).

The profitability of CIS markets has become increasingly important for Gazprom and the willingness to provoke a crisis by cutting off Belarus in February 2004 was, at least in part, a refusal to tolerate continued subsidies unless there was a quid pro quo in terms of ownership of pipeline assets. In the Ukrainian relationship, the restriction of Gazprom's deliveries to payments for transit reduced the scope for commercial disagreement following the adoption of a formula equating a gas sales price of $50/mcm with a transit tariff of $1.094/mcm/00km. But such agreements on prices and tariffs with little analytical justification in terms of costs or market values leave gas trade subject to the changes in bilateral political relationships, or power plays by either side, which in turn complicate long-term security of transit.

The refusal of Russia to ratify the Energy Charter Treaty and its Transit Protocol is, at least in part, a determination to resolve transit at a bilateral level rather than lose control of the process to an international legal regime with independent dispute settlement.[183] This determination risks continued instability and insecurity in transit relationships unless Gazprom – backed by the Russian government

– can succeed in the future where it has so far failed to achieve a stable commercial framework of sales and transit. Future stability will, at a minimum, require sales and transit tariffs based on values that can be independently determined and verified by each side.

In the Caucasus, the gas supply position changed significantly between 2002 and 2004. Up to 2002, all three republics received their external supplies exclusively from Itera; whereas by 2004 the latter had been excluded and supplies had been taken over by Gazprom, with Gazexport as the commercial intermediary. Despite this change, there was some continuity in the source of supply in that Gazprom delivers Central Asian gas to these republics; although this involves more gas from Kazakhstan, compared with Itera's supplies which involved more Turkmen gas.

However, in the late 2000s the position of the Caucasus republics may change again, breaking with the Soviet past in terms of gas supplies. By 2010, Azerbaijan should be self-sufficient and supplying part (and perhaps the majority) of Georgian gas requirements, while Armenia should be taking part (if not the majority) of its gas from Iran. In Georgia and Armenia, much may depend on Russian – Gazprom and UES – ownership of important gas consuming assets.

Gazprom's strategy challenge in the CIS is about how to manage increasingly complex interdependence relationships with three groups of countries:

1.   Central Asia – where Gazprom will depend increasingly on supplies but will also be providing transit to markets.
2.   Caucasus countries where, in advance of competing gas supplies from Azerbaijan and Iran later this decade, Gazprom is trying to secure and retain market share by buying equity in power and industrial enterprises which are large gas users.
3.   Ukraine, Belarus and Moldova – where Gazprom will be (i) selling gas; (ii) providing transit services for Central Asian gas to Ukraine (and potentially other countries in the future); (iii) depending on transit services to Europe.

This has been a difficult balancing act in the post-Soviet period and shows signs of being even more complex in the future until and unless the trade can be moved to a cash basis with a cost/market value foundation, and a contractual basis that is respected by all governments. In 2005, the questioning and possible unravelling of Gazprom's carefully constructed contractual basis for future sales and transportation between Turkmenistan, Ukraine and Russia suggested that long-term stability in these contractual relationships continued to prove elusive.

CHAPTER 3

EXPORT STRATEGY AND CHALLENGES: EUROPE, ASIA AND LNG

The first Soviet gas exports to Europe were delivered to Poland in the mid-1940s, but large-scale gas exports to Czechoslovakia began in 1967 with Austria receiving its first gas the following year.[1] Russia is thus well into its fourth decade as a major gas supplier to Europe, and its second decade as a supplier to post-Cold War reunified Europe. In 2004, eight of Gazprom's customers, which were former Soviet Republics or European socialist allies, became member states of the European Union and were therefore required to implement both EU competition rules and directives on liberalising gas (and electricity) markets. Russia's European exports were therefore becoming increasingly governed by EU regulation overseen both by national regulators and by the European Commission in Brussels across a pan-European space. For Russia and Gazprom, the history of gas exports has been one of pipeline gas exports to Europe. The future will be more diverse, with increased opportunities to export gas to Asia and the potential to become an LNG supplier not just to Asia, but also to North America. This chapter therefore examines not only the recent history of Gazprom's exports to Europe, but the prospects for the company to become a 'global gas player'.

Europe

Table 3.1 shows Russian gas exports to Europe during the period 1990–2003. In aggregate terms, the expansion of Russian gas exports to Europe has not taken a smooth upward path. Volumes did not exceed 1990 levels until 1995, and have risen thereafter, but not continuously. From 2002–2004, exports rose by nearly 20 Bcm, almost entirely due to increases in deliveries to western Europe. But the country by country figures in Table 3.1 do not correspond with the Gazprom data according to which exports in 2003 were 140.3 Bcm of which 132.9 Bcm was gas of Russian origin and 7.4 Bcm was from Central Asia.[2] Neither do the country by country figures identify spot sales to the UK and Belgium which began in 2001, and rose to 4.14 Bcm in 2004; these deliveries are included in the French and German export data.[3]

Table 3.1: Russian Natural Gas Exports to Europe 1990–2004*** (Bcm)

	1990	1991	1992	1993	1994	1995	1996	1997	1998	1999	2000	2001	2002	2003	2004
Former Yugoslavia	4.5	4.5	3.0	2.7	2.3	2.0	4.0	3.9	3.7	3.1	3.5	3.47	3.8	4.071	4.43
including:															
"Yugoslavia"							2.11	2.06	1.80	1.1	1.5*	1.65	1.7	1.87	2.25
Croatia							0.97	1.14	1.20	1.2	1.9**	1.17	1.2	1.23	1.14
Slovenia							0.49	0.50	0.50	0.6		0.57	0.6	0.68	0.65
Bosnia & Herzegovina							0.42	0.14	0.20	0.2		0.15	0.2	0.21	0.32
Macedonia								0.001	0.002	0.04	0.1	0.09	0.1	0.08	0.07
Romania	7.3	5.4	4.4	4.6	4.5	6.1	7.15	5.09	4.70	3.2	3.2	2.87	3.5	5.1	4.14
Bulgaria	6.8	5.7	5.3	4.8	4.7	5.8	6.03	4.95	3.80	3.2	3.2	3.32	2.8	2.94	3.01
Hungary	6.4	5.9	4.8	4.8	5.2	6.3	7.71	6.52	7.30	7.4	6.5	8.03	9.1	10.36	9.25
Poland	8.4	7.1	6.7	5.8	6.2	7.2	7.14	6.75	6.90	6.1	6.8	7.51	7.3	7.36	6.33
Czech Republic	6.6	}13.7	6.8	}13.2	}13.8	8.4	9.44	8.43	8.60	7.8	7.5	7.46	7.4	7.38	6.84
Slovakia	6.0		6.0			6.5	7.04	7.09	7.10	7.5	7.9	7.52	7.7	7.29	7.77
Total Central/Eastern	46.0	42.3	37.0	35.9	36.7	42.3	48.5	42.7	42.2	38.34	38.7	40.3	41.6	44.5	41.77
Greece							0.01	0.16	0.90	1.5	1.6	1.52	1.6	1.90	2.21
Turkey	3.3	4.1	4.5	5.0	4.7	5.7	5.63	6.70	6.70	8.9	10.2	11.12	11.8	12.85	14.51
Finland	2.7	2.9	3.0	3.1	3.4	3.6	3.73	3.64	4.20	4.2	4.3	4.64	4.6	5.11	4.95
Austria	5.1	5.2	5.1	5.3	5.1	6.1	6.02	5.57	5.70	5.4	5.1	4.91	5.2	6.03	6.01
Switzerland	0.3	0.4	0.4	0.4	0.4	0.4	0.39	0.40	0.40	0.4	0.4	0.34	0.3	0.3	0.34
France	10.6	11.4	12.1	11.6	12.2	12.9	12.35	10.91	10.90	13.4	12.9	11.15	11.4	11.24	14.02
Italy	14.3	14.5	14.1	13.8	13.8	14.3	13.99	14.22	17.30	19.8	21.8	20.2	19.3	19.75	21.55
Germany	26.6	24.4	22.9	25.8	29.6	32.1	32.87	32.52	32.50	34.9	34.1	32.61	32.2	34.97	40.87
Netherlands												0.1	1.4	2.27	2.70
Total Western	63.0	62.9	62.1	65.0	69.2	75.1	75.0	74.1	78.5	88.5	90.3	86.49	87.8	94.43	107.32
TOTAL EUROPE	109.0	105.2	99.1	100.9	105.8	117.4	123.5	116.8	120.5	126.8	129.0	126.7	129.4	138.93	149.09

* Bosnia and Yugoslavia; ** Slovenia and Croatia; *** excluding Baltic countries.

Source: Gazprom

All Gazprom's sales to Europe are handled by its wholly-owned subsidiary Gazexport which either directly or through its affiliates, such as ZGG, sells gas throughout Europe.[4] Prior to 1990, a sharp division was made between 'western' Europe, essentially the member-countries of the OECD whether or not they happened to be located in the west of the Continent and 'eastern' Europe, the socialist countries of Warsaw Pact/Comecon.[5]

With the unification of Europe and the expansion of the OECD, the European Union and NATO to include countries in 'eastern' Europe and the former Soviet Union, it becomes more logical to look at Russia's gas trade with the whole of the geographical space known as 'Europe'. The section looks at how Gazprom's export strategy towards Europe evolved in the 1990s and early 2000s through the development of joint ventures and trading houses, the issues of diversification and transit in central Europe and the importance of transit-avoidance pipelines. It highlights the financial importance of exports to Europe and the impact of the liberalisation and competition initiatives of the European Union, the Energy Charter Treaty and the accession of the Russia Federation to the World Trade Organisation. It also discusses the perennial issue of security of Russian gas supplies for European customers.

Joint Ventures and Trading Houses

During the late 1980s, Gazprom devised a strategy of moving 'down-stream' into European gas markets, since its practice of selling gas at the border of the importing country meant that the dominant importing company was able to capture a large amount of the profit from the sale of gas. The folklore of the European gas business has it that in 1989 Victor Chernomyrdin, then Chairman of Gazprom, proposed to the Chairman of Ruhrgas that the two companies should form a marketing joint venture to sell gas in Germany, and was rebuffed in a manner that gave serious offence to Gazprom. Whatever the truth of this story, the consequence was that in October 1990, Wintershall announced a co-operation agreement with Gazprom at the heart of which was a joint venture company to market Russian gas in the eastern part of Germany.[6] The alliance − earlier known as Wintershall Erdgas Handelshaus or WIEH, later to be supplemented by another joint venture, Wingas − was thus able to start by building two major pipelines: STEGAL carrying Russian gas from St Katheriny on the German-Czech border, to join the MIDAL line south of Kassel.[7] Over the next decade, the Wingas venture built major pipelines and storage facilities in Germany, in particular the Jagal and Wedal pipelines and the Rehden storage facility.

For Gazprom the Wingas joint venture was an opportunity to operate in a foreign commercial organisation as equal partners, with its
executives in senior management positions. It also provided market
intelligence as to true costs and margins involved in the German gas
market. No longer did Gazprom have to accept the view of the importing company on how Russian gas should be priced, it could form a view
based on first-hand knowledge. But perhaps the principal advantage
of the Wingas experience was that it struck fear into all of Gazprom's
other traditional partners in European countries. If Gazprom could
find, and form an alliance with, a company prepared to compete with
Ruhrgas − whose position, prior to 1990, had seemed unchallengeable
− it could do the same to its traditional partners in other countries.
An early success of that strategy is illustrated by the Italian Volta joint
venture (with Edison Gas), announced in 1995, to move an additional
10 Bcm into the Italian market. This was an indication of Gazprom's
ambitions in terms of expanding deliveries to one of its largest export
markets. In May 1998 Edison announced that the project had been
postponed, but from Gazprom's perspective, the threat of taking on a
new partner had the desired effect of persuading SNAM (Gazprom's
long-time Italian partner) to sign contracts for additional volumes.[8]

The principal drawback for Gazprom from the Wingas experience
was the resulting pipeline to pipeline competition between Ruhrgas
and Wingas, which drove down prices in the German market. To some
extent, Gazprom found that its supplies sold by Wingas, were competing
with Russian gas supplies being sold by Ruhrgas, resulting in reduced
prices and therefore margins on sales. In the early years of competition,
this was an acceptable price to pay for market entry, market intelligence
and as an important demonstration to other European gas companies.
But by 1998, these advantages had been established and Gazprom's
German strategy changed fundamentally with the signing of a new
cooperation agreement with Ruhrgas. The principal elements of the
agreement were the extension of existing contracts by twelve years,
Gazprom rights to transit gas through the Ruhrgas network and an extension of technical co-operation between the companies.[9] In December
1998, Ruhrgas purchased a 2.5% share of Gazprom's equity at a price
reported at $1bn followed, in May 1999, by the purchase of another
1.5% of the company.[10] By 2004, Ruhrgas − which had become part
of the E.ON group − had increased its stake in Gazprom to 6.4%.[11]

During the 1990s, Gazprom established joint venture marketing
companies or 'trading houses' (the term by which they are often described by Gazprom), throughout Europe. By 2005, the company listed
a significant number of 'associated undertakings' in 18 European

countries (Table 3.2). Excluded from this list is Gazprom's 10% share in the Interconnector (IUK) pipeline (which runs between Britain and Belgium) and previously established joint ventures, Yugorosgaz

Table 3.2: Gazprom's Principal Associated Undertakings in Europe

Country	Name of Organisation	Equity %	Nature of Operations
Germany:	GASA Zarubezhgaz Import-Export	30	Distribution
	Wingas	35	Transportation and sales
	WIEH	50	Sales and marketing
France	Fragaz	50	Distribution and trading
Italy	Promgaz	50	Marketing and distribution
Switzerland:	Baltic LNG	80	Development and sale of LNG
	Gas Project Dev't		Production and development of oil
	Centre Asia	50	and gas fields in Central Asia
	WIEE	50	Marketing and delivery
Slovakia	Slovrusgaz	50	Transportation and marketing
Austria	GWH	50	Marketing and trading
Finland	Gasum	25	Transportation and marketing
Poland:	EuroPol Gaz	48	Transportation (Yamal Pipeline)
	Gaz Trading	16	Marketing and trading, gas and LPG
Serbia	Progresgaz Trading	25	Distribution
Bulgaria	Overgas	50	Marketing, construction, TSO
Czech Rep	Gas-Invest	37.5	Marketing, distribution, trading
Turkey:	Turusgaz	45	Marketing
	Bosphorus Gas	40	Transportation and distribution
Hungary:	AEB	26	Banking
	Panrusgaz	40	Marketing and distribution
Greece	Prometheus Gas	50	Marketing and construction
Lithuania:	Stella Vitae	30	Transportation and distribution
	Lietuvos Dujos	37.06	Marketing and transportation
Estonia	Eesti Gaas	37.5	Market and transportation
Latvia	Latvias Gaze	34	Marketing of gas and LPG
BSPC	Netherlands	50	Construction and gas transportation

OAO Gazprom, *IFRS Consolidated Financial Statements*, 31 December 2003, p.20; Gazprom, *Financial Report 2003*, p.78; *Loan Notes 2005*, pp. 150–151.

(Yugoslavia) and Wirom (Romania). It is difficult to generalise about
the role and activity of these ventures. They can be arranged in three
groups:

1. Those involved principally in pipeline construction and operation,
    such as Europol Gaz;
2. Those which are already handling (or will in future handle) sub-
    stantial amounts of gas under long-term contracts sold in their
    respective countries. Wingas, Gasum, Panrusgas, Wirom and Pro-
    gresgaz Trading come under this heading;
3. Those which principally trade gas outside the framework of long-
    term contracts with Gazprom's major partner in their respective
    countries: GWH, Gaz Trading, Fragaz, Slovrusgaz and Promgaz.

It is difficult to obtain information regarding how much gas these
marketing ventures buy or sell. Each case is different; for example
Panrusgas is believed to have exclusive rights to handle all Russian
gas deliveries to Hungary.[12] Promgas has a long-term contract for 2
Bcm/year and has also sold gas on short-term contracts. It is not known
whether Fragaz has ever sold any gas.

Central Europe: Diversification, Security and Transit

In the immediate aftermath of independence from the Soviet Union
and the break-up of the socialist economic area (Comecon or CMEA),
the former European member-countries of that organisation were
placed in an extremely difficult financial situation. Gazprom demanded
that energy deliveries should be paid for in hard currency and at 'world
prices'.[13] Of considerable assistance to the former Comecon members
was that they had all participated in development co-operation projects
connected with the Orenburg and Yamburg gas fields. These included
intergovernmental agreements guaranteeing deliveries of gas under soft
currency and/or barter arrangements until the late 1990s, which proved
immensely useful for central and eastern European countries in partly
smoothing the path to full commercial relationships with Gazprom.
Nevertheless, gas imports fell sharply under the combined pressure
of adjusting to hard currency payments and economic reform and
restructuring programmes, briefly exceeding 1990 levels in 1996 before
falling again. In 2004, total deliveries to these countries remained below
1990 levels with the collapse of exports to Bulgaria, and significant
reductions to Romania and Poland not offset by increases to Hungary
and Slovakia (Table 3.1).

In the transition to hard currency payments at European price levels immediately following independence, it was difficult to believe that Central European countries would be able to afford the prices needing to be paid in hard currency to bring non-Russian gas through new pipelines to this region. But within five years of independence, the economies of the Czech Republic, Hungary and Poland began to recover, and energy and gas demand began to rise. In the mid 1990s, the perception was that Russia's economic and political hold over these countries would be too strong and that Gazprom would seek to punish those who were intent on diversification away from Russian supplies.

Contrary to these perceptions, gas companies in these countries began active consideration of projects that would bring non-Russian supplies to the region. When the Hungarian company MOL signed a ten-year contract in 1995 with Ruhrgas for the delivery of 0.5 Bcm annually (starting in 1996), it was viewed more as a security measure than as real diversification. The major breakthrough for diversification arrived in April 1997 with the agreement between the Czech company Transgas and Norway's GFU. The agreement provided for the almost immediate start of deliveries and the eventual increase in deliveries to 3 Bcm/year by 2000.[14] Decisive factors in the eventual choice made by the Czechs were a political threat made by the Russian ambassador to Prague regarding the Czech application for NATO membership, and a desire for a source of gas physically separate from Russian production and delivery systems. In late-1998, the new relationship was formalised when Gazprom and the Czech transmission company Transgas signed long-term contracts for supply and transit.[15]

Negotiations between Gazprom and the Czech authorities were notable for the steadfastness with which the Czechs resisted the formation of a joint marketing company with Gazprom in the country, the only major buyer of Russian gas to have taken such a 'hardline' stance, despite the fact that it eliminated the possibility of anything other than hard currency cash payment. In 1997, Gazprom appointed Gas-Invest as an agent with exclusive rights to supply additional quantities of gas to the Czech market, but its activities were limited to trading marginal volumes, pipeline rehabilitation and export of equipment.[16] When the Czech transmission company Transgas and majority stakes in the distribution companies were bought by the German company RWE in 2001, there was no suggestion that Gazprom had even been allowed to bid.[17] In 2005, the Gazexport subsidiary ZMB Zarubezhgaz acquired 37.5% of Gas-Invest.[18]

Gazprom's freedom of action in the Czech Republic is constrained

by the importance of the country as a transit route for Russian gas to
Germany and beyond. Yet Slovakia is an even more important transit
country for Russian gas to the rest of Europe and it would be hard
to find a greater contrast with the Czech Republic than Gazprom's
relationship with the Slovak gas industry, in particular the transmission company SPP.[19] In 1997, a joint Gazprom/SPP trading house
– Slovrusgas – was created, which was intended to purchase all Russian
gas, on-selling to SPP.[20] However, most of Slovakia's gas is obtained
as payment for transit, almost all the rest is purchased by SPP, leaving
Slovrusgas in a marginal role. In 2002, 49% of SPP was sold to Ruhrgas
and Gaz de France with Gazprom retaining an option to subsequently
purchase 12.5% of the equity from those companies.[21]

Poland was another example of a country with a strong desire to
diversify away from Russian gas supplies but extreme difficulty in
achieving this aim. The past decade saw a stream of diversification
announcements about bringing pipeline gas from Netherlands, Norway
and Denmark.[22] The reality has been endless discussions, negotiations
and even signed contracts, but failure to dislodge the commercial reality
that – particularly since the building of the Yamal pipeline (see below)
– Russian gas is by far the cheapest supply alternative for Poland. The
only exceptions to this have been 0.5 Bcm/year imported from Norway,
starting in late 2000, via the German Netra pipeline, and a roughly
similar volume of short-term supply imported from Germany.[23] Plans
for a 5 Bcm/year long-term contract with the Norwegian company
Statoil were finally abandoned in 2003.[24] Meanwhile, the Polish Oil
and Gas Company (PGNiG) – despite concerns about dependence on
Russia – imported around 2 Bcm/year of Turkmen gas from Eural
Trans Gas (ETG) in 2003 and 2004, and issued a tender for supply
of 3.4 Bcm from July 2005 to end-2006.[25] Extreme political sensitivity
in Poland to dependence on Russian gas supplies, which has been in
evidence regularly during the post-Soviet era, especially during the
February 2004 Belarus crisis (see Chapter 2), has also focused on the
Yamal pipeline (see below).[26]

Difficult problems also arose in Bulgaria in the mid 1990s, with the
principal points of disagreement being the role that Gazprom should be
allowed to play in transportation to, and sales of gas in Bulgaria, as well
as the price that the company should pay for transit through Bulgaria
to Turkey. Political instability in Bulgaria led to significant changes in
government policy and greatly increased sensitivity to the sovereignty
issues connected with foreign, especially Russian, commercial activity
in the country. The fall in Russian deliveries after 1996 reflected a
change in the terms of trade to cash and gas for transit, following the

settlement of debts under the Yamburg intergovernmental agreement. In April 1998, after two years of often bitter negotiations, Gazprom signed sales and transit agreements for the period up to 2010 with the Bulgarian government which involved increasing transit capacity to nearly 18.7 Bcm (13.5 Bcm of Russian gas transited Bulgaria to Turkey, Greece and Macedonia in 2002).[27] The outcome was a severe contraction in the Bulgarian gas market due (in some accounts) to Gazprom's insistence on using Topenergy – a company which eventually became 100% owned by Gazprom – as an intermediary.[28] Meanwhile, the Overgaz joint venture (50% Gazprom/50% Bulgargaz) has become a significant gas supplier with licences to build transmission networks in 26 Bulgarian cities.[29]

In Romania, desire to diversify was signalled when Romgaz signed a declaration of intent with Ruhrgas for delivery of 0.5 Bcm/year starting in the winter of 1999, with an option to increase to 2 Bcm by 2005, but no transportation route was created. Negotiations with Gasunie to import Dutch gas similarly came to nothing.[30] Subsequently, the state-owned monopoly Romgaz was privatised and restructured into production, storage, transmission and (five) distribution companies. While Gazprom failed in its bid to purchase shares in the country's gas distribution companies, it has continued to cooperate with Wintershall in marketing, as well as developing transmission and storage projects.[31]

During the 1990s, diversification of gas supplies in central and east European countries appeared to be as much connected with an assertion of economic independence, national sovereignty and a demonstrative break with the Communist era, as with gas supply security i.e. the risk that Russia would force adverse policies on these countries by threatening to cut off gas supplies. In 2005, with most countries having either already become EU members or likely to achieve membership status by the end of the decade, such motivations may become less strong. For most countries, the objective is less that of achieving 'independence', and more about restructuring commercial relationships in order to achieve a more politically acceptable framework of economic and energy interdependence. Nevertheless, contractual diversification – while it may have had additional costs – achieved three important goals. First, it was an important symbol of economic (and hence political) independence. Secondly, it provided a security assurance that, should any supply problems occur with respect to Russian gas, others have a contractual commitment to deliver alternative supplies. Thirdly, it was a means to compel Gazprom to remain competitive with other suppliers.

Transit Avoidance Pipelines: Yamal-Europe, North European Pipeline and Blue Stream

Yamal-Europe. The post-Soviet problems of transit through Ukraine during the 1990s (discussed in Chapter 2) became sufficiently serious that Gazprom – with no solution in sight and fearful of jeopardising its main source of revenues and its reputation for reliability – set out to develop transit alternatives. Its field development options on the Yamal Peninsula were described in Chapter 1. Part of the original plan for the Yamal development was that two export lines would follow the existing Northern Lights system through Belarus, branching at Brest into Poland and thence to Germany. The official Gazexport history of the Yamal-Europe pipeline states that in 1992 Gazprom began to develop the idea of creating a new export corridor. Two important milestones were:[32]

- the signing in 1993 of inter-governmental agreements between Russia, Belarus and Poland on the implementation of construction;
- the naming of Yamal-Europe as a 'priority investment project' under the Trans-European Networks Programme, at the Energy Charter Treaty Conference in Lisbon in December 1993.

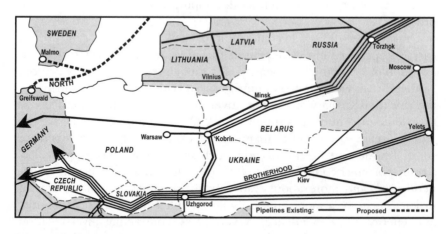

Map 3.1: Pipelines Bringing Russian Gas to Europe

By 1994, the export pipelines through Belarus and Poland had moved significantly ahead of any domestic development and provided a connection between the new export network and existing pipelines delivering gas from existing fields. When Wingas started to build the first sections of pipeline in Germany in 1994, Yamal was said to be being built 'from the market to the fields'.[33] The crossing of the Oder river and the addition of 117 km of new pipeline in the transit countries allowed small quantities of gas to reach Germany at Frankfurt on Oder in 1997.

The first export line, intended to carry 29.3 Bcm into Germany, was significantly delayed. It was not until the end of 1999 that the Belarus section became operational and even by 2004 the pipeline carried only 24 Bcm. There were many reasons for the delays in constructing the pipeline, of which Gazprom's shortage of capital (plus the lack of any funding from Belarus) may be the most important. However, it became increasingly clear, even in 1993/94 when Gazprom first tried to sell Yamal gas, that buyers had no immediate requirement for additional long-term contract gas in such large quantities. Contracts covering more than half of the initial capacity of the line were signed in 1996 with PGNiG (up to 7 Bcm/year), Wingas (10 Bcm/year), and Gasunie (4 Bcm/year but under special circumstances, see below) in 1996 all with very long build-up periods.[34] For these various reasons, Gazprom's urgency to complete the Belarus-Poland (Yamal) pipeline was much reduced. The Yamal pipeline is intended eventually to reach its full capacity of 33 Bcm/year in 2005 when the remaining compressor stations are scheduled to be completed.[35]

During the 2000s, the Belarus-Poland route became problematic for Gazprom not just because of financial difficulties in completing the line and the February 2004 incident in Belarus (see Chapter 2), but also because of the political difficulties in the gas relationship with Poland. The Polish section of the Yamal pipeline was organised as a joint venture to be built and operated by Europol Gaz – a joint venture between Gazprom and the Polish Oil and Gas Company (PGNiG). But detailed examination revealed the joint venture to be owned 48% by PGNiG, 48% by Gazprom, and 4% by the joint venture company Gas Trading. Gas Trading is owned 43% by PGNiG, 16% by Gazexport, 2.73% by Wintershall, 2.27% by Weglokoks and 36% by Bartimpex – a trading company with close historical links to Gazprom. This led Polish politicians to claim that the joint venture was majority Russian-owned – or at least Russian-influenced – and therefore not under the control of the Polish government.[36]

By the early 2000s, Polish gas demand projections had been scaled down substantially, principally due to a failure to develop gas-fired generation, with an expected requirement of 12.7–13.7 Bcm for 2006, compared with 1996 projections above 18–20 Bcm for 2005 rising to 22–28 Bcm by 2010.[37] After a protracted negotiation between Gazprom and PGNiG, the volumes in the 1996 contract were reduced by more than a quarter and the contract period extended.[38]   The much-reduced requirement for gas in Poland, combined with the problems of Belarus transit in early 2004, had eliminated the prospects for a second string of the Yamal pipeline for the foreseeable future. By 2004, Gazprom's strategy for the next major expansion of export capacity to Europe had shifted decisively in favour of the North European Pipeline via the Baltic Sea.

The North European Pipeline. This pipeline (shown in Map 3.2) is designed to run from north west Russia – Vyborg is the most usually stated starting point for the offshore section – through the Baltic Sea to three possible landfalls in Germany, with Greifswald the most likely.[39] According to Gazexport, the UK, the Netherlands and Scandinavian countries (Sweden and Denmark) are the key markets to be served by this pipeline; on some maps the line is drawn with a physical extension as far as the UK.[40] As with the route, the throughput of the pipeline remains uncertain with 20 Bcm being the likely minimum, but with the possibility of expanding this either through compression or – depending on how fast demand may develop – by building additional lines.

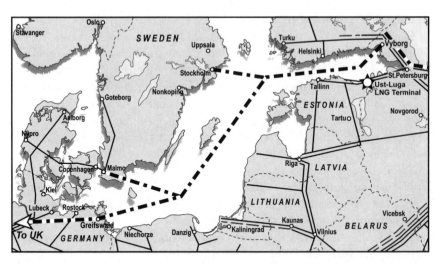

Map 3.2:   The North European Gas Pipeline and the Ust Luga Liquefaction
Terminal

The North European Pipeline (NEP) will be built by the 'North Transgas' company. The original joint venture was established between Gazprom and the Finnish company Fortum (formerly Neste) in 1997 to carry out a detailed study of the offshore section of the project, concluding that it was both technically feasible and commercially viable. The project was awarded Trans-European Network status by the European Commission, followed at the October 2001 EU-Russia Summit by the designation of the NEP as a project of 'common interest' within the EU-Russia energy dialogue (see below). Ruhrgas, Wintershall and Fortum signed an agreement expressing interest in participating in the NEP, since when, according to Gazprom, Gasunie, Shell, TotalFinaElf, British Petroleum, Centrica and PowerGen (the UK subsidiary of E.ON) have also expressed an interest in participating.[41]

In January 2004, Prime Minister Fradkov approved a proposal by the Ministry of Energy and Gazprom to appoint financial, legal and engineering consultants, with a view to taking a final investment decision by the end of the year.[42] However, the original proposed start-up date of 2007 proved to be over-ambitious, and in 2005 NEP was planned to be in operation by 2010. Gazprom purchased Fortum's 50% share in North Transgas, prior to settling the shareholdings of those who will become both owners of, and capacity holders in, the pipeline.[43]

The clear advantage of the NEP from Gazprom's perspective is the avoidance of all transit countries. The clear disadvantages are:

- the lack of any substantial new markets along the route of the line – Sweden and Denmark are small gas markets, while Netherlands and the UK could be reached by other routes;
- the additional cost of the NEP compared with adding another string to the Yamal pipeline

As was noted in Chapter 1, the source of the gas for the NEP was originally intended to be the giant Shtomanovskoye field in the Barents Sea where an international joint venture consortium had been studying the project since the mid-1990s. With the reorientation of Shtokman away from pipeline gas to LNG exports in early 2004, the source of gas for NEP was changed to the South Russkoye field in Western Siberia.[44] This seemed a slightly strange announcement since, if the gas was coming from the NPT region in Western Siberia, there was no obvious reason to designate a particular field as the source. However, it was subsequently revealed that E.ON/Ruhrgas had been offered an opportunity to invest in South Russkoye field – the first western company to be offered the possibility of investing in a West Siberian Cenomanian gas field – as part of a memorandum of understanding with Gazprom.[45] One option under discussion was that equity in South Russkoye would be exchanged for the E.ON/Ruhrgas shareholding in Gazprom which, according to newspaper reports, the latter wants to eliminate.[46] By early 2005, press reports were suggesting that other German companies –

RWE and the chemicals giant BASF (parent company of Wintershall) – were in similar negotiations about participating in South Russkoye production.[47] In April 2005 an agreement was signed between BASF (Wintershall's parent company) and Gazprom which – if it becomes a contractual reality – would provide the basis for building the NEP and substantially enhance the relationship between the companies. The agreement provides for Wintershall to take a 50% minus one share stake in the South Russkoye field in return for Wingas taking an identical share in the NEP; at the same time, Gazprom would increase its share in Wingas from 35% to 50% minus one share.[48] The same day, E.ON and Gazprom signed an agreement which the press release of the Russian company described as follows:

> E.ON is likely to acquire a 25% share in the Yuzhno-Russkoye gas field development project. Gazprom, on its part, is free to purchase the identical share of E.ON's European gas marketing and electricity assets. In addition, the firms will keep on negotiating E.ON's potential involvement in the North-European gas pipeline construction and Russian power generation sector.[49]

The *quid pro quo* for investors is that they will be allowed equity in the South Russkoye field in return for financing a significant share in the NEP. In this way, NEP – which seemed a relatively risky investment given anticipated European gas market requirements around 2010 – could be made attractive to these companies.[50] However, in mid-2005 considerable uncertainty remained as to the status of the agreements reached with the German companies. Despite this uncertainty, NEP had built up a large head of political steam, with the express backing of President Putin who, in a May 2004 speech to the Duma, confirmed the priority attached to the project:

> In export, the construction of the North European Gas Pipeline is most important. It will make it possible to diversify export flows, directly linking the networks of Russia and countries of the Baltic region with the total European gas network.[51]

Such strong endorsement from the president is extremely important and suggests that, whatever commercial reservations may be attached to this project, it is likely to proceed.

Blue Stream (Map 3.3). Having established the legal and commercial basis for the Yamal pipeline in the mid 1990s, Gazprom's attention switched from northern to southern Europe where Turkey had become the fastest growing market of the countries buying Russian gas. Gazprom already had contracts to sell up to 14 Bcm/year to the Turkish company Botas. The gas made the long journey from Russia to Turkey via the 'western

Map 3.3: Pipelines Bringing Russian Gas to Turkey

route' through Ukraine, Moldova, Romania and Bulgaria where, as we have seen in the cases of Bulgaria (above) and Ukraine (Chapter 2), significant transit problems were experienced during the 1990s.

In the late 1990s, Botas was projecting that demand would grow from less than 10 Bcm in 1997 to 54 Bcm by 2005 and 80 Bcm by 2020.[52] With such significant growth prospects and such strong competition elsewhere on the Continent, the Turkish market attracted a great deal of attention from aspiring gas suppliers. As well as its Russian supplies, Botas signed pipeline import contracts with Iran and Azerbaijan, and LNG import contracts with Algeria and Nigeria. Despite the possibility that the Turkish market might not grow as fast as expected during the 2000s, particularly if the power generation market expanded more slowly than anticipated, it was very important for Gazprom, given the competition from other suppliers, to secure a large share of this market for Russian gas.[53]

Another important motivation for Gazprom to develop Blue Stream was to establish the security credentials of Russian gas to the satisfaction of Turkish politicians and the Turkish military who had expressed concerns about the country's overwhelming dependence on Russia. There were concrete reasons for such concern given that, prior to the commissioning of its LNG import terminal, Turkey suffered physical shortages of gas in the mid 1990s due to Ukrainian diversion of transit volumes:

- In early 1994, daily deliveries of Russian gas were reduced by about 50%.
- In March 1995, one of the existing gas-fired power plants had to switch the majority of its input to fuel oil, and two fertiliser plants were put on standby.[54]

If Gazprom was to convince Botas and Turkish politicians that Russian gas would be secure it needed to create a route avoiding transit countries. The solution was a pipeline 1213 km in length running from Izobilnoye, north of Stavropol in Russia's North Caucasus region, across the Black Sea to Ankara. It is supplied with Siberian gas and uses a storage facility at Stavropol for back-up supplies. The offshore section of this pipeline comprises two 372 km lines taking slightly different sea routes from Dzhubga to Samsun, which provides additional security in the event of technical problems. Such problems could be anticipated for a pipeline laid at record depth – up to 2150 metres – in very difficult water conditions.[55]

The crucial commercial step was taken in December 1997 when Gazprom and Botas signed a long-term contract for 16 Bcm/year commencing in 2000.[56] For Gazprom the commercially groundbreaking aspect of Blue Stream was the creation of a joint venture giving the Italian company ENI a 50% share in the capacity of the pipeline, allowing for the possibility of that company selling Russian gas on its own account in Turkey. Gazprom was forced to concede these capacity rights – unprecedented in a major export pipeline – in order to obtain financing for the project. With the signing of a strategic alliance between Gazprom and ENI in early 1998, which included specific mention of the joint development of the Astrakhan gas field on the north west shore of the Caspian Sea, there seemed to be a clear opportunity for the Italian company to develop its own Russian gas for Blue Stream, although no significant new development of that field has since taken place.[57]

With ENI providing the majority of the $3.2bn financing, the laying of the offshore lines started in late 2001 and the entire pipeline was completed in October 2002, somewhat behind the original schedule but well within acceptable limits for such a challenging project.[58] However, as the project was being completed, a political crisis combined with a severe economic recession in Turkey made it evident that the gas demand projections of the late 1990s had been seriously over-optimistic.[59] Even before the Blue Stream was completed, Botas was seeking to scale down volume and price commitments, particularly given the gas liberalisation programme that had been introduced on the initiative of the IMF and the World Bank requiring Botas to reduce its share of imported gas to 20%.[60] Less than a month after the start of commercial flows of gas through the pipeline, Turkey stopped taking gas through the pipeline and both the Botas management and Ministry officials responsible for negotiating the project were replaced.[61]

Following the stoppage of deliveries, Gazprom-Botas relations worsened with talk of international arbitration from both sides and the prospect of Russian sanctions against Turkey. In the event, this did not happen and by July 2003 – when the take or pay element of the contract was due to be implemented – both sides had agreed that a solution was possible.[62] By the end of that year, a new contractual agreement had been established which reduced the immediate volumes that Botas was required to take, unified and reduced the prices of gas in all the Russian contracts with Botas, and settled tax issues relating to the project.[63] Press reports subsequently suggested that Russian deliveries to the Turkish market through Blue Stream had in fact been reduced from 16 Bcm to 8 Bcm up to 2020, and this may account for Gazprom's interest in exports to Israel and Syria which could require agreement between the parties on re-exports of gas.[64] In preparation for liberalisation of the Turkish market, Gazprom bought a 40% stake in Bosphorus Gas – a distribution company through which Russian gas can be sold directly to customers.[65]

Overall, the building of transit avoidance pipelines has thus far not proven to be a conspicuous success for Gazprom and has come at relatively high cost. Experience with the Yamal-Europe pipeline does not suggest that Belarus will necessarily prove a more reliable transit partner than Ukraine. Moreover, with the Yamal line not due to reach full capacity until end-2005, partly due to lower than expected demand in European markets, it is uncertain why there was such a rush to build it. Blue Stream proved useful as a way of keeping Central Asian competitors out of the Turkish market in the 1990s. But subsequent reduction of market opportunities within that country and the lack of markets along the route – not to speak of the substantial costs of the project – suggest that increasing the capacity of the existing western export pipeline route would have been a lower cost option.[66]

The Yamal and Blue Stream experiences can be applied to the North

European Pipeline where a determination to build the line by 2010, combined with a lack of immediate demand for additional gas in Europe, and the lack of substantial additional markets along the route, is reminiscent of both the previous projects. While Gazprom's dislike and distrust of transit is understandable – given its experiences in the 1990s – much of the success of its European export business will rest on successful long-term resolution, rather than avoidance, of these issues which are addressed in the Transit Protocol of the Energy Charter Treaty (see below).

The Baltic Countries

Latvia, Lithuania and Estonia were first to leave the Soviet Union and as a consequence of this, and their refusal to join the CIS, were by 1992, required to pay prices in hard currency at levels between those of CIS and European border prices. These higher price levels combined with economic restructuring, and the availability of lower cost (principally Russian) gasoil and high sulphur fuel oil, caused Russian gas deliveries to these countries to fall to less than half of their Soviet-era levels. Table 3.3 shows that exports to Estonia and Lithuania remained around these levels while exports to Latvia in 2003 were just over three-quarters of 1990 volumes.[67] During the immediate post-Soviet period, non-payment caused gas to be restricted for short periods, but the Baltic countries made the transition to a market economy much faster than other former Soviet republics and this was reflected in the signing of five-year supply contracts with the Estonian and Latvian gas companies at a time when all other former Soviet importers remained on annual contracts.[68]

Table 3.3: Russian Gas Exports to Baltic Countries 1990–2003 (Bcm)

	1990	1991	1995	2000	2001	2002	2003	2004*
Lithuania	6.0	3.2	2.5	2.57	2.8	2.7	2.94	2.9
Latvia	3.2	1.6	1.2	1.36	1.7	1.4	2.44	1.2
Estonia	1.9	0.9	0.7	0.79	1.3	0.6	0.81	0.9
TOTAL	11.1	5.7	4.4	4.72	5.8	4.7	6.19	

* Gazprom deliveries only; preliminary figures

Sources: see Chapter 2, Tables 2.1 and 2.2.

During the post-Soviet period Gazprom concentrated on acquiring equity in Baltic gas companies. The company has owned equity in the

Latvian gas industry since 1997 and in 2004 purchased a further 9% of Latvias Gaze from Itera (which owned a 25% share) in exchange for transportation services, bringing its stake to 34% plus one share.[69] Gazprom's ownership in the Estonian gas industry started even earlier in 1993 and it owns 37% in Eesti Gaas. In Lithuania, resistance to Gazprom's equity ownership in the national company Lietuvos Dujos led Gazprom to establish the marketing company Dujotekana in 2002 and also to acquire 30% of the gas (and oil product) marketing company Stella Vitae. By the following year, Dujotekana had taken over around 60% of the Lithuanian gas market from Lietuvos Dujos. Gazprom also purchased the Kaunas combined heat and power plant which is the second largest power plant in Lithuania.[70] By 2004, Gazprom had increased its equity in Lietuvos Dujos to more than 37%.[71]

Gazprom has therefore established significant ownership stakes in all of the Baltic countries, devoting more attention to them than might be considered warranted given the small size of their markets. When they became members of the European Union in 2004, the Baltic countries institutionalised their European status in a region of significant political and strategic sensitivity for Russia. The status of the enclave of Kaliningrad has been a particularly difficult issue in negotiations between Russia and the EU, and the fact that Russian gas supplies to Kaliningrad need to transit Lithuania gives that country additional importance for Gazprom.[72]

The Financial Significance of Exports to Europe

The financial significance of exports to Europe for both Gazprom as a company, and Russia as a country, can scarcely be overestimated. Table 3.4 shows Gazprom's earning from its three major sales markets: domestic, CIS and European. These figures illustrate the magnitude of the company's earnings from European gas sales which (at an average exchange rate of $1 = RR30 net of all taxes) were in excess of $14bn in 2003; 2004 earnings were estimated at $19.4bn. In 2003, European gas sales accounted for 65% of total Gazprom sales receipts and more than half of total sales earnings. Both of these percentages increased compared with 2002, and are likely to have increased again in 2004 with the continuing rise in (oil and) gas prices. There is a striking asymmetry between percentages of sales volumes and percentages of revenue earnings between Russian sales to domestic and European markets. In 2003, Russian sales accounted for 62% of the sales and less than 30% of the revenues, while European sales were less than 30% of the volumes but 65% of the revenues.

Table 3.4: Gazprom Sales to, and Receipts from, Different Markets, 2002–03 (net of all applicable taxes)

| | *2002* | | | *2003* | | |
	Volume (Bcm)	*Receipts (Rbn)*	*Prices RR/Mcm ($/mcm)**	*Volume (Bcm)*	*Receipts (Rbn)*	*Prices RR/Mcm (S/mcm)**
Russia	298.0	142.8	505.0 (16.8)	308.2	186.7	668.7 (22)
CIS	42.6	51.1	1444.2 (45)	42.6	44.0	1256.6 (41)
Europe	128.6	335.1	3369.0 (112)	144.7	422.3	3782.3 (126)
Total Gas Sales	469.2	529		495.5	653	
Condensate and other products		56.6			92.2	
Transportation services		18.0			28.2	
Other		41.0			46.3	
TOTAL SALES		644.7			819.8	

*   actual realised sales prices (not commercial contract prices)

Source: Gazprom *IFRS Consolidated Financial Statements*, 31 December 2003, *Management's Discussion and Analysis of Financial Condition and Results of Operations*, pages 4, 5, and 15

Table 3.5 shows the importance of fossil fuel exports in total Russian foreign currency earnings. The figures demonstrate the importance of 'mineral products' (fuels, electricity and metals) in total Russian export earnings and particularly exports of those products to non-CIS countries. In the 2000s – with the huge increases in oil and gas prices – exports of mineral products to non-CIS countries reached more than two-thirds of total Russian export earnings. Of this figure, fossil fuels – and specifically crude oil, oil products and natural gas – constitute the overwhelming majority of export earnings. The natural gas figures are partly estimated (see note to Table 3.5) and are high in comparison to the Gazprom figures in Table 3.4 (converted into dollars), probably because they include taxes paid on exports. They show that in the 2000s, Gazprom has accounted for 13–16% of total Russian export earnings – more if CIS exports are included, but the currency convertibility of the latter may not be comparable with non-CIS earnings. Although oil exports during the same period have been much larger at 30–35%, these are diversified across a number of companies. Gazprom as the sole Russian gas exporter to Europe is Russia's largest foreign currency earning company.

Table 3.5: Russian Gas Export Earnings From Non-CIS Countries ($Bn)

	1997	1998	1999	2000	2001	2002	2003
Total Exports	85.1	71.3	72.9	103.1	100.0	106.2	133.5
Total Mineral Product Exports	41.1	30.5	32.7	55.5	54.7	58.9	76.5
Total Non-CIS Exports	68.5	57.6	62.2	89.3	85.4	90.5	113.0
Total Non-CIS Mineral Product Exports	32.2	23.2	27.1	48.7	48.3	51.6	67.8
Natural Gas*	10.5	9.5	8.4	13.6	16.4	14.0	18.3
Crude Oil	13.4	8.8	12.9	23.6	21.6	25.3	33.9
Oil Products	7.0	3.9	5.1	10.2	8.9	10.8	13.4
Coal, lignite and coke	0.8	0.5	0.4	1.0	1.0	1.0	1.5
Electricity	0.2	0.2	0.2	0.1	0.2	0.2	0.3
Oil and Gas Exports as a % of total non-CIS Exports	45.5	38.4	42.3	53.0	54.9	55.4	58.1
Gas Exports as a % of total non-CIS Exports	15.6	16.4	13.4	15.2	19.2	15.5	16.2

* The Russian statistical yearbook does not give data for natural gas revenues, this is the only mineral product for which revenue earnings are not given. However, because figures for all other mineral products are given, natural gas can be calculated as a residual by subtracting the total of mineral product earnings from the sum of the other mineral products.

Source: *Rossiskii Statisticheskii Ezhegodnik*, Moscow, Rosstat Rossii: 2004, Tables 25.10, 25.11, 25.13, pp. 654–661.

The European Union Dimension

Liberalisation and Competition Policy. The liberalisation of European gas and electricity industries, by means of creating access to transmission and distribution networks along with the de-monopolisation of markets, and the abolition of exclusive rights of utility companies has been an extremely long process and in 2005 was far from being either complete or successful in many, if not most, countries.[73] The details of why this process has been so extremely long are complex and need not be explained here. However, at virtually every stage prior to agreement in 1998, key principles of the Gas Directive were fiercely opposed by a majority of gas utility companies – and many important governments – of major European Member States and most gas-producing companies.[74]

After lengthy discussions and negotiations, the first EU 'Common Rules' Gas Directive was finally agreed by Member States in August

1998. The Directive required the opening of markets to competition – so-called liberalisation or 'deregulation' – commencing in August 2000.[75] The second Common Rules Gas Directive – the 'Acceleration Directive' – was ratified by the European Parliament in July 2003 and provided for complete opening of markets by July 2007, as well as further corporate separation ('legal unbundling') of network assets and regulated access to networks.[76]

Partly in response to the first Common Rules Directive and the start of electricity and gas liberalisation, a wave of mergers swept through the European utility sector. The requirement for the EU Competition Authorities (DG COMP) to approve these mergers exposed the contractual detail of the gas sector to the regulatory spotlight for the first time in several decades. Merger approval combined with complaints that had been lodged with DG COMP led to significant action, in support of the liberalisation Directive(s), to accelerate the pace of competition in the sector.

In June 2004, the EU increased its membership to 25 states, all of which are expected to operate liberalised gas markets according to the 2003 Gas Directive.[77] Bulgaria and Romania intend to join the Union in 2007 with Turkey keen to follow soon thereafter and Croatia having expressed the intention to apply within the same time frame. EU competition rules also apply to the European Economic Area (EEA) countries – Norway, Iceland and Lichtenstein – through the Treaty between the two organisations. The expanding EU membership, combined with the EEA countries, therefore means that EU liberalisation and competition regulation has become pan-European, encompassing virtually all significant European nations bordering Ukraine and Belarus in the east and North Africa and the Middle East in the south.

Long-term take or pay contracts and destination clauses. The renewed application of EU competition rules to gas sector contracts (noted above) appeared to threaten the future existence of long-term contracts, and highlighted the existence of 'territorial sales restrictions' – more generally known as 'destination clauses' – in those contracts. In this connection, the most important legal instrument is Article 81 which prohibits companies from entering into agreements that are intended to, or have the effect of, restricting competition.[78]

European merchant gas transmission companies traditionally purchased wholesale gas using long-term – 15–25 year – take or pay contracts. This type of contract had been widely used and accepted by all parties over several decades and no significant questions had arisen about its use. Long-term contracts suddenly arrived on the agenda of the EU not because of the Gas Liberalisation Directives, but because the Exxon-Mobil merger caused DG COMP to look specifically at contractual structures in the gas industry. The negative conclusions about the impact of long-term contracts on the development of competition contained in the Exxon-Mobil merger decision were potentially far-reaching for the entire European gas industry.[79] They were further elaborated by the Head of the Energy Unit at DG COMP who made clear that competition law should be used to reinforce and accelerate progress towards the creation of community-wide markets, and that long-term contracts could create barriers to those developments.[80]

For this reason, during the early 2000s, the European Commission was believed by many market players, including non-European producers, to be 'against long term contracts'. This position gave rise to extremely strong protests by important players in the European gas industry. Companies, in many cases supported by their governments, insisted that long-term contracts were essential to underpin the future of the gas industry and that multi-billion dollar projects could not be financed without these types of contracts. Gazprom was among the strongest opponents of the Commission's reasoning. In 2000, the Gazprom Board Member responsible for exports to Europe expressed the company's opposition to the Gas Directive:

> The EC Natural Gas Directive ideology is based on a simple logic: the TPA system starts functioning. On the basis of certain criteria, the consumers will be able to choose their suppliers. As a result of increased competition the end consumers will get gas price reductions. The spot market is under development and already many questions have been raised as to the existence of long-term contracts for new volumes as well as of earlier signed long-term gas supply contracts.
>
> The above logic is based on the assumption that available quantities of cheap natural gas exceed the demand. In reality there is no cheap gas and there will not be any.
>
> Under the present conditions, the long-term gas supply prospects would largely depend upon maintaining the balance of interests between the long-term contracts and short-term business. Those who declare the need to eliminate the long-term contract system must answer at least one question: how could the financing of super-large projects be arranged in low investment rating countries? We know from our own experience that so far there are no ways of doing it without long-term contracts.[81]

With the launch of the EU-Russia Energy Dialogue (see below), gas contracts featured as a point of disagreement, even in the first report:

> Investment decisions related to gas production and transport from Russia to Europe are based on long-term contracts and a sharing of risks between

producers and importers. Russia notes that past investments have not yet been fully recovered and therefore believes that it is necessary to preserve existing contracts in force and unchanged until their expiration. While the European Commission recognizes that long-term contracts are an essential element for energy security and should continue to supply the European market, these must necessarily evolve with the effective disappearance of boundaries within the EU. *The current discussions about existing long-term contracts, in the context of the completion of the EU internal energy market and its forthcoming enlargement need to be concluded swiftly.*[82] (emphasis in original)

Immediately following that report, the First Deputy Chairman of Gazprom gave a speech to a conference in Paris in 2001 which included some very strong criticisms of gas market liberalisation. Specifically, he argued that the EU Gas Directive ignores the interest of gas suppliers; will lead to the disintegration of long-term take or pay contracts; encourages new players lacking motivation to preserve the gas market; and encourages price reductions for EU consumers at the expense of gas suppliers.[83]

He further asserted that:

...gas market liberalization will do serious damage to European energy security. The interests of long-term security demand the adoption of policies which maintain a balance of interests between consumers and producers.

In respect of long-term contracts, Gazprom and the rest of the European gas establishment prevailed over DG COMP as demonstrated by the Gas Security Directive, passed in April 2004:

Long-term take or pay contracts have played a very important role in securing supplies for Europe and will continue to do so. The current level of long-term contracts is adequate on the Community level and it is believed that such contracts will continue to make a significant contribution to overall gas supplies as companies continue to include such contracts in their overall supply portfolio.[84]

Article 18(3) of the Acceleration Directive was slightly more even-handed in terms of the balance between long-term contracts and competition rules: 'The provisions of this Directive do not prevent the conclusion of long-term contracts in so far as they comply with Community competition rules.'

However, the 'victory' of the industry in the long-term contract debate was to be counterbalanced by territorial and other sales restrictions within those contracts. Territorial sales restrictions in European gas contracts − commonly known as 'destination clauses' − involve two separate types of restriction:

- prohibiting a buyer from re-selling gas purchased under contract to buyers in a different country;
- preventing a buyer from re-selling gas to other customers in the same country e.g. power generators, which are not already customers of the buyer.

If a buyer does re-sell gas in a contract which includes a destination clause restriction, the sale will only be allowed subject to a '*profit-sharing*' (known within the Commission as '*profit-splitting*') *mechanism* – a contractual commitment which obliges the buyer to share with the producer a part of the profit from the resale. The competition authorities stated: 'Both types of clauses are considered incompatible with European competition law as they prevent the creation of a single market, but are considered necessary by certain market operators.'[85]

The Commission therefore set out to eliminate all destination clauses in gas contracts with considerable success, but the problem with Russian (and Algerian) contracts proved particularly acute. Having started to address the problem within the framework of the EU-Russia Dialogue in 2001, it was not until October 2003 that the European Commissioner for Competition announced that the issue of destination clauses in the contracts between Gazprom and the Italian company ENI had been resolved.[86]

In May 2004, it was reported that destination clauses had been removed from Gazprom's Austrian contracts and the Commission confirmed this in February 2005.[87] Subsequently, Gazprom announced that it had completed the elimination of the clauses in its contracts with German companies, although the Commission had not yet given its formal approval.[88] There is also the issue of how these clauses will be dealt with in the new EU Member States. Here the position is somewhat more complicated since these contracts form part of intergovernmental agreements, signed during the Soviet era, which are international legal documents with (arguably) similar authority to the EU Treaties. Whatever the eventual outcome may be, destination clauses are a transitory problem which will pass with the expiry of existing contracts.

Moreover, Russian attitudes towards contracts have demonstrated a growing flexibility as evidenced by the determination to capture 10% of the UK gas market by 2010 (around 13 Bcm). For the UK, a new subsidiary has been set up which operates under the general contractual framework of short-term commodity sales at spot prices. In terms of capacity, the company has also shown itself able to adapt by securing 4.9 Bcm of capacity in the Interconnector pipeline (IUK) and (via Wingas) up to 2 Bcm in the BBL pipeline.[89] In order to reach its target of 10−13 Bcm of sales per annum, there have been indications that Gazprom would like to see BBL capacity increased in future and this would be a much lower-cost option than the physical extension of the NEP to the UK.[90]

The EU-Russia Energy Dialogue.[91] At the EU-Russia Summit in Paris in October 2000, a high level Energy Dialogue (known in its early months as 'the Prodi initiative') was created with the following objectives:[92]

- to make progress on the definition of an EU-Russia energy partnership
- to contribute to energy security
- to cooperate on energy saving
- to help rationalise production and transport infrastructure
- to facilitate investments
- to contribute to producer/consumer relations
- to support the Energy Charter Treaty

The institutional background to the Energy Dialogue is the 1994 EU-Russia Agreement on Partnership and Cooperation which covers the period 1996−2006. Article 65 of that Agreement covers energy and mentions many of the above objectives, albeit in rather more general terms. From the EU side, the Energy Dialogue demonstrated the new form of relationship that Brussels intended to create with the Union's major energy suppliers. This followed from the recommendations of the Green Paper on Security of Energy Supply which, having anticipated major increases in import dependence over the next several decades, recommended an ongoing dialogue with producer countries.[93] The institutional aim of the Energy Dialogue is to develop a long-term Energy Partnership within the framework of the overall Partnership and Cooperation Agreement (expanded in 2004 to include the new member states).

As far as gas is concerned, the Dialogue process reinforced the EU Trans-European Networks initiative which had already designated the Yamal pipeline, the Shtokmanovskoye field and the North European Pipeline (NEP) as EU 'priority projects', and also as projects of 'common interest' which means that they are eligible for funding under the Trans-European Networks for energy (TEN-E) framework.[94] The EU decision to co-finance the feasibility study of the NEP was taken under this framework.

The Dialogue was clearly the right forum in which to deal with the disagreements over long-term contracts and destination clauses. The success in confirming the legitimacy of long-term contracts (with the proviso that these were required to conform to EU competition policy) was noted above. The destination clause issue is somewhat more problematic. The November 2004 Progress Report makes no mention of the issue and the 2004 Communication simply notes the October 2003 agreement between ENI and Gazprom suggesting that no further progress had been made since then.[95] As we noted earlier, the scope of the destination clause problem has widened considerably with the expansion of EU membership in 2004. Nevertheless, the fact that these contractual issues have been contained, and partially resolved, counts as a positive achievement for the Dialogue.

After four years of discussions, the Commission made an assessment of the Dialogue which, unsurprisingly, was relatively upbeat. In particular it claimed that the intention of the November 2000 Green Paper on security 'to strengthen competition in the internal energy market, to defend sustainable development and guarantee external security of supply – has been translated into concrete action in the framework of the Energy Dialogue with Russia.'[96] It claimed that the Dialogue had made possible investments of EU companies in Russia, and Russian companies in the EU, and resolved problems that companies could have encountered. It also claimed that the dialogue had put in place conditions for long-term energy supplies by supporting building and modernisation of infrastructure and establishing safety rules.[97]

However, the Russian side attached considerable priority to the expectation that the Dialogue would '...create mechanisms for financing important infrastructure projects of common interest', with a specific focus on the NEP.[98] After four years, the financing mechanisms associated with the Dialogue are limited to providing investment guarantees and go no further than the possibility of an 'Energy Desk possibly associated with an investment bank, which...would play an active role in setting up banking syndicates.'[99] It is not clear whether such activity is significant enough to maintain the interest of the Russian side. The conclusion of the November 2003 report that '[t]he time has come to reflect on the establishment of an institutionalised relationship between Russia and the EU in the field of energy, which would pave the way for the creation of a real Energy Community', was not reflected in the November 2004 report, suggesting that the Dialogue had not moved forward significantly and this may be a matter of some concern for the future of the process.[100]

The Energy Charter Treaty.[101] The Energy Charter Treaty was signed in 1994 and entered into force in 1998. Originally conceived in a European context as a legal conduit to facilitate energy flows from east to west, the Charter Treaty subsequently broadened considerably in scope and geographical reach.[102] By 2004, the Treaty had been signed by 51 European and Asian countries plus the European Union; of those 51 countries, only five have failed to ratify the Treaty.[103] This means that the majority of OECD states and former Soviet republics have ratified with the notable exceptions of the Russian Federation and Belarus.[104] The Treaty covers four main areas of activity: investment, trade, transit and dispute settlement. Here, the focus will be almost exclusively on transit which, as is shown throughout this study, is a very important security issue for Russian gas exports.

During the late 1990s, the Charter Conference membership came to regard transit as a major issue and in 2000 formal negotiations began on a Transit Protocol which would create an international legal regime for energy transit across multiple borders with enforceable dispute settlement. As we saw in Chapter 2, and earlier in this chapter, substantial gas transit problems were encountered during the 1990s and have continued in the 2000s, but on a much smaller scale. Nevertheless the growing volumes of gas trade and transit within the European/CIS geographical space elevated the necessity of uninterrupted gas transit for both Russian exports to Europe, and Central Asian exports to CIS and European countries, to guarantee security of supply and revenues for all parties. International gas transit creates unusual multilateral mutual dependence relationships:

1. They are multilateral because by definition they involve more than two parties, and in the case of exports of Turkmen gas to EU countries, for example, may involve up to five transit states.
2. They are about mutual dependence because if any of the parties interrupts the flow of gas either by withholding gas or transportation services, it will suffer financial penalties in the short, and perhaps also the longer, term.
3. They are unusual relationships in the sense that there are win/ win and lose/lose outcomes for the parties but no win/lose outcome.[105]

Bilateral transit negotiations between governments or companies are likely to fail because:

1. They will at some point in time become hijacked by political problems between the two countries.
2. They cannot encompass the full range of relationships in the trade which are, by definition, multilateral rather than bilateral.

Unlike many of the issues that arose in the immediate aftermath of the Cold War and the collapse of the Soviet Union, gas transit is becoming substantially more important as export volumes, and therefore the costs of transit failure, increase.

It is for these reasons that the transit protocol of the Energy Charter Treaty is a unique and essential international instrument with the potential to provide much greater certainty for both participants and investors in gas commerce.[106] While the transit context of this study is Russian and CIS gas exports to Europe and Asia (see below), the relevance of the Transit Protocol extends globally to wherever gas (and general energy) trade is limited by transit considerations, and this accounts for the number of Charter Conference observers from outside the European and CIS regions.

The lack of Russian – and to a lesser, but still important, extent Belarusian – ratification of the Treaty and the Transit Protocol is therefore a crucial gap in the natural gas and energy relationship between the EU and Russia. While there are many reasons for this failure to ratify, opposition from Gazprom to the Transit Protocol has been important in creating opposition to ratification in the Russian Duma. During the late 1990s and early 2000s, Gazprom opposition was based on an interpretation in which acceptance of the Transit Protocol would require mandatory access to Russian gas pipelines by third parties. After 2001, its opposition became less strident as the focus of attention on energy transit moved to the government and particularly Russia's application to join the World Trade Organisation (WTO).

In December 2002, when only three issues remained to be resolved, which focused on differences between Russia and the European Union, multilateral negotiations were concluded. During 2003, efforts continued between the EU, the Russian Federation and the Charter Secretariat to find a resolution but that proved impossible by the time of the December 2003 Charter Conference Meeting, partly because of the ongoing EU-Russia negotiations on WTO accession. Further work on the Draft was therefore suspended.[107] The issues that remained unresolved at December 2003 were:[108]

- the European Union's proposal for a Regional Economic Integration Organisation (REIO) clause (Article 20 in the draft Protocol) which would treat the EU as a single entity rather than as national entities;
- the Russian proposal for a 'right of first refusal' for existing transit shippers which, at the conclusion of an existing transit contract, would allow an existing transit shipper – namely Gazprom – the right to continue to extend the existing transit contract prior to the

offer of that transit capacity to other parties. This would, for the term of the existing contracts, deal with the 'mismatch' of transit and supply contracts: if a long-term transit contract finishes prior to the expiry of a long-term supply contract, the remaining term of the latter cannot be honoured without the extension of the former;
– charging methodology for transit tariffs.

It is uncertain how – and indeed whether – these outstanding issues will be resolved and the Transit Protocol and Energy Charter Treaty will be ratified. The official Russian position is that when these issues are resolved to its satisfaction, it will ratify the Transit Protocol and then, 'options will open up with regard to the ECT in general', suggesting that ratification of the Treaty itself would follow.[109] But for as long as the Protocol (and the Treaty) is not ratified, a legally binding resolution to transit problems will remain elusive. In this situation (and indeed possibly even if the Transit Protocol is ratified), Gazprom may continue to regard transit-avoidance pipelines (such as the NEP) as a necessity despite the additional investment costs associated with such infrastructure.

However, when the issue of transit surfaced in the Russia-EU WTO negotiations it was interesting that from the Russian side the primacy of the ECT as the forum within which transit should be negotiated was firmly expressed. Referring to the attempt to include transit issues within WTO negotiations, the Russian Deputy Prime Minister said:

> From our point of view this is impossible as a matter of principle: to leave aside the Charter which has been established especially to deal with such issues, and take the topic to negotiations on the WTO. Our position is simple – WTO in no way resolves the transit problems. This theme is not covered by WTO norms and rules.[110]

Irrespective of whether this is a correct legal interpretation, the expression of a Russian commitment to deal with transit within the ECT process is important in institutional terms; although by no means a guarantee that Russia will ratify the Protocol (and the Treaty).

During the early years of the Transit Protocol negotiations, Gazprom's dilemma was that while it would effectively provide international sanctions against any transit violations by Ukraine and Belarus, it would also open the door to uncontrolled transit of Central Asian gas to Europe. In 2005, with Gazprom having made such strenuous – and partly successful – efforts to contractualise control of Central Asian gas (Chapter 2), this risk appeared somewhat reduced. Nevertheless, the February 2004 incident in Belarus was a sharp reminder of how a transit crisis can suddenly arise and the impact that any interruption of deliveries, however short, can have on Russia's reputation as a secure gas supplier to Europe.

Moreover transit is not simply an issue of security but also an issue of commercial significance. Transit costs are the biggest single element of Gazprom's operating expenses accounting for 13−16% of total costs in 2002−03.[111] Transit costs in 2003 amounted to RR108bn, slightly less than $4bn at the then current rate of exchange and increased by 6% during the period 2002−03.[112] European transit tariffs tend to be confidential but as part of its financial disclosure Gazprom noted the sharp increase in (US dollar denominated) Polish transit tariffs from $1.35/mcm/00km in 2002 to $2.68/mcm/00km in 2003.[113] A near-doubling of transit tariffs in a single year in a country where transit is of increasing importance to Gazprom shows the potential for commercial volatility in the absence of a cost-based commercial framework.

EU-Russia WTO Negotiations. As noted above, in late 2003 the Transit Protocol negotiations were to some extent 'derailed' by the negotiations between the EU and Russia over the latter's application to join the World Trade Organisation (WTO). A significant number of the key conditions laid down by the EU trade negotiators for approval of the Russian Federation related directly to the gas industry:[114]

- the abolition of gas export tariffs – currently 30%;
- the raising of Russian gas prices for non-residential customers because of EU concerns that subsidised gas prices (see Chapter 1) would allow those exporting gas-intensive products an unfair advantage on international (specifically European) markets;
- an ending of Gazprom's monopoly on exports to Europe; although this was a *de facto* monopoly[115] the EU was seeking formal abolition of Gazexport's dominant position, and official approval from the Russian government for other companies – Russian and foreign – to export gas;
- the lifting of restrictions on gas transit – principally transit of Central Asian gas and
- the establishment of non-discriminatory transport/transit tariffs for delivery of gas to domestic users and export markets;
- the right of foreign investors to obtain access to Gazprom's network for the transport of gas, and to build their own pipelines.

In May 2004, the two sides agreed terms for Russia's WTO accession. Just as in the case of the negotiations, little detail was made available on the terms agreed and most of that focused on the domestic price increases that were discussed in Chapter 1.[116] In Chapter 4, we return to the issue of what remains to be clarified in terms of Russian price commitments. On other issues, the Russian side made a commitment not to increase export tariffs beyond the level of 30%. No concessions were made on Gazprom's de facto monopoly of exports to Europe, 'the single export channel'. EU Trade Commissioner Pascal Lamy was quoted as saying: 'it was a red line for Putin. In these sorts of negotiations, there are red lines, and I can tell you that it will remain a red line for Mr. Putin'.[117] While foreign investors appeared to gain the right of access to Gazprom's pipeline network, it was never clear that this was denied to them but, given the refusal to concede any ground on Gazprom's export position, clearly this right does not apply to export pipelines. The main concession which the EU appeared to have extracted from Russia in the WTO negotiations involved support for ratification of the Kyoto Protocol on Climate Change. Following the conclusion of the negotiations President Putin said:

> The fact that the European Union has met us halfway at the [WTO] negotiations…cannot but influence Moscow's positive attitude towards ratification of the Kyoto Protocol. We will accelerate our movement towards ratifying this protocol.[118]

The Russian Duma duly ratified the Kyoto Protocol in late 2004, allowing it to come into force in 2005. This led some to speculate that the EU negotiators – unable to force Russia to make substantial concessions on gas market liberalisation – were prepared to settle for Kyoto ratification which was far less politically problematic for the Russian president to agree, and (arguably) far more important for European interests, than any considerations surrounding gas trade.

Security of Supply – The Changing Geopolitical Context. From the start of Soviet gas deliveries to Europe, the issue of security of supply has been very important for European companies and governments from an import perspective, and their counterparts in Russia from an export perspective. During the Cold War era, the strategic context of security discussions was ultimately reduced to the question, 'is it advisable to import a growing proportion of a strategically vital commodity from your primary military and strategic adversary?' Disagreements with the US (Reagan) administration on this question created significant tensions in the Atlantic Alliance in the early 1980s. These tensions were the origin of the widely quoted, but never formally agreed, policy that no West European country should be dependent on Soviet gas for more than 30% (or one-third) of its gas demand.[119] But even during the Cold War, West European governments tended to regard Soviet gas imports in a positive political context of 'engaging' the USSR in a dialogue, and for West Germany there was the additional issue of engaging the German Democratic Republic in the (for decades vain) hope of the reunification of Germany.

For gas utilities, the issue was somewhat more practical: increasing quantities of Soviet gas were being produced in a remote, harsh environment and needed to travel thousands of kilometres to reach European markets. It was therefore necessary to ensure that shortfalls, for whatever reason, could be managed without causing inconvenience to customers. This was achieved by building storage reservoirs and additional pipeline connections allowing gas to be brought from other sources – notably the Netherlands – at short notice. While these arrangements, which also met the concerns of politicians and their strategic advisers, tended to focus on Soviet gas, they were equally important for dealing with shortfalls of gas from any source, domestic or imported.

With the end of the Cold War and the unification of Europe, the military/strategic context of gas security became less important and greater emphasis has been placed on the potential for political and policy disagreements, accidents, facility failures and – in the post 9/11 world – terrorist acts.[120] Perhaps paradoxically, as the Russian Federation came closer to Europe politically, so a number of disagreements about gas surfaced that had never been considered during the Cold War era. The most important of these from a commercial perspective have been the disagreements on EU liberalisation and competition policy detailed above. Concerns about the creation of the Gas Exporting Countries Forum (GECF) – of which Russia is a founder member – surface periodically but so far they have been tempered by that organisation's lack of institutional focus and its repeated disavowal of any desire to become a 'Gas-OPEC'.[121] President Putin's suggestion to create a Eurasian gas organisation composed of CIS countries (see Chapter 2) has made little progress since it was first suggested in 2002.

The greatest concern about post-Cold War Russian gas security has been caused by transit problems in CIS countries and particularly problems in the Ukraine and Belarus which were detailed in Chapter 2. Russian management of transit problems is strongly connected to Gazprom's determination to be seen as a reliable supplier to Europe. The only blemishes on the track record of Russian gas supplies have been as a result of transit incidents in Ukraine (see above in relation to Turkey) and Belarus. These incidents and the threat of more serious problems in the future, account for the emergence of the 'transit avoidance pipelines' such as Yamal, Blue Stream and the North European pipeline. The importance of the transit countries to Gazprom explains why in the 2000s:

- it has taken back full control of gas supply and transit arrangements from Itera and Eural Transgas;
- it is important that initiatives such as the Ukraine Consortium succeed not simply in building new capacity, but in refurbishing the existing transit pipelines which for many years will continue to carry the majority of Russian gas to Europe;
- it would be advantageous for the Transit Protocol of the Energy Charter Treaty to be ratified by Russia and Belarus in order to create an international legal framework with enforceable dispute resolution to deal with future problems.

Russian gas supplies to Europe are required to travel many thousands of kilometres from the point of production from and through an extremely harsh physical environment. Production operations and the requirements of the Russian domestic market are affected by the harshness of winter conditions. A range of potential technical problems and market conditions which might both restrict supply and increase demand have caused Gazprom to put in place commercial arrangements to deliver physical gas to European storages during the summer, which are then available to meet contractual requirements in winter. Some of these arrangements relate to storage part-owned by Gazprom (for example in Wingas' Rehden facility) but the contract signed with Dutch company Gasunie provides for deliveries from Gazprom – which started in 2001 – of up to 4 Bcm/year thereafter.[122] Under this contract, Gasunie provides 'hub services' for Russian gas in the form of transit, quality conversion, storage, technical support and back-up services.

Despite huge changes in the post-Cold War political and geopolitical landscape, the security aspects of Russian gas exports to Europe continue to surface both in official discussions, and whenever political problems arise either in Russia or transit countries. The continued, real or imagined, existence of the '30% rule' discussed above, led the European Union – within the framework of the EU-Russia Energy Dialogue to state that:

> Russia can help the EU to diversify its fossil fuel supplies. It is therefore inconceivable that the EU should impose quantitative restrictions on its imports...a Joint Declaration on EU enlargement and relations between Russia and the EU stated that there were no longer any restrictions on imports of gas and oil into the EU.[123]

In reality, as Table 3.6 shows, European dependence on Russian gas is a complex statistical issue and varies from country to country. The often-quoted statistic that Russia provides 26% of European gas supplies

Table 3.6: European Dependence on Russian Gas Supplies, 2003

	% of Total Imports	*% of Total Consumption**
Austria	77	65
Finland	100	100
France	24	23
Germany	37	33
Greece	76	76
Italy	32	26
Netherlands	17	6
EU15	28	18
Czech Republic	74	73
Hungary	86	66
Poland	85	58
Romania	91	29
Slovakia	100	97
Slovenia	60	60
Central/Eastern Europe**	87	60
Turkey	61	60
TOTAL EUROPE***	38	26

* including exports and stock changes; ** 12 countries; ***28 countries

Source: Calculated from Cedigaz, Trends and Figures in 2003, from *Natural Gas in the World 2003.*

is largely meaningless as a measure of the vulnerability of individual countries or regions. In Central and Eastern Europe, except Romania, the legacy of high dependence on Russian gas from the communist era remains, despite – as we saw above – attempts at diversification. In the main European gas markets (Germany, France, Italy, Netherlands) the share of Russian gas in total gas demand varies from 6% in the Netherlands (and in reality zero because of that country's status as a gas exporter), to 33% in Germany. Other major European gas markets such as Spain, UK and Belgium have little or no dependence on Russian gas although, as we saw above, this is changing with Gazprom's intention to supply up to 10% of the UK market by 2010.

When political problems arise, such as the Ukrainian election crisis in late 2004 which raised the possibility of a division of the country, this is immediately linked to the security of Russian gas supplies to Europe, with the Executive Director of the International Energy Agency warning that political instability would jeopardise EU energy security.[124] In the minds of many European politicians and bureaucrats, any suggestion that Europe is becoming more dependent on imported gas supplies produces the immediate conclusion that such import dependence carries with it a threat of increased insecurity of supply – and this tends to focus on Russia as the largest external source of European supply. Such a conclusion is neither necessarily well-reasoned nor based on empirical evidence, but it is extremely popular with European politicians and media.

Much has been written about the importance of security of Russian gas supplies from a European perspective. Less well appreciated is how important the security of European gas sales has been, and continues to be, from a Russian perspective. For much of the 1990s – as we saw in Chapters 1 and 2 – Gazprom was required to supply much of the Russian domestic and CIS market at a loss, due to a combination of low prices and lack of payment. During this period, the Russian gas industry was financially maintained by the revenues from European exports. The future will be different as exports to CIS countries become profitable (the February 2004 Belarus incident can be seen as evidence of Gazprom's determination in that context) and in 2004, for the first time in many years (and perhaps ever), the company did not lose money on sales to the Russian market. Nevertheless, the financial security of the revenues from European gas sales shown in Tables 3.3 and 3.4 will continue to be of enormous importance for the Russian Federation and Gazprom. That need for financial security goes a considerable way towards guaranteeing the security of Russian gas supplies to Europe. Only if Russian earnings from European gas imports are reduced from the current 15–20% of import revenues to a much lower percentage will it be time to question whether Gazprom, and the Russian government, can afford to jeopardise security of gas supplies to Europe.

Asia[125]

The prospect of Russian gas exports to Asia has been treated by many as a new development in the 2000s. In fact, plans to export Soviet gas to Asia by pipeline and LNG, and LNG to North America date back to the 1960s.[126] During the Soviet era, gas export projects to Asian markets failed to make progress because of a mixture of political, commercial and institutional obstacles. Until 1990, Japan was seen as the only realistic Asian market for Soviet gas, but the lack of a Peace Treaty between Japan and the Soviet Union after the Second World

War was a serious political obstacle. An equally serious obstacle to any improvement in bilateral relations has been the territorial dispute over four small islands in the Kurile chain which were occupied by the Soviet Union after the Second World War.[127] Japan's tendency to follow the political lead of the United States reinforced the lack of trust between the two countries during the Cold War era, and produced only a very slow improvement in relations over the past decade. Problems with the political relationship were mirrored in the lack of enthusiasm of Japanese gas utilities to import Russian supplies. The attitude of these buyers to (Soviet and) Russian gas contrasted sharply with their much greater keenness to develop LNG trade with south east Asian (and Middle East) countries. While, as this section shows, progress has been made in Russo-Japanese gas trade, the post-Cold War era has not yet seen any definitive resolution of the outstanding political issues – the Peace Treaty and territorial dispute. Meanwhile other potential Asian buyers of Russian gas have entered the picture.

The Resource Base

The Eastern Siberian and Far Eastern gas resource base is straightforward. Multi-trillion cubic metre gas resources that are substantially in excess of the potential domestic requirements of the regional population of roughly 11 million are largely concentrated in four regions: Krasnoyarsk, Irkutsk, Sakha and Sakhalin.[128] However, numerically and conceptually, resource estimations are misleading for several reasons: new and conflicting data constantly increase the resource potential; there is seldom any estimation of the proportion of resources that may be economically and technically recoverable at different price levels; and there is rarely any estimate of whether such resources could be considered commercially viable when delivered to markets via transportation systems requiring investments of \$10–20bn. Table 3.7 shows the known gas resources of the different East Siberian and Far Eastern regions, as well as some West Siberian resources more likely to be oriented east than west.

The Sakhalin Projects[129]

During the Soviet era, interest in gas exports to Asia centred largely on the oil and gas fields offshore Sakhalin Island. In the immediate post-Soviet period, there was renewed interest from international companies in the region because – unlike many other potential development opportunities within Russia – export of these resources did not require

Table 3.7: Main gas supply sources for Northeast Asia

Region	Field (Licensed Company)	Reserves (C1+C2)
Sakhalin	Odoptu, Chaivo, Arkutun-Dagi (Sakhalin I project))	485 bcm + 307 mt
	Piltun-Astokskoye, Lunskoye (Sakhalin Energy Investment Corp)	800 bcm + 185 mt
Irkutsk	Kovyktinksoye (Rusia Petroleum)	1,932 bcm + 90 mt condensate + 2.3 bcm helium
	Verkhnechonskoye	280 mt
Republic of Sakha*	Chayandinskoye*** (Sakha Republic Gov)	1240 bcm + 50 mt
	Sredne-Botuobinskoye (Sakhaneftegas)	171 bcm
	Taas-Yuriakskoye (Sakhaneftegas)	114 bcm
	Talakanskoye (Surgutneftegas)	124 mt + 50 bcm
Krasnoyarsk**	Yurubchonskoye (Yukos)	282 mt + 374 bcm + 29 mt condensate
	Kuyumbinskoye (Slavneft)	154 mt
	Sobinskoye (Gazprom)	159 bcm
West Siberia	Palkliahinskoye, Bolshehetskaya (Gazprom)	3,021 bcm, of which C1 751 bcm, C2 596 bcm, and C3 1,203 bcm

*   As of 2002, the estimated recoverable oil and gas reserves in Sakha Republic are 2.39 billion tonnes of oil, 9,420 bcm of gas, and 409 million tonnes of condensate respectively.

**   The geological oil and gas reserves of Yurubchen-Tokhomskaya area composed of Yurubchen, Kuyumbinskoye, and Tersko-Kamovskoye fields stand at 1.2 billion tonnes and 1,000–1,200 bcm respectively.

*** license is being auctioned in 2005.

Source: *Keun-Wook Paik, Pipeline Gas Introduction to the Korean Peninsula,* 2005.

long distance transportation through Russia and other CIS countries
to export borders. There are a number of different Sakhalin projects,
known by their numbers 1–6 (see Table 3.7 and Map 3.4), but the most
advanced are Sakhalin 1 and 2 which are the largest foreign investment
projects in Russia.[130]

Sakhalin 1, 3, 4 and 5 involve consortia of Russian and foreign
investors. There are no Russian partners in Sakhalin 2, and no foreign
partners in Sakhalin 6. The commercial parties in the various consortia
have changed several times due to mergers of international oil companies (e.g. Exxon/Mobil, BP/Arco) and withdrawal/buy-out of some of

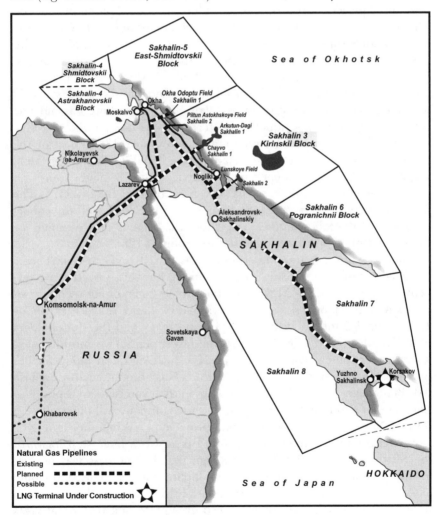

Map 3.4: The Sakhalin Projects

the original partners (e.g. McDermott and Marathon from Sakhalin 2). Further issues of ownership, particularly in terms of Gazprom's future role in these projects, are discussed later in this Chapter. Sakhalin 1 and 2 operate under production sharing agreements (PSAs) with a legal status approved by the Duma. Sakhalin 2 received its PSA in June 1994, and Sakhalin 1 in June 1996, along with assurances that the PSAs would not be affected by subsequent legislation. None of the other projects received PSA approval.

Sakhalin 2. Sakhalin Energy Investment Corporation (SEIC) divided the Sakhalin 2 project into two phases.[131] Phase 1 focused on oil production which began in 1999. Phase 2 is gas development and in July 2001 the Corporation's supervisory board approved a plan to move ahead with 'an integrated oil and gas development that will be the world's largest LNG project'.[132] Pipelines are to be built to shore from Piltun-As-tokhskoye – an oil field with associated gas; and Lunskoye – a gas field with condensate and an oil rim. A single 840 km onshore gas pipeline will bring the gas to a liquefaction terminal (with a parallel pipeline carrying oil to an export terminal) at Prigorodnoye (13 km east of the city of Korsakov) on the ice-free Japan Sea. The liquefaction terminal will consist of two trains each with a capacity of 4.8 million tons (mt) per year reaching a total capacity of 9.6 mt or 13.3 Bcm/year.[133] The first LNG cargo is due to be loaded on November 2007 with full capacity achieved the following year. By 2004, the original cost estimate for the project of $10bn had increased to around $12bn.[134]

The Sakhalin 2 marketing strategy was to sell LNG to Asia Pacific markets (Japan, Korea, Taiwan and China), but this proved more difficult than expected. In May 2003, the project signed long-term agreements with the Japanese companies Tokyo Gas and Tokyo Electric for 1.1 mt and 1.2 mt per year of LNG respectively and the shareholders made the decision to proceed with the investment. Two months later, a further agreement was signed with Kyushu Electric in Japan for 0.5 mt/year of LNG for 21 years, and Toho Gas committed to purchase 0.3 Bcm/year. Tokyo Electric subsequently exercised an option to purchase an additional 0.3 mt/year and the company will buy up to 0.8 mt of LNG in 2007–08, earlier than projected.[135] While the signing of agreements with the major utilities in Tokyo was a huge step forward, the relatively small volumes were a sign that Russian gas was not yet a fully accepted source of supply for Japan. This is, at least to some extent, a reflection of the general relationship between the countries, noted earlier, which has not improved greatly despite reciprocal visits of the Russian President and the Japanese Prime Minister to each other's countries.[136] In the 2000s, there has been little sign that either side feels any urgency to resolve these outstanding issues of the Peace Treaty and the Northern Territories, certainly not to the point of making concessions.

In October 2004, 37 mt of LNG over a 20-year period (with an anticipated plateau volume of 1.6 mt/year) were sold to an affiliate of Shell, to be shipped to the Costa Azul terminal on the west coast of Mexico where Shell is a partner in a joint venture with Sempra Energy.[137] In early 2005, Sakhalin 2 was one of the winners of a tender issued by the South Korean company Kogas, to supply 1.5 mt of LNG per year with an option to supply another 0.5 mt.[138] In addition, management revealed that discussions were ongoing with Sinopec in China and stated confidently that the full 9.6 mt/year capacity would be sold by end-2005.[139] Nevertheless, the length of time it has taken to sign contracts with Asian buyers combined with the sales to the North American market reflect the difficulties of selling Russian LNG in Asia. This is caused by a combination of reduced demand, market uncertainty due to the prospects for deregulation and restructuring, and severe competition between suppliers.[140] The purchase of LNG by Asian buyers from Australia, East Timor and Indonesia over the same period must, to some extent, reflect the attractiveness of those sources in the eyes of buyers, compared with Russia.

The other issue that remains to be decided is the future of the shareholding in Sakhalin 2 which is the only major energy project in Russia with no Russian partner. Over the years there have been sporadic discussions with Gazprom about bringing the company into the joint venture. In 2004, negotiations recommenced about the possibility of Gazprom taking a significant equity stake, and seemed to be near finalisation in early 2005, with Gazprom taking a 25% share in the project in exchange for equivalent Neocomian reserves in the Zapolyarnoye gas field, where the two companies have a joint venture which had been dormant for several years.[141]

Sakhalin 1. In October 2001, the Sakhalin 1 partners declared the commerciality of Phase 1 of the project involving the start of oil production in late 2005 with 'limited gas supplies available to help meet Russian domestic demand'. As far as gas exports are concerned, the press release which announced commerciality described the position thus:

> Gas market development and sales remain a high priority for the project. An assessment of gas export markets in Japan and China has been completed and the Consortium has concluded that a pipeline, built to international design standards, would be the most cost-effective method to deliver gas

to these export markets. Discussions with potential export customers are under way, along with a framework for developing commercial gas sales to Russian domestic purchasers.[142]

Thus Sakhalin 1 adopted a completely different marketing strategy compared with Sakhalin 2, concentrating on pipeline gas rather than LNG. A feasibility study of pipeline exports from the Odoptu and Chaivo fields to Japan, which for many years was the only market considered by the operator Exxon Neftegas, was completed in spring 2002.[143] Only in late 2004 with no progress in negotiations and no likelihood that Japan would develop a significant gas pipeline network in the foreseeable future, did the Sakhalin 1 partners announce that they had commenced negotiations with the Chinese company CNPC.[144] There has been no public discussion of selling pipeline gas to Korea. This could be commercially feasible but is impossible without a political settlement of the North Korean problem to the satisfaction of the United States.[145]

In late 2004, for the first time since the Sakhalin 1 joint venture was created, the CEO of Exxon-Mobil said that the joint venture would consider the possibility of exporting LNG instead of pipeline gas.[146] But the only immediate progress for Sakhalin 1 gas marketing has been the sale to the local gas and power companies Khabarovskkraigaz and Khabarovskenergo for the start of the 2005–06 winter season.[147] Interestingly, the gas will be sold at the Chayvo onshore processing facility with transportation via regional pipeline networks to be arranged by the buyers. Volumes could start as early as the 2005/06 heating season and increase to 3 Bcm/year by 2009.[148]

Sakhalin 3. Unlike Sakhalin 1 and 2, which are based on fields already established during the Soviet era, the other Sakhalin projects are located in acreage believed to contain substantial hydrocarbon deposits but requiring further exploration. Corporate mergers and acquisitions determined that by 2004, the Sakhalin 3 partners – which originally involved very different companies – were the same as the Sakhalin 1 partners with the addition of Chevron/Texaco (see Table 3.8). However, perhaps for that reason, there was very little progress on Sakhalin 3. A key official in the local Sakhalin administration writing in 2001 noted: 'The Kirinsky block PSA has been in a state of lengthy deliberation by the negotiations committee for 8 years while the Ashansky and East Odoptu blocks have not been included in the list of subsurface areas to be developed on a PSA basis yet.'[149]

In January 2004, the Russian government annulled the results of the 1993 Sakhalin 3 tender and withdrew the exploration licence from

Table 3.8: The Sakhalin Projects and Shareholders: 2004

Sakhalin 1:

Fields: Odoptu, Chaivo and Arkutun-Dagi

Partners: Exxon-Neftegas - operator 30%, Sodeco 30%, Sakhalinmoreneftegaz
    – Shelf, Rosneft 20%, ONGC Videsh 20%

Proven Reserves: 485 Bcm of gas, 307 mt of oil

PSA agreed June 1996.

Sakhalin 2 (Sakhalin Energy Investment Corporation SEIC):

Fields: Lunskoye, Piltun-Astokhskoye

Partners: Shell – operator 55%, Mitsui, 25%, Mitubishi 20%.

Proven reserves: >500 Bcm of gas, >150 mt oil.

PSA agreed June 1994.

Sakhalin 3:

Fields: Kirinsky, East Odoptinskii and Achanskii Blocks.
Partners: Exxon-Neftegas 33.3%, Chevron/Texaco 33.3%, Sakhalinmorneftegaz
    16.6%, Rosneft 16.6%

Projected recoverable reserves: 713 Bcm of gas, 62 mt of condensate.

Sakhalin 4:

Astrakhanovskii and Schmidtovskii Blocks
Partners: BP 49%, Rosneft 25.5%, Sakhalinmorneftegaz 25.5%
Projected recoverable reserves: 440 Bcm of gas and 110 mt of oil.

Sakhalin 5:

Blocks: Kaigan-Vasuygan, East- Schmidtovskii, Elizaveta, Khanguzinskii Blocks
Partners: BP 51%, Rosneft 49%
Preliminary estimate of reserves: 432 Bcm of gas and 783 mt of oil.

Sakhalin 6:

Fields: Sakhalin VI Block including PetroSakh License area
Partners: Rosneft 50%, Alpha-Eco 50%
Preliminary estimate of reserves: 510 mt of oil equivalent of which two thirds gas
    and one third oil.

Source: adapted from: Keun-Wook Paik, *Pipeline Gas Introduction to the Korean
          Peninsula*, 2005.

the group with the intention of auctioning the licence. Deputy Prime Minister Khristenko was quoted as saying:

> There are no grounds for granting Exxon-Mobil a licence to develop the Sakhalin 3 field under production sharing conditions or under regular taxation conditions. This means that the development of the field, if it is considered expedient, may take place according to the usual scheme, that is, based on an auction.[150]

The Natural Resource Ministry was even more negative about the performance of the Sakhalin 3 partners, and this may be related to what they perceive as overly slow development of the Sakhalin 1 gas resource.

Sakhalin 4 and 5. These can be considered together since they have similar partners (Table 3.8). Much of the detail as to how and when the projects may proceed is uncertain because they are still in the exploration phase. The major foreign company BP, after some hesitation (partly related to the takeover of Arco, the original partner in Sakhalin 4) formed a partnership with Rosneft and Sakhalinmorneftegaz to develop the Astrakhanovski field (Sakhalin 4) and to tender for some part of the East Schmidtovskii block (Sakhalin 5). However, there was little progress until mid-2004 when the first well on Sakhalin 5's Kayaganskii and Vasuyganskii blocks was drilled and both oil and gas were found.[151] *Sakhalin 6* is unique in having only Russian shareholders – Rosneft and Alpha-Eco; the licence has changed hands several times.

Sakhalin is a province of substantial proportions, particularly as far as gas is concerned. Sakhalin 2 and 1 have established proven reserves of more than 500 Bcm and 485 Bcm respectively, giving a total of 985 Tcm.[152] Taking into account the indicated reserves at Sakhalin 3–6 of nearly 2 trillion cubic metres (Tcm), the resource base could support a production of more than 100 Bcm/year which could be shipped by pipeline to Asia Pacific markets or in liquefied form to those markets and the west coast of North America.

The Kovyktinskoye (Kovykhta) Project

In addition to the Sakhalin projects, there are a number of pipeline gas export projects to East Asian countries. Of these, the most advanced is the project to export gas from the Kovyktinskoye field, located 430 km north of Irkutsk to China, Mongolia, Korea and potentially also Japan, which was first unveiled in late 1994 by the Russian company Sidanco. The licence to develop the field was awarded to Rusia Petroleum with

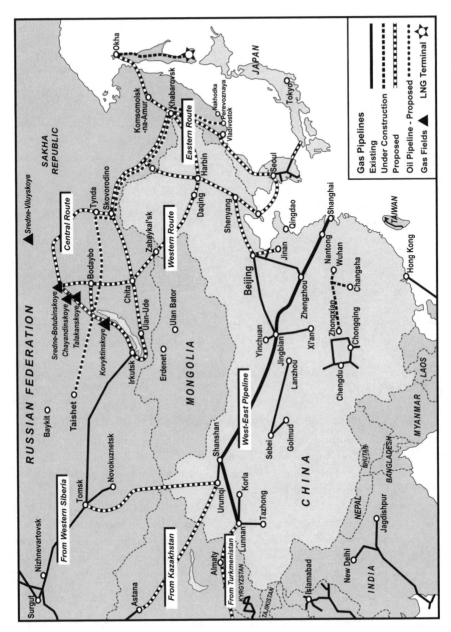

Map 3.5: Gas Pipelines from Russia and Central Asia to East Asia

Sidanco as its main shareholder; other shareholders included the local Irkutsk government and energy companies, and Korea's East Asia Gas Company. In late 1997, British Petroleum bought a 10% shareholding in Sidanco – specifically targeted at participation in Rusia Petroleum and (oil and) gas exports to China.[153]

A combination of Asian (1997) and Russian (1998) economic crises cast shadows over the prospects for development and the finances of the Russian and Korean shareholders. The bankruptcy of Sidanco and some questionable corporate governance involving subsidiaries of that company,[154] followed by the merger of BP's Russian interests with the company TNK, finally led to the position that by late 2004 the equity holders in Rusia Petroleum were TNK/BP 63%, Interros 25.82%, Irkutsk State Property Committee 10.78%.[155]

A trilateral agreement to conduct a feasibility study was signed in late 2000 by representatives from Rusia, Kogas and CNPC. Up to 2000, three main pipeline routes were considered, a route through Mongolia and two eastern routes:

- one which followed the Russian-Mongolian border through Buryatia and Chita into north Eastern China and then through North Korea to South Korea;
- another which travelled offshore through the Yellow Sea to bypass North Korea.[156]

According to the feasibility study completed in November 2003, starting in 2008 and building up to 30 Bcm in 2017, the project would deliver 20 Bcm/year to China and 10 Bcm/year to Korea; 4 Bcm/year would also be delivered to local markets in Irkutsk, Buryatia and Chita.[157] The 2003 feasibility study estimated the project cost at $17bn. The selection of routes for the Kovykta project was strongly influenced by the extremely negative stance taken by the Chinese authorities to the Mongolian route. The Russian parties were well disposed towards the Mongolian route, which was around 1000 km shorter with a capital cost saving of around $1bn and provided opportunities for sales to Mongolia.[158] But the Chinese were unwilling to compromise and it was impossible for other parties to oppose their wishes.

There has been constant speculation over the past decade that CNPC (of China), JNOC (of Japan), Kogas (of Korea) and a variety of Russian companies, including Gazprom, would take equity in Rusia Petroleum. As early as November 2001, BP announced that it was ready to offer Gazprom participation in the venture.[159] Periodic discussions have taken place between the companies and these have intensified since 2004 as it became increasingly apparent that Gazprom had gained the upper hand in the negotiations.[160] Earlier in the year, Rusia established a company for domestic development of gas for local consumers with production of 0.3 Bcm in 2006 rising to 2.2 Bcm in 2009.[161] In addition, Gazprom appeared to be conciliatory to TNK-BP by inviting it to join the existing Gazprom/Rosneft/Surgutneftegaz consortium for joint development of East Siberian oil and gas resources.[162]

By late 2004, the mood had changed as the government questioned whether the Rusia partners had infringed their licence conditions, with the threat that the licence could be withdrawn.[163] Following the announcement of the Gazprom/Rosneft merger, Gazprom was quoted as 'losing interest' in Kovykta although some believed this was simply a negotiating ploy.[164] With the collapse of the merger, progress may depend on how quickly Gazprom takes equity in the project combined with how quickly Chinese buyers indicate serious interest in purchasing pipeline gas.

Sakha Republic Projects

The other group of fields relevant for exports to Asia are those in the Sakha Republic of which Chayandinskoye is by far the most important in terms of reserves (see Table 3.7). The development of Sakha gas fields for export dates back to the Soviet period (when the region was known as Yakutia). A number of possibilities for pipeline and LNG exports of Sakha gas include routes:

- to Japan either as part of a Sakhalin pipeline project or a free-standing pipeline project or as LNG;
- to DPRK (North Korea) and South Korea via Russia;
- east and south to China (possibly via Mongolia) with a possible extension to Korea;
- west and south to link with a pipeline from the Kovyktinskoye field.

Sakha Republic resources are less advantageously located than those of either Sakhalin or Kovykta gas in respect of export markets. While Sakha resources could 'back up' projects based on either of these other regions, this will not be necessary in the first stage of either project and the likelihood that additional gas will continue to be discovered offshore Sakhalin and confirmed at Kovykta could render Sakha resources surplus to requirements. Prior to the Gazprom-Rosneft merger, the advantage for Sakha gas was that this was the only major gas resource in the region in which Gazprom could be involved via its strategic alliance with the government of the Sakha Republic, as well as its alliance with Rosneft and Surgutneftegaz.[165]   A key development will be the result of the auction of the Chayandinskoye licence in 2005.[166] Following the collapse of the Gazprom-Rosneft merger, early development of Sakha gas appeared somewhat more likely. But much will depend on the outcome of the Chayandinskoye auction and Gazprom's negotiations with other resource holders in the region, particularly the Kovykta partners.[167]

The Role of Gazprom and the Russian Government

An overview of the status of different projects in late 2004 suggests a rapidly changing situation in terms of project alliances and priorities. Much will be decided by market opportunities, but the preferences of Gazprom and the Russian government will clearly determine the strategic direction and control of exports to Asia. In the early years of the post-Soviet era, Gazprom failed to demonstrate any substantial interest in Asian gas export initiatives. Part of the reason for this can be attributed to the company's Soviet-era disillusion with Japanese gas buyers.[168] Another part was due to lack of top level management time for a prospective, but uncertain, set of markets in contrast to the more immediate opportunities for increasing deliveries to Europe.

From 1997 onwards, Gazprom management began increasingly to mention Asian gas exports as part of their general export strategy.[169] Chairman Vyakhirev devoted an entire section of his speech at the 1997 World Gas Conference to the 'East-Asian Gas Market' mentioning all of the potential projects.[170] At the APEC Summit in November 1998, Gazprom's Chairman announced a plan to link the fields of the Yamal Peninsula with Shanghai, a distance of 7,100 km, with a route via Tomsk, Barnaul, Irkutsk and Urumchi. Gazprom officials also spoke of the Zapolyarnoye field as a possible source of gas for China (although not since the field started production in 2001) as well as fields in Krasnoyarsk region such as Bolshekhetskaya.[171] Two years later, Gazprom's Chairman was more specific about projects and timing:

> The Far East region, China, Korea and Japan is a new promising market for Russia's pipeline gas. Various options of Russia's involvement in this market development are under discussion. At the first phases, the Far Eastern gas transmission system project is supposed to be realized with gas pipeline supply up to 30 Bcm annually. Gas flow will go from the fields in the Irkutskaya oblast and the Republic of Sakha. Gas produced from Sakhalin offshore (Sakhalin 2) will mainly go to liquefaction...as an alternative, construction of a gas transmission system to deliver gas to China and

Korea via Khabarovsk is under consideration. Annual deliveries of Sakhalin gas could reach 12−15 Bcm by 2010 and 20−25 Bcm by 2020.[172]

Evidence of Gazprom's increased attention to gas development prospects in Eastern Siberia and the Far East and Asian gas export potential can be seen in the creation of its Vostokgazprom subsidiary in 1999 which became involved throughout the gas chain with an annual production of 3.5 Bcm.[173]

The institutional basis for gas development in Eastern Siberia and the Far East changed in June 2002 when the Russian Government issued Decree No 975-r instructing the Ministry of Energy and Gazprom to draw up a programme for a unified system of production, transmission and distribution of gas in Eastern Siberia and the Far East, taking into account the possibility of exports to China and other Asia-Pacific countries. Critically, the Decree named Gazprom as the coordinator of the programme thereby placing the company in control of all future projects in the region.[174] Since then, the basis on which Gazprom has proceeded appears to have been that if a project does not fit into its programme for the region, it is unlikely to be able to make significant progress.

The 2003 Russian Energy Strategy placed significant emphasis on the development of Far Eastern gas resources, with the possibility that production could expand up to 106 Bcm by 2020 (Table 3.9) and a projection that in the same year the region would account for 15% of total Russian gas exports.[175]

Table 3.9: Projected Gas Production in Eastern Siberia and the Far East (Bcm)

	2000	2005	2010	2015	2020
Central	7	8	31	86	95
Optimistic	7	8	52	97	106

Source: *Russian Energy Strategy, 2003*, Figure 11, p.72

Chairman Miller's speech to the World Gas Conference in Tokyo in June 2003 was a milestone in Gazprom's Asian policy.[176] Miller laid stress on both domestic gas development in Eastern Siberia and the Far East, and the prospects for exports to the Asia-Pacific region emphasising Gazprom's coordinating role; but the most interesting feature was the map of the region that he presented. In Map 3.6, the West Siberian pipeline network is extended east from Novosibirsk to Irkutsk, with the Krasnoyarsk fields (Yurubchenskoye and Sobinskoye) connected to that pipeline. At Irkutsk, a pipeline is projected from Kovyktinskoye north

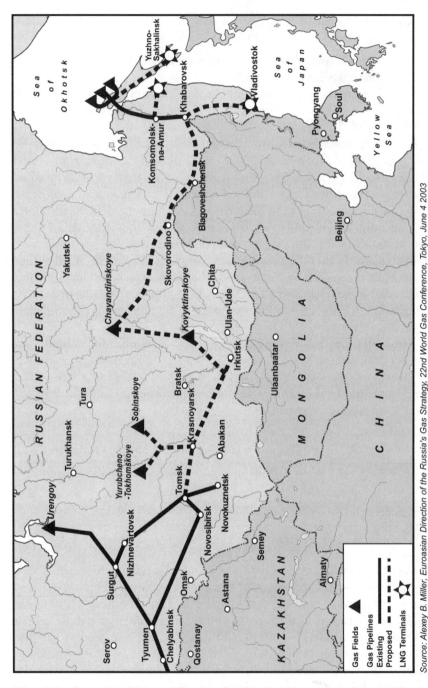

Map 3.6: Gazprom's Vision of Russian Gas Pipeline Networks in Eastern Siberia
and the Far East

Source: Alexey B. Miller, Euroasian Direction of the Russia's Gas Strategy, 22nd World Gas Conference, Tokyo, June 4 2003

to Chayandinskoye and east to Sakhalinsk, meeting a pipeline from the Sakhalin fields and proceeding further south to an LNG plant at Vladivostok.[177] The Sakhalin 2 pipeline to the LNG plant at Yuzhno Sakhalinsk is the only ongoing export project acknowledged on the map. With hindsight, this representation – it was not a proposal and the text of the paper does not discuss any specific projects – signalled a significant change in policy towards regional development.

The 2003 presentation of Alexey Miller suggested parallel development of gas and oil pipelines. During the early 2000s, there has been competition between two proposals for major oil export pipelines to Asia: the Angarsk-Daqing pipeline, and a pipeline from Taishet to Perevoznaya Bay on the east coast (Map 3.5).[178] The choice between these pipeline routes has been determined largely by Russian internal politics – Angarsk-Daqing being a Yukos-sponsored project at a time when that company began to experience serious political and commercial difficulties with the Russian government. But the oil pipeline options also highlighted differences in export strategy, specifically the view that a pipeline with China as its sole destination would both limit the scope of oil exports and place those exports at the commercial mercy of a single buyer. A pipeline from Taishet to a Pacific location, however, would open up a range of markets in Asia and allow Russian sellers to exploit competition between buyers. Estimated total cost of a Taishet to Perevoznaya pipeline was $12.5bn in 2005, but there were insufficient established oil reserves in Eastern Siberia for a large diameter pipeline carrying 80 mt/year (necessary to keep unit costs down). Nevertheless, by early 2005, the Russian government had opted for the Taishet-Perevoznaya line to be built by Transneft (the Russian state-owned oil pipeline company) in three phases. In Phase 1, a pipeline with a capacity of 24−30 mt will be built only as far as Skovorodino, from where the oil will be moved by rail to the coast (with a possible spur line to China); there is an intention to complete this phase by 2008.[179]

The Miller concept of a Far East gas pipeline network to a large extent mirrors the approach to oil exports but, from a domestic perspective, goes further as expressed by another Gazprom board member:

> The mainstay of eastern Russia's future gas supply network is said to be the so-called Central Gas Main that will unite basic fields of Eastern Siberia and the Far East, to be linked with Russia's United Gas Supply System (UGSS). Based on the Central Gas Main, eastern Russia will see before 2020 already the construction of a united gas production and transmission system which may possibly be built in several stages, allowing the optimisation of capital investments for all the main gas fields for a diversity of regional markets while avoiding competition between the projects.[180]

This would mean that, at least in theory, East Siberian gas could flow in either direction: east to domestic or East Asian markets; or west via Western Siberia to markets in western Russia. The main problem with the 'Central Gas Main' concept of joining up the Chayandinskoye, Kovyktinskoye, Krasnoyarsk (Yurubcheno-Tokhomskoye and Sobinsko-Paiginskoe) and Sakhalin fields with the UGSS, is that it is not clear how such ambitious network developments can be reconciled with profitability if the markets are intended to be domestic, particularly given the relatively poor economic performance of Eastern Siberia and the Far East in the post-Soviet period.[181]

In the wake of the 2002 Decree, it became clear that Gazprom had indeed taken charge of all export negotiations, irrespective of the origin of the gas. In May 2003, it signed a five-year cooperation agreement with the Korean gas company Kogas to examine the prospect of Russian gas supplies to Korea. The agreement, from Gazprom's standpoint:

> ...will lay the legal basis for intensive cooperation between the two companies in the pipeline gas deliveries to South Korea as well as for the realisation of joint projects in third countries...The agreement concluded today means that the principle of delivering gas via a single export route will be effected for the Korean gas market.[182]

One year later, at a meeting with the South Korean Ambassador to the Russian Federation, it was made clear that sales to Korea were being placed within the general development programme for the East Siberian and Far Eastern region which would be based on: '...establishing an integrated export channel and delivering gas from the gas supply network but not from separate fields.' It was anticipated that the Gazprom-KOGAS Working Group would start negotiating a long-term contract for deliveries to Korea with Gazexport.[183] The previous day, at a meeting with the Gazprom chairman, COO of TNK/BP (Victor Vekselberg) had agreed the concept of the 'integrated export channel' i.e. that the Kovykta partners would not be able to make their own contractual arrangements directly with customers and that '... negotiations on gas supply terms and conditions covering gas volumes, supply timing and price calculation formula should be conducted by Gazexport'.[184]

As far as relations with China are concerned, the failure of Gazprom to participate in the construction and development of China's West-East Gas Pipeline was a potential setback. Gazprom (and the other potential foreign partners Shell and ExxonMobil) had imagined that equity in the West-East Pipeline would provide it with the opportunity to supply gas from Western Siberia into the line.[185] With the collapse of all foreign investment in the West-East Pipeline, Gazprom was left to rebuild the relationship.[186] In October 2004, China National Petroleum Corporation (CNPC) entered into a strategic cooperation agreement with Gazprom of a very general nature. While there was general discussion of China needing gas imports of 20 Bcm by 2010, it was stressed by Chairman Miller that the discussions were about 'the resource base and its optimisation, but we did not talk about specific [pipeline] routes...the price formula for Russian gas to be imported to China has not yet been agreed upon either.'[187] Following the Russian government's decision to favour the Taishet-Perevoznaya pipeline over Angarsk-Daqing – a project which the Chinese side regarded as having been agreed – it may take some time to rebuild Chinese confidence in Russian ability to deliver on large-scale pipeline projects.

In March 2005, the Deputy Head of the Fuel and Energy Department at the Ministry of Industry and Trade, in a presentation that seemingly dealt mainly with the Taishet-Perevoznaya oil pipeline, proposed four new options for building a regional gas pipeline network with export options to East Asian countries (see Map 3.5):

1. A 'western route' which would give gas from Irkutsk and Sakha access to the Chinese market via Zabaikalsk, Daqing and Shenyang. This route could also include gas from Western Siberia.
2. An 'eastern route' which would connect fields in Sakhalin to China via Harbin; a link to Western and Eastern Siberian gas would be created at Khabarovsk.
3. A 'central route' from the Sakha fields to Skovorodino and Blagoveshchensk, bringing gas from the rest of Siberia to China.
4. A proposal by Rusia Petroleum which is based on exporting gas from Irkutsk and Sakha, but also from Sakhalin.[188]

The fact that these were the most recent set of proposals available as this study was being completed, in no way suggests that they will have continuing relevance in what has clearly been a very fast-moving situation with many actors jockeying for political and equity positions. Central to any final decision on routes are likely to be the wishes of the importing company or government. In addition, in all of these conceptual proposals there is little discussion of investment requirements, potential shareholders and financing, which are the main building blocks of any actual development.

The proposal and then collapse of the Gazprom-Rosneft merger (see Chapter 4) changed the context for development of substantial

Sakhalin resources. The merger would have brought Gazprom into all of the Sakhalin projects (with the exception of Sakhalin 2 where, as we saw above, it is negotiating for a share). Unlike Rosneft, which has neither financial resources nor commercial/political incentives to mount major greenfield gas developments, Gazprom has definite and influential views on the development of the Far Eastern region and, when the merger seemed likely to go ahead, Chairman Alexey Miller suggested that the Sakhalin region had priority for development over other regions in Eastern Russia.[189] With the failure of the merger, it remains to be seen whether, as in the case of Sakhalin 2, shareholders will invite Gazprom to take equity shares in other Sakhalin projects.

Liquefied Natural Gas (LNG) Exports to the United States

During the late 1970s, projects were planned to export Soviet LNG to both Japan and the United States. However, a combination of the arrival of the Reagan administration and US gas deregulation prevented the progress of those early projects.[190] LNG has for some time featured in Gazprom's long-term plans; in the 1990s, there were occasional references to the possibility of LNG exports from Murmansk and the Yamal Peninsula, which were never followed up. But in the 2000s – and particularly since 2003 – a frenzy of activity has developed around LNG export projects aimed at the United States.

Global LNG prospects during the 2000s were transformed due to a combination of technological advancement and cost reduction throughout the LNG chain; the development of liberalised and competitive gas markets which allow a much greater role for short-term contracting and swaps; the change in the North American gas market from supply surplus and low prices during the 1990s, to shortage and high prices in the 2000s, creating great urgency to reopen and expand existing LNG regasification terminals, and proposals to build dozens of new terminals.[191] In this fundamentally changed commercial context, it was possible for Russian LNG export projects to be considered attractive from both a commercial and political perspective for the first time in thirty years. With North American gas prices fluctuating between $4–9/mmbtu during 2003–05, Gazprom came to believe that failure to pursue LNG projects might be a major missed commercial opportunity. The prospect, albeit expressed in rather general terms, of developing a 'global gas business' encompassing North America as well as Europe and Asia, was clearly attractive. In addition, LNG could be part of the answer to monetising stranded gas at both the Shtokmanovskoye field in the Barents Sea and the Yamal Peninsula, both of which have reserves in excess of any likely immediate pipeline requirements (see Chapter 1).

Politically, there was a desire to develop more than symbolic energy trade between Russia and the USA in order to put some commercial flesh on the bones of the Russian-American Commercial Energy Dialogue, which had been created following the bilateral energy co-operation agreement at the presidential summit of May 2002.[192] The Russian-American Dialogue (which looked suspiciously like a copy of the EU-Russia Energy Dialogue – discussed above) has produced annual energy 'summits' between the two countries but – for reasons of geography and commercial viability – energy trade remains limited and LNG could provide an excellent basis for expanding commercial energy flows.

In his 2003 speech to the World Gas Conference, Gazprom Chairman Miller was optimistic but cautious about LNG prospects:

> ...Russia may consider supply of LNG to the American market in the future [but this] will depend on the demand and supply on the world market. In principle, the unique Yamal and Northern Sea fields provide a basis for implementation of LNG production.[193]

By 2004, the company had become much more aggressive in exploring LNG opportunities. Uniquely for Gazprom, LNG is a business in which partnership with non-Russian companies is essential for technical and commercial reasons. With no experience in the LNG business and a great deal of money at stake, Gazprom embarked on a series of discussions with virtually every major international company involved in the Atlantic LNG business.[194] With Gazprom's huge resource base giving the potential for virtually unlimited supplies of LNG, it was not surprising that large numbers of companies were eager to discuss potential opportunities relating to three possible projects:

1. The Shtokmanovskoye field with a pipeline to a liquefaction plant at the ice-free port of Murmansk or an offshore plant near the field (Map 1.3);[195]
2. A liquefaction plant at Ust Luga, 140 km west of St Petersburg, with gas from Western Siberia (Map 3.2);
3. A liquefaction plant at the Kharasevey field on the Yamal Peninsula (with gas from the Kharasevey field, see Map 1.1).

In 2004, the Shtokmanovskoye field was clearly Gazprom's priority project for LNG exports to the USA.[196] The project has been the subject of agreements with the Norwegian companies Hydro and Statoil which have specific technical expertise in the type of field development (at the Ormen Lange field) and LNG development in an Arctic environment (at the Snohvit terminal) respectively.[197] ConocoPhillips, one of the original partners in the Shtokman joint venture has also signed a memorandum of understanding with Gazprom.[198] The criteria for partners in LNG development are (a) those with the most advanced technology relevant to the development of the Shtokmanovskoye field; (b) those who can easily access the US market, i.e. have access to regasification terminal capacity, and have experience of working in that market; and (c) those who can attract finance to the project.

In line with these criteria, Gazprom initiated discussions with a range of companies owning or developing US regasification terminal capacity including Statoil, BP, ExxonMobil, Repsol, ChevronTexaco and Sempra Energy.[199] Nevertheless, in late 2004, the Director of Business Development at Gazexport was quoted as saying: 'We've been talking to a lot of companies, but there will not be a lot of deals.'[200]

A decision on joint venture partners to participate throughout the value chain from production to marketing is scheduled for the latter part of 2005, followed by conclusion of supply contracts, and a production sharing agreement by early 2006, suggesting that LNG from Shtokman could be reaching US markets by 2010.[201] This seemed over-optimistic simply in terms of lead times involved for negotiation and construction for such a complex project. But evidence of Gazprom's urgency to enter the LNG business can be seen from its discussions with BP (and others), which focused on the possibility of swapping pipeline gas in Europe for spot sales of LNG to the USA in order to enter the US market as soon as possible.[202]

In the first stage of the development Shtokman had been projected to produce up to 30 Bcm of which 22.5 Bcm/year (15 mt of LNG) will be used for LNG exports and the rest will be used locally; annual production will eventually reach 100 Bcm/year.[203] An LNG plant on the Yamal Peninsula may be similarly sized. The Canadian company PetroCanada has focused on Gazprom's idea of building a small – 3.5 mt per year – LNG plant at Ust Luga near St Petersburg and the companies have signed a Memorandum of Understanding which includes a feasibility study of the project.[204] This project, which is much smaller than the Murmansk terminal could move faster with LNG reaching one of the proposed Canadian terminals (at Bear Island or Irving New Brunswick) by 2009. The small size of the project could increase unit costs, but it will use the transmission system that will be built to bring gas to the North European Pipeline.

Much remains to be decided regarding Gazprom's LNG exports to the USA but the determination of the company to establish a project was illustrated by the creation of an LNG business unit headed by a former deputy chairman of the company who is its most experienced gas export executive.[205] There are technical problems in relation to ice conditions at the liquefaction sites, and on the routes between Russia and North America, which will require either the development of ice-breaking LNG tankers or ice breaking vessels to accompany the tankers. There are also problems for all sites in relation to dredging a port with sufficient depth for LNG vessels to dock, which will not be blocked by drifting ice. However, ambient temperatures at the Russian liquefaction sites are quite low for long periods of the year and this will lower the cost of the facilities. All the projects are around 4000 nautical miles from the USA (and less from the Canadian) east coast, and Gazprom has pointed out that only Norway, Algeria, Venezuela and Trinidad are closer to the US market.[206]

All three Russian LNG projects have advantages and disadvantages. In 2005:

- Shtokmanovskoye was the clear priority LNG project for Gazprom, because the field represents a huge stranded gas resource which – if pipeline gas supply beyond local markets is ruled out – can only be commercialised as LNG. Shtokman presents huge challenges in both production and transmission which are at the extremes of technical and economic feasibility. Nevertheless, once the liquefaction facilities are established, additional trains can be added in a second and third phase. Alternatively, once production and a pipeline to Murmansk have been established, additional phases could involve pipeline gas supplies to the domestic market and Europe.
- Ust Luga is a small project but much less technically complex and requiring far less upfront investment than the others. If it is developed as part of the North European Pipeline it could move ahead relatively quickly. However, it is uncertain whether the economics of the project will be adversely affected by the cost of transportation, first by pipeline and then in liquefied form to the North American market.
- Yamal, despite its location, may be considered attractive as soon as Gazprom starts to develop the fields on the Peninsula for domestic consumption. Unlike Shtokmanovskoye, the gas can be produced on land and, unlike either Shtokmanovskoye or Ust Luga, very little transportation investment is needed since the liquefaction plant can be built at the field.

Summary and Conclusions

Exports to Europe

Given the location of Gazprom's current exports and the importance
of those exports for revenue earnings, European exports are clearly
of paramount importance to the future of Russian gas and Gazprom.
Although Russian gas exports will become more diversified in the future
– towards Asian and North American markets – Europe will dominate
Russian gas exports for at least the next two decades and probably
beyond. During the period 2002–04, exports to Europe increased nearly
15% due to a combination of attractive prices and spare transportation
capacity. In terms of volumes, the immediate, and perhaps even more
distant, future is possibly less dramatic than is often portrayed. In public
statements Gazprom limits itself to the observation that by 2008, if
existing contracts are not extended, exports will be 147 Bcm and if
existing contracts are extended the maximum would be 180 Bcm.[207]
The furthest projection the company has made is that pipeline exports
to Europe by 2010 will be 'not less than 180 Bcm'.[208] This projection
simply suggests that Gazprom is seeking to maximise the capacity of
its existing export infrastructure, of which at least the Yamal-Europe
and Blue Stream lines have been seriously under-utilised.

In the period up to 2012, around one half of Gazprom's existing
contracts will expire. The General Director of Gazexport said at the
end of 2004 that '...it was probable that many would be prolonged',
and that he had received 'strong requests from all our major partners
for prolongation'.[209] However, in the future, contract extensions may not
be quite as automatic as they have been in the past and may depend
on development of markets in both Europe and Russia.

Looking further ahead, publicly available projections are remarkably
cautious. The Russian energy strategy sees total exports – including those
to CIS and Europe – rising from 194 Bcm in 2000 to 250–265 Bcm in
2010, and 273–281 Bcm in 2020, suggesting very moderate increases in
the second decade of the century.[210] The International Energy Agency
sees little growth in deliveries to Russia's traditional European markets
with exports to the EU projected at 137 Bcm in 2010 rising to only 155
Bcm in 2030, a smaller increase than would be accounted for by building
the North European Pipeline.[211]

Russia's ability to resist future competition/liberalisation initiatives
of an enlarged European Union has been shown to be limited; the
long-term contract and 'destination clause' debates showed the EU
Competition Authorities in the unfavourable position of retrospectively

objecting to clauses in existing contracts, after those contracts had been in operation for long periods. While DG COMP prevailed on the destination clause principle, these clauses have not yet been eliminated from all contracts, particularly in the new EU Member States.

The EU-Russia Dialogue is a useful political vehicle for discussion and, seen from Brussels, this is a sufficient basis for continuing towards an Energy Partnership Agreement. But unless it can produce tangible benefits as seen from the Russian side, related to investments in gas projects and particularly the North European Pipeline, it remains to be seen whether the Dialogue can be more than a 'talking shop'. The EU-Russia WTO negotiations clearly demonstrated that the Putin administration was prepared to tolerate limited 'interference' by the EU in the Russian domestic gas industry. Thus, there were no significant concessions on liberalisation of access to transportation, no concessions on Gazprom's dominant export position – the 'single export channel' and the agreement on domestic gas price reform were similar to what had already been set out in the 2003 Russian Energy Strategy.

Two substantial problems dominate the future of Russian gas exports to Europe, both of which have arisen in the post-Soviet period. The first of these is transit: a direct consequence of the break-up of the Soviet Union which will continue to remain unresolved until a multilateral agreement covering Eurasian gas markets is concluded. The Transit Protocol of the Energy Charter Treaty is such an agreement but neither Gazprom nor the Russian government has yet come to view the Protocol as a better answer than bilateral negotiations with transit countries.

The second problem concerns the rapid changes in European gas markets, which have been extremely important for Russian gas and Gazprom during the post-Soviet period, but loom even larger in an EU already expanded to 25 member states which will, over the next decade, effectively encompass the entire European energy space including Turkey. In 2005, the EU initiative to liberalise and introduce more competition into gas markets had far to go, but had already changed the European utility landscape with mergers creating a smaller number of gas and electricity mega-utilities. A combination of oil prices in excess of $40/bbl, a surplus of gas supply in Continental Europe, and the likelihood of a supply surplus in the UK after 2007, held out the possibility that significant gas to gas competition could arrive later in the 2000s. Gazprom's challenge, similar to those of other gas suppliers to Europe but more important because of the Russian company's much greater dependence (corporate and national) on revenues, will be to devise strategies that are robust in the event of a genuinely liberalised and competitive European gas market. We return to this issue in Chapter 4.

Exports to Asia and LNG

The first Russian LNG will be delivered to Asia (Japan and Korea) and the west coast of Mexico starting in 2007. China and Korea seem the most likely future pipeline export markets for Russian gas with China as the key player. But in 2005, Chinese attention was fixed on LNG imports and there was disappointment (to the point of disillusion) about the reliability of Russian oil imports by pipeline; no meeting of minds on the future development of pipeline gas seemed possible. In contrast to the popular view in the mid-2000s that China was 'desperate' to import the maximum possible quantity of any available energy supplies as quickly as possible, as far as gas was concerned there was little evidence from corporate or government behaviour to support such perceptions.

This may have been to Gazprom's advantage in cementing its exclusive negotiating relationship with CNPC and its power over the various Russian stakeholders in potential pipeline gas projects. It may not be to the advantage of South Korea – given the likelihood that any pipeline gas would need to pass through China (unless it was to transit North Korea) – but the continuing uncertainties that surround privatisation of KOGAS, and the liberalisation and restructuring of the gas industry, may also suggest a longer time frame.[212] When this is considered in the context of Japanese reluctance – for reasons relating both to demand uncertainties and political antipathy to Russian gas – to import Sakhalin LNG in large quantities let alone even more substantial volumes of pipeline gas (as suggested by Sakhalin 1 partners), the prospects for significant Russian gas exports to Asia appear to be somewhat further distant than is often believed.

With all the pipeline projects under consideration requiring a decade to negotiate and build, the most likely time frame for substantial pipeline gas exports to Asia seemed to be 2020 if negotiations could be completed in the late 2000s. Such negotiations would require all parties – Russian, Chinese and Korean – to resolve corporate structures and internal political problems which, in the mid 2000s, remained either unresolved or in conflict with each other. What the 2000s have established, as far as the Russian government and Gazprom are concerned, is that individual Russian resource holders should not regard themselves as having any negotiating autonomy in relation to export markets. They should regard their resources as feeding into a 'central gas main' which will eventually join all of the major fields in the region and with a link to the Unified Gas Network covering Western Siberia and western Russia. Resource holders should also recognise that their gas will be part of an 'integrated export channel' with Gazexport (Gazprom) negotiating on their behalf with both Chinese and Korean buyers. To the extent that Gazprom does not hold equity in some of these gas fields and projects, this will create very difficult problems. The International Energy Agency projection of only 30 Bcm exports to Asia by 2030 suggests that no more than one major pipeline project will be built during the next 25 years.[213] This is relatively cautious, but in 2005 accurately reflected the complexity of the projects and the relative lack of urgency of key players to advance them.

In 2005, LNG development was still at an early stage but was right at the top of the Gazprom's export agenda. In Asia, the company's negotiations regarding an equity stake in the Sakhalin 2 project were ongoing, but were independent of the over-riding aim of obtaining access to the east and Gulf coast North American market for Russian LNG supplies – principally for gas from the Shtokman field – by the end of the decade.

CHAPTER 4

REFORM, RESTRUCTURING AND LIBERALISATION OF THE GAS INDUSTRY

Ownership and Control

In 1989, shortly before the end of the Soviet era, Gazprom 'Kontsern' was created by Victor Chernomyrdin who became its first president and subsequently, a long-serving prime minister of the Russian Federation. By the end of 1992, Gazprom Kontsern had become Russian Joint Stock Company (RAO) Gazprom – a partly privatised joint stock company.[1] In February 1993, the company was registered as Open Joint Stock Company (OAO). Gazprom and the government issued licences to the company under the Subsoil Law of 1992, granting it the right to explore for and produce hydrocarbons.[2]

From 1993 to 2004, the ownership structure of the company changed remarkably little, with the Russian government holding 35–40%, Russian legal entities 35–40%, Russian individuals (including Gazprom employees) 15–20%, and foreigners 10–12%.[3]

Table 4.1 shows that, aside from the Russian government, the entities that had registered ownership of more than 2% of the company's

Table 4.1: Gazprom Shareholders with More than 2% Equity in the Company, 31 December 2003

Shareholders	Percentage Shareholding
Russian Federation Government	38.37
OOO Gazprominvestholding, OOO New Financial Technologies; OOO Fincom	4.83
Gazprom Finance BV	4.58
Bank of New York International*	4.42
NPF Gazfund	3.17
Ab Gazprombank (ZAO)	3.08
ZAO Gerosgaz	2.93
Ruhrgas AG	2.50

* nominees under the programme for the issuance of American Depositary Shares

Source: *Gazprom Annual Report 2003*, p.14.

share capital were either Gazprom affiliates or foreign investors. An alternative way of viewing the company's share structure in late 2003 was that, aside from the 38.37% government stake, Gazprom subsidiaries held 17.33% of the shares, foreign shareholders 6.92% and other parties (including Gazprom employees) 37.38%.[4] However, this picture is far from the whole story and was about to change significantly in 2005, as we shall see below.

In the late 1990s, two decrees were passed limiting foreign ownership of the company to 14%; the Gas Supply Law also limited foreign shareholdings in Gazprom's charter capital to 20% and by early 2004 it reported the share of foreign equity as 11.5%.[5] The legislation led to a formal separation between the shares that could be owned and traded in the Russian share market, and those owned and traded by foreigners. Following the issue of American Depositary Shares (ADS) in 1996 and subsequent sales in 1999, 2000 and 2001 (on both the London and New York stock exchanges) the domestic shares traded at a huge discount to ADS.[6] This separation – dubbed the 'ring fence' by the financial community – led Russian-based brokerages to purchase large quantities of domestic Gazprom shares on their own account and for foreign clients who in this way could be represented as Russian individuals and legal entities referred to above as major holders of Gazprom equity. These 'grey schemes' meant that neither the identity of Gazprom's shareholders nor the true share of foreign ownership of the company were known with any certainty.

Not only did the ring fence fail to prevent foreign ownership, but it maintained the capitalisation of the company at an artificially low level because of the inability of foreigners to trade openly in the shares. With the need to increase the capitalisation of the company becoming increasingly urgent in the 2000s, the government faced the following problems:

1. How to find a way of abolishing the ring fence without providing a huge windfall to the Moscow-based financial community – and its foreign clients – which had invested in low-price domestic Gazprom shares via the grey schemes;
2. How to obtain a formal majority stake in the company in order to ensure that it could not fall under foreign control.[7]

In early 2003 it was announced that a 'consolidation' of the government shareholding and the shares in the company held by Gazprom and its subsidiaries, meant that 51% ownership had been achieved.[8] But this was clearly not sufficient for a government and a president unwilling to leave anything to chance in terms of control. In September 2004, it was announced that these problems would be resolved by a merger of Gazprom and the Russian oil company Rosneft (see below). However, before entering further into this aspect of Gazprom's future, it is important to review the change in the management of the company in the 2000s.

Gazprom Management and Relationships with Government

During the 1990s, the governance of the company, and specifically how the government's equity stake should be represented, became extremely controversial. A 1996 presidential decree allowed Gazprom (in the person of its Chairman) to vote 35% of the government's 40% share in the company for a period of three years, giving rise to widespread criticism of governance arrangements.[9] Gazprom's involvement in politics was also the subject of significant criticism. The company had provided substantial financial support for the 'Our Home is Russia' Party – of which Victor Chernomyrdin was the founder and leader in the late 1990s. In the 1999 elections Gazprom supported around 130 candidates and provided them with electoral advice from a leading political consultancy.[10]

By the time Chairman Vyakhirev's term of office had expired in June 2001, there had been many rumours as to who would replace him. But when his successor was finally announced it came as a complete surprise. Alexey Miller was a Deputy Minister in the Ministry of Energy who had previously worked with President Putin at the Mayor's Office in St Petersburg; little else was known about him.[11]

Less than four years after Miller became Chairman, most of the former Gazprom management had retired or been replaced. By May 2005, only three out of nineteen members of the Management Committee remained from the previous administration.[12] Aside from Alexey Miller himself, eight of the new management committee members were from St Petersburg or had close links to President Putin or both. In addition, government had a clear majority on the Supervisory Board ('Soviet Direktorov') which included the Minister of Economic Development and Trade, the Minister of Energy, the head of the presidential administration, the (former minister of energy) now adviser to the president on international energy cooperation, and the former head of the Federal Property Fund in addition to Alexey Miller himself.[13] With the arrival of the Miller management Gazprom, which had often been called 'a state within a state', became very much a part of the state with direct links to the president, and accepted its role as an instrument of government policy both domestically and internationally.

Reform: Pricing, Liberalisation and Restructuring

One of the main tasks of the new management – seen both from inside and outside Russia – was 'reform'. However, there are many different aspects of reform and this section considers the subject under three headings: price, liberalisation and third party access, and structural reform.

Price Reform

Pricing of gas for the domestic market is a key issue for the development of the domestic industry, but also became increasingly important in external relations with the European Union in the context of Russia's application to join the World Trade Organisation (WTO). As far as the development of the Russian market is concerned, in the early 2000s there was a consensus among government officials, independent producers and Gazprom that a regulated price of gas in the 5th zone of $35/mcm, would be sufficient to cover short-run marginal costs with a margin for profitability (see Chapter 1). In early 2004, Alexander Ryazanov, Gazprom Deputy Chairman, was specific that at an average price (i.e. across the seven zones) of R810/mcm (roughly $30/mcm at then current exchange rates) excluding VAT and excise taxes 'will enable us to operate without losses, excluding investment expenses and debt servicing expenses'.[14] Since the average regulated industrial price in January 2005 across the twelve zones was RR1076/mcm (approximately $38/mcm, see Chapter 1, Table 1.16), it is clear that Gazprom has incentives to develop new NPT gas for the domestic market.[15]

Despite the projections of the 2003 Russian Energy Strategy that prices would reach $40–41/mcm by 2006 and $59–64/mcm by 2010, the second Putin administration initially took a relatively timid stance towards price increases.[16] In March 2004, in a presentation on short-term economic scenarios, Minister of Economic Development Gref suggested price increases for the period 2005–07 which would amount to an 11% real increase over the 2004 price.[17] This would have meant that by 2007, regulated prices in the 5th zone would reach $36/mcm – well below the Energy Strategy targets.

However, in May 2004 events took a different turn during the negotiations with the European Union over Russian accession to the

World Trade Organisation (see Chapter 3). One of the most important demands of the European Union was that Russian gas prices should increase to eliminate subsidies to industrial customers. After a protracted negotiation, it was agreed between the parties that Russian gas prices would increase to $37–42/mcm by 2006 and $49–57/mcm by 2010.[18] While this was hailed as a great victory by the EU negotiators, Table 4.2 shows that the price range in the WTO Accession Agreement agreed with the EU was somewhat below the 2006, and significantly below the 2010, price projections set out in the 2003 Russian Energy Strategy. The major difference between the two is that the latter is not legally binding on the Russian government whereas failure to implement agreed WTO commitments could lead to recourse to the WTO dispute resolution procedures.

Table 4.2: Projections of Future Regulated Industrial Gas Prices* $/mcm

	Actual	Energy Strategy 5.03	MEDT Short Term Economic Projections 3.04	EU-Russia WTO Accession Agreement 5.04
January 2004	31			
2006		40–41	36** (2007)	37–42
2010		59–64		49–57

* figures assumed to be for Zone 5 up to 2004, Zone 9 from 2005; ** real $2004

Much remains to be clarified regarding the Russian WTO price commitments to the EU:

– Are these real or nominal prices? In order to achieve transparency, they need to be stated in real 2004 dollars. Russian inflation for the remainder of this decade will be an important issue even if these are intended to be real prices.
– Are the prices stated in rubles as well as dollars? If not, the dollar/ruble exchange rate could have a major impact on the price commitment, particularly over a period as long as six years.
– Are the prices only for Zone 9 (which had been Zone 5 up to 2004)? If so, is there any commitment for prices in other zones or has this been left to Russian government (or regulatory) discretion?
– The figures apply to industrial gas prices only – with no commitments on residential prices.

Assuming that the WTO commitments are intended to represent industrial gas prices in Zone 9, in real 2004 dollars at 2004 dollar/ruble exchange rates, then the 2005 price of $40/mcm was already comfortably within the WTO range for 2006 and it seemed entirely plausible that the $49–57/mcm price band for 2010 would be reached. Should prices reach the upper boundary of $57/mcm/00km – somewhat short of the 2003 Energy Strategy levels but still nearly double the 2004 level in real terms and far higher than the Ministry of Economy Development was suggesting two months before the outcome of the WTO negotiations, domestic gas sales would become a significantly profitable business, assuming no significant tax increases. Equally significantly, and taking into account the many qualifications in the discussion in Chapter 1 (most notably the tax regime), domestic prices would approach levels that could make development of Yamal Peninsula fields commercially viable.

Deregulating Prices: Trading and Exchanges. Thus far, this discussion has focused solely on regulated prices. However, only Gazprom is required to sell at regulated prices, whereas independent producers may charge whatever the market will bear. It is very difficult to obtain reliable information about prices charged by independents, the volumes which are sold at these prices and the customers to whom they are sold. The OECD conducted a survey of industrial gas customers in November 2003 with interesting results. Dividing the responses between the industrial and power sectors the survey[19] found that 39% of industrial customers reported paying more than regulated prices for gas; on average they reported buying 11.5% of their gas above regulated prices at an average mark-up of 37%. But 90% of those buying part of their gas at higher prices reported buying all of their gas from Gazprom. Only 7.3% of customers reported direct purchases from independent producers.

In the power sector, 98% of federal power plants paid regulated prices for 98% of their gas in 2003, but regional power companies (energos) paid regulated prices for only 71% of their 2003 gas supplies. The average mark-up was 30% above regulated prices.

These findings reinforce the fact that independents can find profitable markets for their gas although they may still find it commercially convenient, or politically advisable, to sell gas to Gazprom.

During the 2000s, there have been many proposals from Gazprom on price reform. In relation to regulated prices, its argument in 2003 for a reform of the zonal pricing system with an increase in the number of zones to improve cost reflectiveness has been implemented. But the suggestion of a move to winter and summer prices to recognise increased seasonal transport and storage costs has not been taken further by the regulatory authorities.[20] The more substantial part of Gazprom's reform proposals were centred on the deregulation of prices, progressively reducing the portion of the market to which regulated prices would apply.[21]

This line of thinking first surfaced in late 2002 with the suggestion that a gas exchange could be created for trading at unregulated prices, with Gazprom selling 5% of its 2003 production on the exchange. Gazprom also suggested that Mezhregiongaz should be the administrator of an exchange charging commission for its services.[22] By early 2003, Mezhregiongaz was already conducting electronic trading which showed that during winter months some customers were prepared to buy gas at the wellhead for $30/mcm when the regulated price in Moscow was around $25/mcm.[23] However, by mid-2004 the exchange had only transacted 2.2 Bcm of gas, and there was no meeting of minds between Gazprom, the various government departments (in particular the Ministry of Economy and Trade) and the Federal Energy Commission on price deregulation.[24]

Meanwhile trading developed in the unregulated market. In July 2002, a group of companies – principally Itera, Novatek and Centrrusgas – created the Interregional Exchange for Oil and Gas (Mezhregionalnaya Birzha Neftegazovovo Komplekca); the company received its trading licence in September 2003 and the first trades commenced the following month.[25] The Exchange has a website which can be accessed openly and where bids and offers can be viewed. Anecodotal evidence suggests that the exchange has traded less than 5 Bcm/year since its creation, the main problem being uncertainty on the part of customers as to where their purchases will be delivered; and whether onward transportation to their preferred location can be assured and at what price. Nevertheless, despite these problems and small volumes, the very existence of an exchange competing with Mezhregiongaz is significant.

By 2004, Gazprom had developed a three-stage reform concept of which the first stage – break-even (i.e. average price = operating costs) on delivery of gas to industrial customers – had been achieved.[26] As noted above, Gazprom had also proposed that a limited volume of production (5–10%) should be sold at unregulated prices, but the government did not agree. For the second stage, 2006–2008, a gradual expansion of the unregulated market was proposed and by the end of the third stage (2010) customers would have a free choice of suppliers with gas prices stabilising around $50–55/mcm. Gas would be sold at market prices both on a bilateral basis and via the gas exchange. In April 2005, Chairman Miller proposed a substantial acceleration of price reform with an end to regulated prices for industrial customers starting in 2006 and an acceleration of trading. This was described as a 'shift in market relationships' with other fuels:

> Our proposal is to use commodity trading mechanisms starting from 2006 in order to set prices for gas supplies to industrial consumers, and to keep regulated prices exclusively for the housing and communal services, state and local budget consumers and the population.
>
> Natural gas is currently the only primary resource for which price regulation is based on historical indicators and is not set by the demand and supply levels. As a result, the gas industry has been a powerful financial donor for the entire economy, including profitable export oriented consumers supplied with cheap natural gas.
>
> The natural gas share in Russia's energy balance has risen to 50%, even to 80% in some regions, and there is a considerable decline in coal, heating oil and other fuel alternatives utilization. Therefore, there is a slowdown in the development of the corresponding industries on which our country's energy security also relies. [27]

There are a number of problems with this proposal, the principal one being that as long as Gazprom dominates the market, it will be very difficult for competition and market prices to develop. The Miller statement acknowledges this:

> Gazprom has definitely a dominating position in the gas market, but the independent producers and alternative fuel suppliers, including coal and heating oil, will compete with us under equal economic conditions. [28]

But the problem is that, in order for the gas market to be seen as genuinely contestable, Gazprom's share of the non-residential market should probably be reduced below 50%.[29] It is interesting that the statement is very clear about the continuation of regulated prices for state organisations and residential customers about which most reform plans are noticeably silent. Any form of competition in these markets is very far, probably much more than a decade, in the future, particularly since their regulated prices (Table 1.16) remain below those of industrial customers.

Pricing Principles: Netback Market Pricing versus Cost Plus. Even the principles on which Russian gas prices should be based are not obvious. In the absence of a contestable domestic gas market within Russia, an 'economically correct' way to determine the country's gas prices could be to take the export border price and 'net back' to different locations within Russia by subtracting transportation and transit costs. Such a methodology would make Russian producers 'indifferent' between serving domestic and foreign customers. However, there are a number of problems with such a methodology:

1. It assumes that there are no constraints on transportation capacity or export markets which clearly is not the case.
2. Continental European border prices are principally based on, and indexed to, oil product prices; hence these prices also bear only an indirect relationship to gas supply and demand and therefore a 'free market'. When oil prices are high – e.g. the post-2002 period – European gas prices are high, e.g. more than $140/mcm in 2004. Conversely when oil prices are low so are European border gas prices, e.g. less than $70/mcm in 1998. The lack of a competitive gas market in Continental Europe prevents any confident analytical discussion of European border prices as a benchmark for 'market prices' in Russia.
3. Changes in ruble/dollar and ruble/euro exchange rates are important over longer time scales, particularly given growing convertibility of the ruble.
4. Netback values for Russian gas are affected by transit charges that are not necessarily set using cost-reflective methodologies or regulated. Hence they may be subject to change, independent of gas prices, and Gazprom has a limited measure of control over them. These transit charges comprise a significant proportion of total export costs.[30]

An alternative to netback market pricing from European borders is to adopt a cost-plus approach by estimating short- and long-run marginal costs of producing and delivering Russian gas at different dates in the future for different regions of Russia and export markets. While economists, especially academic ones, tend to be scornful of such an approach, understandably in view of the difficulties of accurately defining the cost base, it has considerable appeal to Russian policy makers. As a result, it is more likely to be used than other methodologies. In summary, there is currently no satisfactory methodology to determine Russian gas prices and this is likely to continue until (1) The gas market in Russia is liberalised with unregulated prices for (at least) industrial customers; (2) The gas market in Europe is liberalised with prices set by gas to gas competition. Despite progress towards both of these goals, in 2005 it required significant bravery to forecast a timescale for either development.

In any discussion of regulated prices and how these will evolve, Gazprom's proposals raise the important issue of how rapidly government will allow price deregulation in the industrial sector of the market, and the expansion of the company's role in that price-deregulated sector. The answer to that question depends critically on reform and rebalancing of transportation tariffs and a much less discriminatory third party access regime.

Liberalisation and Third Party Access

Rights of access for third parties to Gazprom's network were established in 1998, before similar rights were introduced by the European Union's first Gas Directive in 2000.[31] Gazprom is required to provide access subject to the availability of capacity, the quality and technical specifications of gas, the availability of input points for gas supplies and delivery points to customers, and the availability of supplies and demand from relevant customers.

Table 4.3: Gazprom's Transport of Third Party Gas 1998–2003

Year	Number of Shippers	Volume of Gas (Bcm)	Including from Central Asia (Bcm)	3rd Party gas as % of total UGSS throughput
1998	6	28.2		
1999	10	83.7		13.5
2000	20	106.2		16.8
2001	24	92.4		14.7
2002	33	103.6	44	16.3
2003	35	110.4	48.8	16.4
2004*	35	111.8	50.2	

* The Gazprom January 25, 2005 press release reports that in 2004, 4 additional independent producers gained access to the network shipping 7.8 Bcm of additional gas compared with 2003, which is not consistent with its previous data. There are conflicting data from Gazprom showing that the company carried 82.9 Bcm for independent producers in 2003 and 87.9 Bcm in 2004. (*Loan Notes 2005*, p.130)

Sources: 'Gazprom is fully satisfying independent gas producers' applications on granting access to its gas transportation system,' *Gazprom press release*, December 11, 2003; 'Gazprom reports its major interim operating results over 2004,' *Gazprom press release*, January 25, 2005.

Given well-publicised instances of Gazprom's reluctance to provide transportation services, it comes as some surprise to discover that substantial quantities of gas have been transported for a relatively large number of shippers. Table 4.3 shows that volumes rose to around 110 Bcm in

2003 or more than 16% of total pipeline throughput. Subtracting from those figures Central Asian gas shipped through the Russian network, Russian gas produced by companies other than Gazprom accounted for more than 9% of total throughput. While Table 4.3 certainly does not suggest third party access on the scale of Britain or North America, it compares favourably with the situation in many Continental European countries over the same period.[32]

The regulated transmission tariffs that Gazprom charges third parties for the use of its network are also the subject of much speculation. These charges were set by the Federal Energy Commission (FEC) which in March 2004 was renamed the Federal Tariff Service (FTS) and placed under the direct responsibility of the Prime Minister's office – the FEC had previously been responsible to the Ministry of Economic Development and Trade.[33] Transportation tariffs differ according to market destination:

– Transport of gas to Russian and CIS customs union countries (Belarus, Kazakhstan, Kyrgyzstan and Tajikistan) since 2004 has been charged at a rate of RR19.37 ($0.69) per thousand cubic metres per 100 kilometres (RR/mcm/00km); prior to that date the rate was RR13.80/mcm/00km.[34]
– Transport of gas to consumers located outside Russia and the CIS customs Union incurs a tariff of $0.92/mcm/00km.

These tariffs illustrate the importance of the location of gas sources and markets for independent producers. With an average transportation distance for gas to a domestic customer of 2400 km, the transportation charge alone would have been RR331.2 up to 2004 and RR464.9 since then. It is not difficult to calculate that at the regulated prices of the late 1990s and early 2000s (see Chapter 1, Table 1.15), it would have been impossible for gas to have been sold profitably to customers even at a relatively low cost of production. In the early 2000s, independent producers maintained that the 'economic radius' for gas sales from the point of production was no more than 1000 km.[35] Table 4.4 suggests that the radius has increased to more than 1500 km and this may be due to the rebalancing of tariffs which we noted in Chapter 1.

A common complaint of independent producers in the 2000s was that they were being forced to pay a regulated transportation tariff far higher than Gazprom was charging itself for transportation. It is not known how Gazprom's internal transfer pricing treats transmission charges, but independents claim that it charges itself between one-third and one-quarter of the regulated tariff. Even if this is correct, in 2004, the year in which

Gazprom began to break even on deliveries to the domestic market, the company projected the net profitability for its transmission subsidiaries at 1.5% (compared with 2.7% profitability for production subsidiaries).[36] Partly as a result of this, Gazprom suggested that the transportation tariff for third parties should be almost doubled from $0.55 to $1.00/mcm/00km, a suggestion which (as we saw above) the regulatory authorities went part way towards implementing. Transmission tariff developments are extremely important for future price and market reform given the aspiration of at least some government and regulatory policy makers that the eventual outcome for the industry should be non-discriminatory transmission tariffs charged to all parties including Gazprom.

Table 4.4: Share of Independent Gas Sales in Russian Regions

Region	Share Of Independent Supplies (%)
Sverdlovsk Oblast	100
Tyumen Oblast	82.4
Kurgan Oblast	69.8
Republic of Komi	28.2
Republic of Bashkortistan	26.0
Arkhangelsk Oblast	21.9
Chuvash Republic	21.4
Samara Oblast	18.2
Republic of Tatarstan	15.2
Chelyabinsk Oblast	13.1
Perm Oblast	12.5

Source: Alexander Ryazanov, *Razvitiye Rinka Gaza v Rossii*, Briefingi i Press Konferentzii, June 1, 2005.

One important aspect of third party transportation about which little information is available is access and network rules, particularly in respect of capacity availability and determination of optimal routes for third party gas. One of the mysteries of Itera's rise to prominence (see Chapter 1) was how that company was able to obtain access to Gazprom's transmission network for large volumes of gas to be transported from and to specific locations. This is something that others – and in the 2000s increasingly Itera itself – have struggled to achieve. Independents often complain that Gazprom claims it has insufficient capacity to carry the volumes for which transportation is requested, or that their gas is delivered by circuitous routes which significantly add to transportation costs and threaten viability of their sales; but no evidence is provided of capacity bottlenecks which would legitimise such actions. While independents can appeal to the Federal Anti-Monopoly Agency, this procedure is too cumbersome to be commercially workable. In the mid 2000s, workable regulations and regulatory oversight had yet to extend to detailed access rules. Similar comments apply to the period over which independents are required to 'balance' their portfolios.[37] Gazprom periodically complains about independents being out of balance, leaving gas in the network which acts as a 'free storage' service. Yet on other occasions, Gazprom appears to benefit from the 'loan' of such gas from independents.

In July 2003, the Commission on Gas Industry Reform proposed the creation of a 'gas market coordinator' (GMC) which 'maintains a balance between the regulated and unregulated segments of the gas market'.[38] The GMC is a non-commercial partnership between Gazprom, producers, consumers and state bodies. It was created to advise on rules for the unregulated market, coordinate tariffs set by the regulatory authorities, help to set up trading and exchanges, and assist in regional tenders for supplies.[39] Interestingly, key independent gas producers such as Novatek and Itera do not seem to be involved in the GMC. Its creators believed that transportation tariff reform would be necessary to create the required degree of access to the network and suggested dividing Russia into zones with entry and exit points as a basis for transmission charges.[40]

Thus far the only discussion has been about access to high pressure transmission networks. Because of the prices and payments problems of the 1990s, particularly the problems of the residential sector, little attention has been paid to third party access to regional and local distribution networks, where Mezhregiongaz has achieved widespread access (see Chapter 1). According to Gazprom, the share of residential customers in the gas sales of independents was only 1.2% in 2004, compared with 14% of Gazprom's sales.[41] This may be because of Gazprom opposition but it is just as likely to be because of unattractive prices and difficulties of obtaining payment from customers. Despite the fact that access to distribution networks has (with the exception of Sverdlovsk) only been utilised by the dominant player, the establishment of legal unbundling in this sector puts Russia far ahead of many European countries in this area of reform in 2005.

Exports. While there is good reason to hope for a continuing liberalisation of gas sales within Russia, the scope for a similar liberalisation of exports – and particularly exports beyond CIS countries – appears much more limited. One aspect of reform on which both government and Gazprom have been adamant has been their determination to maintain Gazexport's monopoly on exports to Europe. From a European perspective, the main institutional change in the immediate post-Soviet period was the renaming of the gas export organisation from 'Soyuzgazexport' to plain 'Gazexport', and its shift in 1991 from the Soviet Ministry of Foreign Economic Relations to a department within Gazprom.[42] OOO Gazexport was established as a limited liability company and a 100%-owned subsidiary of Gazprom in accordance with two resolutions of the Gazprom board in 1997 and 1998 and was registered in Moscow in May 1999.[43] Gazexport has a wholly-owned subsidiary company Zarubezhgaz Erdgashandel Gesellschaft (ZGG) which is the legal owner of its interests in Wingas, Verbundnetz Gas and has other affiliates such as ZMB which sells gas both directly and via other trading houses and affiliates.[44] ZGG also manages some of Gazprom's foreign upstream investments, for example the Shachpachty field in Uzbekistan.

Until the 2000s, Gazexport only dealt with exports to Europe. Exports to former Soviet countries were handled by what was originally called the 'near abroad department' within Gazprom. In the 2000s, CIS trade has been increasingly taken over by Gazexport which manages all of the imports from Central Asia, and exports to the Caucasus countries and Moldova (see Chapter 2). However, exports to Ukraine and Belarus are still managed within Gazprom (by the Department for Marketing and Processing of Gas and Liquid Hydrocarbons), with the exception of small volumes of Central Asian gas sold by Gazexport to those countries (Table 2.7).

As far as exports to Europe are concerned neither Gazexport nor Gazprom before it has ever had a legal monopoly. The original presidential decree establishing Gazprom placed an obligation on the company to 'ensure a reliable supply of natural gas to customers in Russia and to foreign customers, and supply gas abroad under inter-governmental and inter-state agreements,'[45] but did not confer on the company any exclusive rights of supply to either domestic or foreign customers. However, Gazprom's ownership of pipeline capacity to Ukraine, combined with the difficulty of obtaining capacity in the Ukrainian system, constituted a *de facto* monopoly on exports to Europe or, in Gazprom-speak, a 'single export channel'.

This determination was highlighted in 2004 in the WTO negotiations and the organisation of pipeline exports to Asian markets (Chapter 3). Gazexport's general director has called the 'single export channel' (known in an Asian context as the 'integrated export channel') the 'sacred cow' of export strategy.[46] Replying to a press question as to whether other companies would be allowed to export gas, Deputy Chairman Ryazanov responded:

Our position is that Gazprom and independent producers should be on an equal footing: in case domestic gas sales are at market prices, there are unified transport tariffs and equal taxation, there could be equal share structure in exports. This is the point of mutual understanding among all authors of the Russian gas market reform concepts, and there should be a single export sales channel. This is our position. We estimate that under these conditions it is possible to facilitate a maximum export price of Russian natural gas, and a maximum level of return on investment. And it is in the interests of Russia to increase its hard currency sales proceeds.[47]

Structural Reform

Reform and restructuring of Gazprom has been intensively debated since at least 1997. In the early months of that year, a restructuring of the company created a new marketing subsidiary, Mezhregiongaz, to handle all gas sales, suggesting that the transmission subsidiaries would become transportation-only companies with no merchant function.[48] As we saw in Chapter 1 that did not happen but Gazprom then announced a corporatisation of the company which was accelerated by a 1997 presidential decree requiring the conversion of Gazprom's 'daughter companies' into wholly-owned legal subsidiaries.[49]

In the 2000s, there have been a variety of 'reform plans' for Gazprom and the Russian gas industry as a whole, with the same basic recommendations:

- different levels of separation ranging from 'accounting unbundling' to break-up ('ownership unbundling') of the various business units;[50]
- different timetables for separation, ranging from more than 10 years (usually advocated by Gazprom) to immediate and radical action (usually advocated by radical reformers and international financial institutions).

The most structurally elegant of these was the 'Gref Plan' published in 2000 by the Ministry of Economic Trade and Development. This was a plan for the whole economy but the section on gas contained a blueprint for full unbundling and liberalisation throughout the sector.[51]

The next serious set of reform plans − 'Conception for the Development of the Gas Market in the Russian Federation' − appeared very briefly on an internet newspaper website in September 2002.[52] They were apparently prepared jointly between Gazprom officials, from the new management, and the Ministry of Economic Development and Trade (MEDT), with direct input from Minister Gref, and proposed separation of transportation assets into one company and the creation of a separate system operator. Both of these companies would have been owned by Gazprom, at least initially, but with more transparent access to the network for independent producers and Gazprom subsidiaries.

While the Conception was never officially published, it clearly provoked considerable debate not only between MEDT and Gazprom, but also other government departments and regulatory authorities who did not appear to wholeheartedly support MEDT.[53] By early 2003, MEDT appeared to be fighting something of a rearguard action on structural reform, repeating the president's view that a break-up of Gazprom was not on the agenda, but emphasising the virtues of transparency, internal separation and exclusion of cross-subsidies.[54] While MEDT remained insistent on the importance of a separate ('legally unbundled') gas transport subsidiary company in order to assist transparency, during 2003 the focus of reform shifted away from structure towards price, issues of access to networks and creation of exchanges.[55]

By late 2003, gas industry reform had become embroiled in EU-Russia negotiations over Russian Federation accession to the WTO (see Chapter 3) which caused the president to publicly restate his position on important issues:

> The European Commission's demands to open access to the Russian gas pipeline system as a prerequisite for Russia's accession to the World Trade Organisation are unacceptable...We intend to maintain the state's control over the gas pipeline system and Gazprom. We will not break up Gazprom.[56]

During the first part of 2004, the WTO price question dominated reform debates and all Russian government statements need to be placed in that context. Nevertheless, the president's views (coming just before his re-election) were interesting in the emphasis they placed on access:

> Gazprom is an institution on which a large part of our economic growth depends. We are perfectly aware that natural gas in our country is sold to both individuals and industrial customers at a price lower than its cost. Gazprom also ensures economic growth of other sectors to a significant extent. This is a fact we should not forget...we should treat Gazprom with care. We must at least secure a gas market inside the country and definitely provide independent producers with access to the pipelines. However, they should understand that this would not mean free access to the foreign market.[57]

Despite the announcement that the Gazprom board – on which MEDT Minister Gref and other government officials sit – would discuss reform plans and develop programmes during 2004, such discussions were repeatedly 'postponed'. Deputy Chairmen Ryazanov and Ananenkov reinforced Gazprom's opposition to any break-up of its vertically integrated structure, but the fact that all of the production and transportation subsidiaries had become legal entities at least provided a basis for future restructuring.[58] When questioned about the virtues of separation of the network in order to promote transparency of transportation tariffs, Deputy Chairman Ryazanov responded:

> The gas transmission cost structure is already transparent enough. You should know that Gazprom has a separate gas transmission expenditures accounting system. All data is reported to the regulators. All you have to do is refer to it. At the same time, some of our gas transmission companies are involved in other businesses as well, such as gas production, gas treatment and storage, and we are ready to take the necessary steps to reflect transmission business revenues and expenditures in the balance sheets of these companies.[59]

Public discussion of Gazprom priorities in 2004, by the President and Gazprom Chairman Miller, made no mention of reform issues aside from price.[60] But MEDT continued to keep the separation of the company's business units on the agenda, despite the fact that by the end of the year, the Gazprom-Rosneft merger had submerged all other restructuring issues.[61] A Federal Anti-Monopoly Service investigation into Gazprom discrimination against independent producers in relation to pipeline access suggested that the company would need to pay attention to at least this aspect of reform.[62]

The pace of future Gazprom reform, particularly structural, will also depend on a parallel process in the electricity industry which is much further advanced than gas.[63] A crucial issue for gas supply and demand will be whether the new owners of power stations will have incentives to replace old gas turbine stations with new combined cycle gas fired units which would provide much greater efficiency with lower gas usage. In terms of the sequence of reform, in late 2004 Prime Minister Fradkov was clear about the difficulties of pursuing parallel gas and power reforms simultaneously with the clear inference that Gazprom reform will not proceed until after that of the electricity industry.[64]

An additional complication for general reform of the utility sector is that Gazprom has become increasingly involved in the electricity industry holding a 5.3% equity share in RAO UES and a 'preliminary agreement' that would allow the company to control 10.5% of UES voting shares.[65] In addition, Gazprom owns a 25.01% blocking share in (local Moscow electricity utility) Mosenergo, the legality of which was being examined by the anti-monopoly authorities.[66] If Gazprom is allowed to purchase additional electricity assets during the privatisation and restructuring of UES currently scheduled for 2006, it could substantially extend its dominance of the utility sector. Gazprom has itself developed a substantial electricity infrastructure with 1700 power stations and 84,000 km of transmission lines.[67]

Different Concepts of Utility Reform. With firm views held within Gazprom and the Russian government – and with the second Putin administration set to hold office until 2008 – most of the international commentary and 'recommendations' on structural reform of the Russian gas industry is unlikely to be relevant at least in the medium term. The policy recommendations of the OECD (and others), which suggest that the Russian gas industry should be unbundled and liberalised, while analytically interesting and 'economically correct', were nowhere near the policy agenda in Moscow. To be fair, the OECD recognised this: 'Given that there is little or no prospect of Gazprom being broken up in the near term, the sector is destined to remain highly monopolised and therefore highly regulated.' [68]

But even the use of the term 'highly regulated' illustrates a fundamental problem of applying the traditional OECD/World Bank/IMF 'Washington consensus' model of utility industries in a Russian context, which is that the consensus is irredeemably Anglo-North American in character. The gas industry is a creature of the Russian state and is likely to remain so for the foreseeable future. If the Russian government and president had ever been tempted to relax their grip on the industry (which is almost certainly not the case), their experience of the consequences of oil sector restructuring and privatisation in the 1990s would certainly have dissuaded them.

Some western commentary advances the view that, despite the governance problems of the 1990s, splitting the oil industry into a number of companies eventually proved to be a dynamic process which was responsible for the surge in production and exports of the early 2000s. Irrespective of the analytical correctness of this view, it fails to take into account, firstly, that, whatever success may have been achieved, the acquisition of oil assets during the 1990s is still regarded as illegal by a large part of the political establishment who resent the loss of government control over the sector (hence the Yukos episode of the mid-2000s, see below). Secondly, there is an essential difference in Russian administrative/political culture between what can be regarded as 'private industry', and utility companies which are regarded as 'natural monopolies' and therefore subject to direct government control.[69]

Thus the use of the term 'highly regulated' in describing the Russian gas industry is misleading because it suggests that Gazprom is controlled by Anglo-North American-style independent regulatory authorities. While such authorities exist in Russia, there is little likelihood that the state would vest in them sufficient powers to control Gazprom. Gazprom is therefore not 'highly regulated', it is directly controlled by government, and specifically by the president, as evidenced by the individuals who have been appointed to both the management committee and the supervisory board since mid-2001.

In this respect, the Russian approach has much less in common with Anglo-North American models of industrial organisation, and much more in common with the administrative/political culture of utility management found in Continental Europe and Asia. In most Continental European countries – and virtually all countries in Asia – government dominates the utility industries, often directly appointing senior executives to the boards of these companies. An important reason for the relative failure of liberalisation of gas markets in Continental Europe – despite nearly two decades of debate and the passage of substantial legislation – is that politicians fundamentally believe that they should be in control of utility industries, rather than allowing 'market forces' to shape their destiny.

Continental European governments share with the Russian government the desire to maintain – or in some cases create – 'national champion' utility companies. It is therefore more useful to view the institutional future of the Russian gas industry in a Franco-German, rather than an Anglo-North American, context. In 2005, the French gas industry was envisaging partial privatisation and other companies had taken market share from Gaz de France.[70] But the essentially state-owned, centralised nature of the utility, with all important strategic decisions controlled by the government, seemed set to remain. In Germany, the determination of the government to promote national champion utility companies – as seen by its protection and promotion of the E.ON-Ruhrgas merger from the competition authorities which were vehemently against it – had far greater political priority than the introduction of competition and liberalisation into the industry.[71]

Governance and the First Stage of Reform. The first stage of reforms – deemed to have started in mid-2001 when Chairman Miller was appointed – focused on improving governance, regulatory procedures, financial accounting and transparency. During this first stage, the issue of governance loomed large in much of the critique of the previous management. In contrast to Chapter 1, which explained most of the events of the 1990s and early 2000s as a consequence of economic crisis and the transition to a market economy, much academic and journalistic literature explains Russian economic history during the 1990s in terms of 'rent seeking', or in plainer language corruption. The development of Gazprom during the 1990s has been described as an 'insider privatisation to the benefit of its managers and employees',[72] resembling 'a Vyakhirev and Chernomyrdin family business'.[73] Appendix 4.1 explains the non-payment era (detailed in Chapter 1) in these terms. But this literature contains little substantiation of the majority of corruption allegations about Gazprom, which consist of newspaper reportage or simple assertions with little attempt at verification.[74]

In no respect can Gazprom be held up as a model of good governance during the 1990s. Family connections abounded within the company and major transactions with external companies were, at a minimum, insufficiently transparent and lacking checks and balances on management actions. Poor governance resulted in Gazprom assuming majority ownership of NTV, a major media company, as a result of a billion dollar loan to Vladimir Gusinsky, one of the 'oligarchs' forced to leave Russia when Vladimir Putin became president.[75]

Yet on utility governance, much of the criticism comes from those with little comparative perspective on events elsewhere in the world, events that have occurred much closer to where their authors live and work. For those, like this author, who spend a great deal of time studying gas industries around the world, Gazprom's record of financial transparency during the 1990s, was an extreme example of an industry which (outside North America) has been and remains shrouded in commercial 'confidentiality'. On the observation of Gazprom being run as a 'family business', similar observations could be made about a large number of utility companies around the world where decisions are taken by very few individuals at the top of the company, often in close relationships with each other.

A now notorious example of poor governance from North America – which occurred around the same time as the worst of the Gazprom problems – was the apparently inexorable rise of the energy marketing and trading companies during the 1990s, led by Enron. Enron – fêted by energy and business analysts year after year as the most brilliant, entrepreneurial and innovative company of its generation – was subsequently declared bankrupt and its top management accused of financial wrongdoing involving billions of dollars.[76] Many other American energy trading companies suffered similar, if less severe, fates in the 2000s.

Despite the impression given when reading academic literature on Russia, poor governance at Gazprom was far from an isolated case in gas industries around the world during the 1990s. In addition, it is worth pointing out that this was a particularly difficult transition period for both the Russian economy and political system in which a great deal of Russian state property, particularly in the energy sector, was appropriated by those in privileged positions. While the previous management of Gazprom is alleged to have 'stolen $15–20 billion' from the company,[77] in retirement they have become invisible and have not been seen among the international jetset buying foreign football clubs.

The Miller management has made much of its 'asset reacquisition programme' comprising the following:

1. The April 2002 reacquisition of 32% of Purgaz from Itera was achieved via a repurchase option provided for in the 1999 sale of the shares for their nominal value. The repurchase price was RR33,000m in cash and the financing of RR6,594m which Itera had spent on the development of the field. Gazprom thereby reacquired an asset which had produced nothing at the time of its sale and contributed 11.2 Bcm of supply in the nine months following its repurchase.

2. In February 2003, Gazprom acquired the remaining 51% interest in Severneftegazprom, the licence holder for the South Russkoye field which was subsequently chosen as the source for the North European Pipeline (see Chapter 3). In return, Gazprom sold Itera a 10% stake in the Sibirsky Oil and Gas Company and a 7.8% stake in Tarkosalneftegaz.

3. In February 2003 – well after the Miller management had assumed control of the company – Mezhregiongaz, violating internal company procedures, sold 40.1% of ZAO Agrochemical Corporation to other shareholders in the company. Gazprom has subsequently reacquired most of its interest and litigation is ongoing to recover the remainder.

4. 48% of Achimneftegaz – an affiliate of Urengoygazprom – was acquired by ZAO CTI Sigma, an affiliate of Itera. Gazprom is taking steps to reacquire this stake.

5. Gazprom never accepted the legality of its exclusion from Nortgaz and in 2005 appeared to have re-established its monopoly shareholding in the company (see Chapter 1).[78]

Not mentioned in this list was the 4.83% of Gazprom's shares repurchased in 2002 from Stroytransgaz – a major gas industry contractor which carries out a huge amount of construction and engineering work for Gazprom. One estimate suggests that Gazprom recovered the

Stroytransgaz shares for 22% of their average (local) market price that month.[79] Gazprom's December 2003 Consolidated Financial Statement made reference to transactions with Stroytransgaz entered into in the period 2000–2003, '...under contracts which had been executed by certain prior representatives of the Group's Board of Directors and members of their families who at that time owned significant share-holdings in OAO Stroytransgaz.' [80] In 2003, Gazprom purchased a 25.9% stake in Stroytransgaz.[81] The company made exactly the same statement about Interprocom which acted as an agent for Gazprom in Hungary.[82]

The Miller management came under serious criticism for extending financial guarantees to Eural Transgas (ETG), the company which suddenly became the shipper of Turkmen gas to Ukraine in January 2003 (see Chapter 2). Gazprom's December 2003 Consolidated Financial Statement records that:

> In August 2003 credit facilities in the amount of $227 million were provided to Eural Transgas by Vnesheconombank and guaranteed by the Group. The guarantee extends through December 2007. The credit facilities are for the purchase of natural gas in Central Asia which is then sold to the Group. Guarantees to NAK Naftogaz Ukraine in the amount of $100 million were also provided by the Group in connection with purchases of natural gas from Central Asia. [83]

There are potentially respectable reasons for such guarantees, for example that ETG did not have sufficient credit rating to borrow such sums of money at short notice and that Gazprom was obliged to ensure that the purchase and shipping of Turkmen gas to Ukraine continued without interruption. But the same table which shows the ETG guarantees also shows significant guarantees to Itera which are not explained in the text.[84] This gave some commentators the opportunity to suggest that the Miller management was continuing the poor governance of its predecessors:

> ...the initial optimism of investors that the company would become more efficient and transparent soon dissipated. Despite vast investment spending, it was unable to raise the level of gas production. Cosy new deals were signed with obscure companies. Calls for oil companies to gain access to Gazprom's monopoly control over the pipeline network, and to liberalise the domestic gas market, went nowhere. A private near-monopoly had been replaced by a state one. Miller has proved a loyal bureaucrat and a statist first of all. [85]

Irrespective of the factual accuracy of these comments, there is an interesting link between criticism of poor governance and criticism of lack of reform. Those who were quick to criticise the former Gazprom management for failing to provide access to the transmission network, and equally quick to condemn the governance shortcomings in the relationship between Gazprom and Itera, failed to recognise that Itera's development of Russian and Central Asian gas supplies for delivery to CIS markets marked the beginning of large-scale third party access in Russia. Likewise, those who condemned Gazprom's continued 'monopoly' of exports to Europe, and the sudden appearance of Eural Transgas (ETG) as the main intermediary for Central Asian gas in 2003,[86] failed to appreciate that ETG had broken the Gazprom export monopoly to Europe. When confronted with these contradictions, there is a tendency to claim that Itera's business did not constitute 'real' third party access – and ETG did not represent 'real' export diversity – because these companies were just 'Gazprom management under other names'. Whatever the truth of such allegations, they miss the point that where Itera led the way in terms of access to Gazprom's network, others have followed. It remains to be seen whether others can follow ETG's example in terms of exports to Europe.

Corporate Restructuring and the Second Stage of Reform. In March 2004, Chairman Alexey Miller declared the first stage of corporate restructuring to be complete and the second stage to have begun.[87] Figure 4.1 shows the corporate structure of Gazprom in 2004. But the six production and seventeen transmission companies do not provide a clear picture in terms of function with many 'transmission' companies producing significant quantities of gas (and oil). The second stage of Gazprom's internal reform is a significant corporate restructuring of the subsidiaries of the company such that they concentrate on a single activity:

> Each subsidiary must run its core business, fulfil one function and not squander resources to related and sometimes non-core activities. We want the core businesses to be consolidated within separate companies…achieving full transparency of financial flows. [88]

The centrepiece of this reform is the assurance that, starting in 2005, all Gazprom's transmission subsidiaries will focus only on transmission (and transmission-related) business. These subsidiaries will be forced to divest their non-core activities (e.g. production and social infrastructure) with the consequence that costs of transmission will become much more transparent and allow for greater accuracy in setting tariff levels. This focus on core activities is intended to extend to all main functions: transmission networks, distribution networks (with the creation of Gazpromregiongaz, see Chapter 1), storage, and processing.

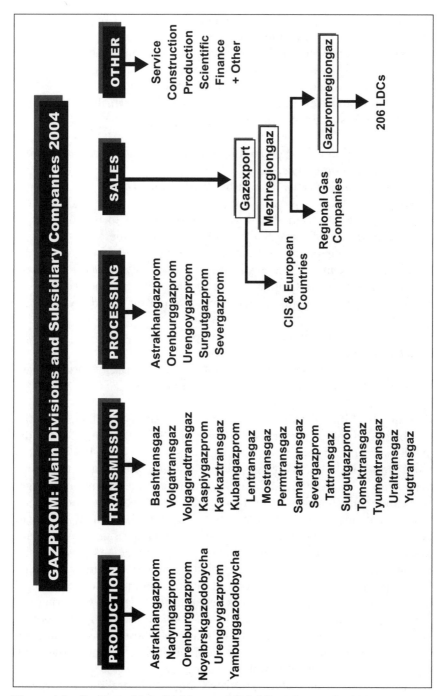

Figure 4.1: Gazprom: Main Divisions and Subsidiary Companies 2004

Well servicing and pipeline maintenance services will be taken out of production and transmission subsidiaries and consolidated into service companies which will sell their services, possibly on the basis of competitive tendering. Non-core activities, such as social infrastructure, will either be maintained as separate subsidiaries or sold off.

Early indications from the restructuring process which was ongoing in early 2005, suggested the following: [89]

- Gas production will be divided into *Gazpromdobycha* (literally Gazprom production) companies.
- The transmission network will be divided into *Gazpromtransgaz* companies with those at Ukhta, Surgut, Kuban, Astrakhan and Moscow (region) already decided and probably others yet to be announced. Each of these will have 8000–9000 km of pipelines.
- The processing plants at Sosnogorsk, Surgut and Urengoy will be amalgamated into a single subsidiary – *Gazprompererabotka*, but there is no suggestion that Sibur will be included in this business unit[90]
- Gas storages will be amalgamated into a separate subsidiary *Gazprom-PKhG*
- There will be an oil and condensate production subsidiary, *Gazprom-neftedobycha*.[91]
- Three well servicing and repair subsidiaries – *Gazprompodzemremont* Centre, North and South – will be established.

Part of the aim of this restructuring is to increase efficiency. The number of employees reached 391,000 in 2003 up from 323,000 the previous year and corresponding staff costs rose from RR65.7bn to more than RR100bn, a very significant cost increase for a single year.[92] Seen from the perspective of financial analysts, there is urgency to get costs under much stricter control in order to increase productivity.

Restructuring should provide a boost to liberalisation of access to networks by improving transparency and removing a significant barrier to entry. There is far to go before the transmission network (or networks) operates using transparent tariffs which do not discriminate between Gazprom production subsidiaries and independent producers. But legal unbundling of Gazprom's network subsidiaries is laying the structural foundation for a non-discriminatory access regime. It is a measure of how far reform has progressed that many of these measures are being taken on the initiative of management, rather than mandated by regulators or 'reformers' within government.

The progress of gas reform, restructuring and liberalisation in Russia up to 2005 has some of the features of the same process within the

European Union following the passage of the Gas Directives.[93] The first Directive, which came into force in 2000, allowed member states to choose between negotiated and regulated access to networks; only 'accounting unbundling' (i.e. separate accounts for different divisions of vertically integrated companies) was required under the first directive.[94] The second Directive, which came into force in July 2004, requires member states to operate a system of regulated access overseen by an independent regulator. It also requires the subsidiaries of vertically integrated companies to be 'legally unbundled' (i.e. different divisions of vertically integrated companies must be placed in separate subsidiary companies) and for the operators of transmission and distribution networks to be legally separated from the owners of the networks.[95] In 2004, the Commission proposed a gas regulation, to be introduced in 2006, that would codify common rules of access to networks.[96]

In 2005, Russian reforms, which started somewhat earlier than the first Gas Directive, are located somewhere between the two directives: access to networks is operational but with weak regulation that appears to involve significant elements of negotiated, as well as some elements of regulated, access. Only accounting unbundling is required but legal unbundling is being introduced and there is discussion about the possibility of a separate transmission system operator. Given this rather weak regulatory framework, the dominant player remained firmly in control of access to networks, and without its cooperation it was almost impossible for independent producers to achieve such access. This aspect of the industry was described by the Head of the Federal Anti-Monopoly Service in the following way: '[it is]...semi-feudal. You have to take the vassal oath. The big monopoly allows only work on its conditions.'[97] However, in late 2004, despite the introduction of the Directives, some of the same observations could be made about access to networks in many EU Member States and it seemed unrealistic to expect that Russia would have made substantially greater progress than the majority of EU countries, given how much longer the latter had been supposed to be working to open up their gas markets.[98]

The Oil Dimension: The Failure of the Rosneft Merger. Gazprom's oil production increased slowly but steadily during the 2000s to 12 mt in 2004.[99] Similarly its reserves, calculated according to international standards, at the end of 2002 were 634 mt of condensate and liquids and 165 mt of oil.[100] In September 2004 it was announced that, in order to provide the Russian Federation government with a majority of Gazprom's equity which (as we saw above) the government believed it needed to secure before the company's share ownership is liberalised, Gazprom would be merged with the 100% state-owned oil company Rosneft. In 2004, Rosneft's oil production was 21.8 mt and the company had an expectation that it would be able to increase production to 45 mt by 2015.[101]

Prior to the merger announcement, Gazprom had already decided to create a separate oil company – Gazpromneft – consistent with legal unbundling of subsidiaries concentrating on a single core business.[102] Putting together Gazprom and Rosneft's existing production would have created a company with production of around 30 mt/year, making it a significant (but not large) producer. However, the Russian government and tax authorities forced Russia's largest oil company Yukos to sell Yuganskneftegaz – its main oil producing asset – in order to pay tax debts. At an auction conducted in December 2004, Yuganskneftegaz was purchased by the unknown Baikal Finance Group, which turned out to be a proxy for Rosneft, used as subterfuge in an attempt to avoid litigation by the Yukos/Menatep Group.[103] As a result of the latter's litigation in the American courts, Gazprom was forced to sell Gazpromneft as a shell company with no assets. Gazprom's oil assets were transferred to its new oil and condensate production subsidiary Gazpromneftedobycha.

A merger of Gazprom and Rosneft/Yuganskneftegaz would have created an oil company with a production of more than 85 mt in 2005 and, according to one estimate, 120−125 mt by 2010.[104] The merger would also have placed Gazprom in a much more advantageous position in Eastern Siberia and the Far East. Chapter 3 showed that Gazprom was in the somewhat anomalous position of being the coordinator of gas development in Eastern Siberia and the Far East without being a partner in any of the major export projects aimed at Asian markets, and also that the acquisition of Rosneft would have brought Gazprom into five out of the six Sakhalin projects.

However, in May 2005 the company announced that the Rosneft merger had been abandoned and that the government would obtain its majority shareholding by purchasing additional Gazprom equity, financed by a flotation of a minority stake in Rosneft/Yuganskneftegaz.[105] The impact of this decision on Gazprom's future strategic direction will be discussed in Chapter 5. Here, the most important observation is that the collapse of the merger leaves Gazprom as a significant, but not substantial, oil producer with liquids production likely to increase to 16 mt by 2010 and 25 mt by 2020.[106] The increase in production will be mainly associated with gas production from the Achimov and Valengenian layers of the NPT fields (see Chapter 1) and the Prirazlomnoye field in the Kara Sea which Gazprom and Rosneft had been jointly developing prior to Gazprom's purchase of Rosneft's share in Sevmorneftegaz.[107]

Without acquisition of additional assets, this would not give Gazprom any claim to significant oil status either domestically or internationally. Its prospects in this regard, however, could be significantly changed by potential oil linkages between Gazprom and Chinese energy companies, which were already apparent in 2004 even before the Yuganskneftegaz affair, but have subsequently been made explicit at the highest political level.[108] In addition, Gazprom's Chairman undertook a wide range of international visits with no apparent relevance to gas, but significant potential for cooperation in the oil sector.[109] It remains to be seen whether Gazprom's – and also the Russian president and government's – vision of itself as a major international oil player has ended with the collapse of the Rosneft merger, or whether it will be resuscitated by future acquisitions.

Summary and Conclusions

Reform in the Russian gas industry resumed in the 2000s with significant price increases for both industrial and residential customers, and substantial increases in the volume of gas carried by Gazprom for third party users of the transmission network. Little progress was made towards the bold structural reforms proposed in the late 1990s and by 2005 Minister of Economic Development and Trade Gref, was the only remaining high level government supporter of such reforms. With the president having made it clear that break-up of Gazprom was not on the agenda, structural reform has been reduced to 'legal unbundling' i.e. separation of Gazprom's subsidiary companies and especially the network companies. In 2005, there was a serious commitment to third party access at the highest level, although this did not extend to export pipelines to Europe. Nevertheless, the extent to which independent gas producers and oil companies continue to require Gazprom's goodwill and patronage to use its networks should not be minimised, and this seems likely to continue for the foreseeable future.

The post-2001 management, under Alexey Miller, reclaimed assets that had been sold or loaned in unclear circumstances to other companies. The new management developed even closer links with the government and the president to the point where, price reform excepted, it was hard to see any differences. In terms of ownership, 2005 will be remembered as the year in which Gazprom became a majority government-owned company and increased its capitalisation with the removal of restrictions on trading in its shares (the ring fence). However, this will not be achieved by a merger with Rosneft through which Gazprom could have become a major oil-producing company. This is seen by some as a positive development since the addition of a major oil business could have complicated Gazprom's management and planning processes, slowing down reform of the gas sector due to management time and attention being diverted elsewhere. It remains to be seen whether the failure of the merger means the end of Gazprom's large-scale oil ambitions.

Appendix 4.1: Governance-related Explanations of the Non-payment Era

Academic economists writing about the economic transition in Russia have tended to see non-payment as a deliberate criminal act by those in positions where they could profit from illegal activity. One of the principal proponents of this view explains low regulated prices of commodities (including gas) in the following way:

> Rent seekers claimed that industrial production would collapse if faced with world market prices and a broad post-Soviet public concurred out of ignorance. In reality, rent seekers bought large volumes of these commodities privately and sold them abroad at world market prices. Their profitable arbitrage was made possible by price controls, their exclusive access to these commodities, and their export privileges.[110]

Specifically in the gas sector Aslund claims that:

> One reason for the surge in barter was that it allowed natural monopolies to differentiate their prices, as barter prices tended to be 40–50% higher than ordinary prices. The natural monopolies also accumulated arrears to extract substantial discounts in their taxes through offsets against their unpaid taxes. Thus, they kept loss-makers going by extracting implicit subsidies from the government for themselves.[111]

Gaddy and Ickes's work on the 'virtual economy' of the 1990s highlights deliberate 'value destruction' in the Russian economy for the benefit of 'rent seekers'. They suggest that:

> The ultimate 'value pump' in Russia today is the fuel and energy sector, above all one single company, Gazprom…In exchange for the rights to keep what it earns from exports, Gazprom pumps value into the system by supplying gas without being paid for it (or, more generally, at a cost that is low enough to keep enterprises operating). Gazprom subsidies – which then lead to arrears to the government – are the primary way in which unprofitable activity is supported today in Russia.
>
> The system survives because it meets the needs of so many actors in the economy. Workers and managers at industrial dinosaurs benefit because

the virtual economy postpones the ultimate reckoning for loss making firms. Government, especially at the sub national level, where much of the important action takes place, benefits because it maintains employment and continues providing social services. Gazprom also benefits however; the value transfers it makes to the virtual economy are the price it pays to be able to appropriate the massive rents from exports. [112]

The general theme running through this work is the notion of Russia as a kleptocracy and the explanation of most economic phenomena is that 'they are all crooks' or, in more acceptable academic jargon, 'rent seekers'.[113] The specific gas-related argument is that Gazprom was a willing party to non-payment in return for being allowed to keep revenues from exports. But it is important to ask whether the problems in the domestic market were the creation of Gazprom or successive governments struggling through an economic transition. Viewed by this author over the past decade, Russian governments bore overwhelming responsibility for the non-payment crisis. Not only did Gazprom have little control over pricing policy, but government decrees prevented the company from cutting off whole categories of non-paying customers. Furthermore, it is somewhat misleading to claim that Gazprom 'appropriated' the revenues from exports to Europe. The government clawed back a substantial proportion of these revenues – via excise taxes and from 2000 via a more direct (although relatively small) export tax. But with Gazprom's losses on the domestic and, for a period of time the CIS market, export revenues were the sole means of keeping the company financially viable.

Non-payment (or at least its worst excesses) could certainly have been avoided by the type of radical economic reform advocated by Aslund. But successive Russian governments rejected that solution and Gazprom bore the brunt of that decision. If these governments had had the political courage to impose hard budget constraints on enterprises and accept the economic and political consequences of the bankruptcies that would have ensued, then economic reform and restructuring might have happened earlier; but so might political chaos and collapse of government and institutions. Gazprom undoubtedly tried to make the best of its rather difficult position and pursued economically undesirable policies in terms of acquiring stakes in enterprises in return for gas debts. However, this situation was largely forced upon Gazprom, it was not of the company's own making. While academic commentators have seemed to suggest that Gazprom was a major beneficiary from non-payment and 'the virtual economy' era, the reverse is probably the case. Had Russian governments adopted radical economic reform with prices equivalent to (at least short run, moving rapidly towards) long-run

marginal cost and strict payment discipline, the likely consequences
would have been that:

- domestic gas demand would have fallen sharply, due to bankruptcies
  and enforced conservation and efficiency measures;
- as a result, there would have been far less pressure on gas production
  which Gazprom could have allowed to fall much more significantly
  than actually happened;
- profitability from domestic sales would have come close to that of
  exports to Europe (particularly during the period of low European
  prices in the late 1990s), reducing the pressure to build new and
  expensive infrastructure to increase exports.

Consequently, the company's core business would have been dramatically simplified, management would have had market signals that would
have made business planning and project selection relatively simple in
comparison with the situation it actually faced during this period. This
would have been accompanied by demands for the reform of Gazprom
itself, which would not have been welcomed by a majority of the then
management of the company, but would have had some credibility. In
the circumstances of the 1990s they did not have credibility.

CHAPTER 5

THE FUTURE OF RUSSIAN GAS AND GAZPROM

The theme of this study is that what lies ahead for both Russian gas and Gazprom constitutes a significant break with the past. This final chapter summarises the arguments of the preceding chapters and presents some conclusions on the future.

Resources and Supply

Since the late 1990s, it has become increasingly important to consider Russian gas resources and supply under two headings: Gazprom and non-Gazprom. Gazprom's total reserves are huge but when the figures from the Yamal Peninsula (not yet in production) and the Shtok-manovskoye field (now aimed at LNG export markets) are subtracted, the available resource base to support annual production at the level of the early 2000s appears more modest. Taking Gazprom's proved and probable reserve (international classification) figures for end-2004 (Table 1.1) – subtracting the Yamal Peninsula and Shtokman – and dividing by 2004 production, gives a figure of 24 years of remaining reserves; using Russian $A+B+C_1$ classification this increases to 38 years. Neither of these figures gives any cause for immediate concern but they are much less impressive than those quoted in the general literature.[1]

A time horizon of 25−35 years for reserves at fields currently in production, and available from producing regions close to existing infrastructure, does not convey the urgency for Gazprom to open up the fields on the Yamal Peninsula and adjacent offshore regions, if the company is to maintain production at 530 Bcm/year (let alone the higher figures it has set itself) over the next decade. Delay in the development of these fields may have already cost it the ability to maintain production at this level by 2010. However, this does not necessarily mean that delaying Yamal development was the wrong policy, or that it will lead to major problems in future.

As the 2000s unfold, it becomes increasingly apparent that the production investments that were made before 1991 (the 'Soviet gas dowry' to the Russian Federation) are within sight of the end of their productive lives. Gazprom's production is therefore moving from dependence on three fields (Urengoy, Yamburg and Medvezhe), to a larger number of smaller fields requiring more complex and costly development of gas and liquids, and therefore more complex and costly transportation options. The main domestic tasks for the Russian gas industry and Gazprom over the next twenty years are to replace the production capacity of those fields, and to carry out large-scale refurbishment of the Unified Gas Supply System (UGSS) bringing that gas from Western Siberia to domestic and export markets.

In the first part of the 2000s, the consequences of decline in the existing large fields were masked by the start-up of the supergiant Zapolyarnoye field, which reached its plateau of 100 Bcm/year in 2005. As a result, Gazprom production, which had fallen during the period 1998−2001, increased again in the early 2000s. But as Zapolyarnoye and other smaller new fields reach their peak, Gazprom's production will plateau and decline before 2010. With an average rate of production decline at the three major gas fields of more than 22 Bcm/year during the period 1999−2004, there is some urgency for Gazprom to establish a future supply strategy containing a clear plan for the timing of new large-scale supplies, particularly from the Yamal Peninsula and Ob/Taz Bay fields.

Capital investment requirements of $20−25bn for the first phase of onshore Yamal development made such a commitment impossible in the economic and political environment of the late 1990s and early 2000s; even in 2005, it was not on Gazprom's immediate investment agenda. Lead times for field development and pipeline construction suggest that production of 100 Bcm/year cannot be achieved in less than eight years. Thus even if a decision is taken to begin Yamal development in 2006, the earliest date that the Bovanenko field can be producing 100 Bcm/year would be 2014, and even this may be optimistic in terms of the logistical challenges and environmental difficulties likely to be encountered in such a remote and ecologically fragile region.

Those who criticise the company for failing to invest sufficiently in new production have not understood that, despite the fact domestic gas prices have risen sharply in real terms in the early 2000s, Yamal gas could not be sold profitably in Russia at 2005 prices – and possibly not even at prices of $60/mcm foreseen for 2010.[2] While this justifies the commercial wisdom of Gazprom's decision not to develop Yamal for production in the 2000s – even if this was mainly driven by financial constraints − it does not provide a future supply 'road map' for the company.

To the extent that Gazprom does not move towards rapid, large-scale development of the Yamal Peninsula, it must, by design or default, rely on:

- a larger number of smaller fields in the NPT region (including offshore fields in the Ob and Taz Bays), close to the existing pipeline network which could provide around 80 Bcm/year, but with plateau volumes in many fields only able to be maintained for around a decade. Developing these fields could be a crucial part of a low cost supply strategy;
- deliveries from other gas producers which, with adequate incentives, could increase from a 2004 level of nearly 90 Bcm to as much as 150 Bcm/year by the early 2010s, and perhaps more than 200 Bcm by 2020;
- imports from Central Asian countries where Gazprom has long-term agreements in place envisaging more than 100 Bcm/year of imports by the early 2010s.

The outcome will depend both on a view of costs, time schedules and levels of security attached to these different options; and the margins available from the different markets for Russian gas – domestic, CIS and European – which in turn will depend on the prices they will be willing to pay over the next decade. The latter two options would introduce a level of dependence on other suppliers never before experienced by Gazprom.

Non-Gazprom producers (oil companies and gas independents) which already supplied nearly 90 Bcm of gas in 2004, could increase production to as much as 150 Bcm by the early 2010s and exceed 200 Bcm by 2020, but only if prices are attractive and access terms are 'reasonable'. Although there is a tendency to refer to 'independent producers' as if they were a significant number of companies, in 2005 only five companies appeared to have the ability to substantially increase gas production for sale to markets west of Siberia: Lukoil, Rosneft, TNK/BP, Surgutnefte-gaz and Novatek. Lukoil's production should be around 30 Bcm by the early 2010s and its projection of 80 Bcm by 2020 is entirely possible in terms of reserves, but questionable because of the required investments. Rosneft has the resource base to develop production of between 45−50 Bcm in the 2010s but its merger with Yuganskneftegaz seems more likely (particularly in its initial stages) to focus investment resources on oil, rather than gas. TNK/BP production could be around 20 Bcm in the early 2010s. But much will depend on its success in developing major projects in Eastern Siberia (Kovykhta) and Sakhalin which – if they were to go ahead over the next decade − could swallow much of the company's available budget for gas development elsewhere in Russia. Surgutneftegaz's ambitions seemed limited to gas associated with its oil production, and the company's potential for increasing gas production is significant, particularly if flaring can be reduced. The independent gas company Novatek is projecting production of 50 Bcm in the late 2000s and early 2010s based on current developments, and has no significant oil business to compete with its gas investments. The company has demonstrated the ability to attract international investment which will support its development ambitions.

Of the other current and potential gas producers, the case of Itera is the least easy to predict. Its production ambitions are similar to those of Novatek but, since 2001, have been limited by the Gazprom management under Alexey Miller. If it could resolve its differences with Gazprom, it could increase production significantly, but in 2005 its future seemed more likely to be as a downstream gas marketer purchasing from Gazprom, Novatek and others. No other companies seemed likely to have future production or sales significantly in excess of 10 Bcm, although Itera – assuming it can resolve its disagreements with the Gazprom management – could achieve production of twice that figure. Of the other oil companies, Sibneft seems to have little interest in gas, and the demise of Yukos has removed a potentially significant future player from the market, although the latter's properties will undoubtedly be purchased and developed by other players.

The other main source of supply for Russia and Gazprom could be imports from Central Asia – Turkmenistan, Kazakhstan and Uzbekistan – which together could provide more than 100 Bcm/year by the early 2010s. But these sources present cost and security problems for the company. If the presidents of Central Asian countries are unwilling to provide a secure source of supply at prices that make it profitable to sell in Russian and CIS markets, imports will remain limited as it will be commercially unattractive for Gazprom (or other Russian marketers) to import more than marginal quantities of this gas. The four-month cessation of supply to Russia in early 2005, which resulted in a significant increase in the price of Turkmen gas, could prove a major setback to any Gazprom supply strategy involving large volumes of Central Asian gas. If Gazprom is forced to pay prices for Central Asian imports that make this gas uncompetitive in the Russian market, it is most likely to regard these as 'balancing supplies' to be purchased as a last resort when necessary, rather than as long-term baseload supplies. To the extent that Central Asian gas supplies prove to be problematic, domestic Russian gas producers will become even more important than currently anticipated, accelerating the need for liberalised access to markets.

Demand and Prices

During the period 1998–2005, the Russian industrial gas sector was transformed from a commercially loss-making nightmare to a modestly profitable business for Gazprom selling at regulated prices. In 2005, it seemed likely that sales to residential customers could become profitable within ten years. Further reform of regulated prices is needed not just to remove subsidies to residential customers, and to increase prices to all customers closer to long-run marginal costs, but also to increase cost-reflectiveness (in terms of location and customer demand profile). However, full deregulation of even industrial prices, with further development of trading and exchanges, will be difficult as long as Gazprom is the overwhelmingly 'dominant player' in both production and sales.

Lack of detailed data on gas demand and price elasticity means that it is very difficult to estimate the impact on demand of increasing industrial prices, two to three times higher in real terms than five years previously, with a requirement to pay on time, in full and in cash. Thus in terms of price levels and payment enforcement, in 2005 the industry is in uncharted territory. It is probable that significant conservation and efficiency measures will take place, threatening the traditional assumption that demand will continue to increase at 1–2% per annum indefinitely. The problem is to know when structural change and large-scale replacement of old inefficient plant will begin. To an important extent this will depend on reform in the power sector and whether the new owners of power stations will have sufficient confidence in their property rights to make substantial investments in new, energy efficient, plant. Substantial inertia may lead to a continuing increase in gas demand for the remainder of this decade, but the 2010s may see a different picture. If large-scale replacement of Soviet-era plant does not take place in the 2010s, this will suggest a bleak future for Russian economic growth.

A combination of market reforms and industrial restructuring may bring about the kind of improvements in the country's energy/GDP ratio which are foreshadowed in the 2003 Russian Energy Strategy, and indicated by comparisons of Russian levels of energy demand with those of comparable industrialised countries. The faster the pace of industrial restructuring within Russia, the more likely it is that heavy industrial sectors with old, highly inefficient plant will be replaced by new and far less energy-intensive industries. At the same time, replacement of plant in energy-intensive sectors including power generation will, in itself, be a huge source of natural gas savings and efficiency for which carbon credits may be available via the joint implementation mechanism of the Kyoto Protocol.

If Gazprom encounters problems in obtaining additional supply at prices which allow it to be profitably sold in the domestic market, either prices will need to increase, or supplies will need to be more tightly rationed; both will depress future growth in demand. If industrial prices exceed $60/mcm by the early 2010s, then gas demand in western Russia might not increase significantly even in the event of healthy GDP growth.[3] A scenario in which Russian gas demand stays at its 2003 level or falls slightly over the next two decades, would reduce gas demand by up to 70 Bcm in 2020 compared with the 'business as usual' scenario (Table 1.19).

Price, Demand and Supply Scenarios

As noted above, the key to judgements as to whether it would be profitable for Gazprom to pursue new sources of supply, how quickly and for which markets, is based on prices that consumers will be willing and able to pay in those markets. Table 5.1 shows four simple outcomes for Gazprom based on a combination of high and low gas prices in Russia, and high and low European border prices, and hypothesises the likely impact on Gazprom's commercial decision making and investment programme.

These scenarios suggest that price developments in the domestic market are likely to be the key to decisions to develop new supplies, domestic and imported. Of the risks facing Gazprom and other producers the most serious are:

1. The price risk that the domestic market does not become sufficiently profitable to warrant development of new higher cost sources of gas, specifically gas from the Yamal Peninsula fields. This risk relates both to price levels and payment terms; the period 1996–2001 serves as a reminder of how much money can be lost by selling gas in unprofitable markets (Figure 1.1). In order to support development of the Yamal fields and/or large-scale imports of Central Asian gas in the 2010s, industrial customers in Moscow will need to be paying at least $60/mcm (in 2004 dollars and at 2004 exchange rates) in cash and without significant delays. Even at these prices there would be little or no tax revenue available for the Russian government from new domestic gas development and no profit for Gazprom on resale of Central Asian imports. These price levels – roughly 50% above 2005 prices in real terms – are dependent on government determination to deal with the political consequences of such substantial increases. Any suggestion

Table 5.1: Gas Price Scenarios for Russia and Europe in the 2010s –
Consequences for Gazprom

*EUROPEAN BORDER PRICES**	*RUSSIAN REGULATED INDUSTRIAL PRICES***	
	HIGH	*LOW*
HIGH	Demand in both Europe and Russia is low but revenue and profitability is high allowing for domestic new, large scale supply to be developed (eg Yamal) or imported from Central Asia. In this scenario the major risk for Gazprom is that volume growth in both domestic and export markets may be uncertain. In that situation, flexible, ie non-Gazprom, supply sources would be preferable.	Close to the situation in 2003–04. Expansion of Russian exports to Europe with strongly increased revenue earnings. Market expansion prospects are uncertain at these price levels. Developing new large scale supply or imports for the domestic market, where demand is still expanding due to low prices, is impossible as both would incur significant losses.
LOW	Additional exports to Europe become unattractive, especially through new infrastructure, such as NEP. Sales to the domestic market become extremely profitable. Investment in large scale new supply and imports is problematic because of uncertain domestic demand at high prices. If low European gas prices continue into the 2010s renewal of some long term contracts may be questioned.	Close to the situation Gazprom faced in the period 1997–2000 (except that the domestic price was much lower). Very difficult to make a case for more than marginal investments or new infrastructure, domestic or imported

*   high European border prices = above \$120/mcm; low border prices = below
\$80/mcm; prices in 2004 dollars at the German border; 1Euro = \$1.15;
** high regulated domestic prices = above \$60/mcm; low regulated domestic prices
= below \$30/mcm. Prices for industrial customers in 2004 dollars in the zone
which includes the city of Moscow; \$1= RR30

that industrial gas prices will not reach those levels, either because
of government unwillingness to impose them or because of customer inability/unwillingness to pay, will make it very unwise for
Gazprom to commit to large-scale additional supply.

2.   The market/volume risk that if prices are raised to these levels and above, there will not be sufficient demand for these very large volumes of gas. These risks are particularly acute for Yamal Peninsula gas where Gazprom might find itself in a situation of having invested up to $25bn to produce large volumes of gas that it is unable to sell profitably in its major markets.

Table 5.2 translates the outcomes in Table 5.1 into very simple numerical scenarios for demand and exports in 2020 (based on the discussion in Chapters 1–3). These scenarios are presented not as projections of likely outcomes, but as illustrations of the complexity of the investment decisions facing Gazprom over the next decade. The figures in Table 5.2 include only domestic demand from Western Siberia westwards, and pipeline gas exports to Europe and CIS countries (an additional 6.5% has been added to these figures to allow for pipeline fuel).[4]

Table 5.2: Russian Gas Demand and Export Requirements in 2020* (Bcm)

		*RUSSIAN DOMESTIC PRICES***	
*EUROPEAN BORDER PRICES***		*HIGH*	*LOW*
	HIGH	593	761
	LOW	657	825

*   demand in western Russia plus pipeline exports to CIS and Europe, plus 6.5% for pipeline fuel;
** see Table 5.1 for definitions and assumptions

From the figures in Table 5.2 we can derive a requirement for additional gas supply in 2020. The principal building block for this requirement is the 2020 projection of 344 Bcm of likely Gazprom production from existing fields and those expected to be brought into production (Table 1.10). Table 5.3 shows the remaining Russian gas requirements when 344 Bcm of likely Gazprom production from existing fields is subtracted from the figures in Table 5.2.

We can then compare the figures in Table 5.3 with the potential availability of gas from independent (non-Gazprom) production, Yamal Peninsula on- and offshore production (mainly Gazprom), and Central Asian imports (Table 5.4).

Tables 5.3 and 5.4 suggest that Russian gas supply requirements in 2020 additional to those of Gazprom's fields, will be 248–478 Bcm; compared with a potential availability of 305–505 Bcm from inde-

Table 5.3: Additional Russian Gas Supply Requirements in 2020 (Bcm)

DOMESTIC/EXPORT PRICES*	*HIGH*	*LOW*
HIGH	249	386
LOW	313	478

* see Table 5.1 for definitions and assumptions

Table 5.4: Likely Additional Potential Gas Supply Availability for Russia by 2020 (Bcm)

Independent Production	125–210*
Yamal Peninsula on and offshore (Gazprom)	80–175
Central Asian Imports	100–120
TOTAL	305–505

* this reduces to 0–85 Bcm assuming a minimum of 125 Bcm of production already committed for 2020

pendent Russian producers, Yamal Peninsula fields and Central Asian imports. It needs to be stressed once again that these are illustrative figures based on the analysis set out in the foregoing chapters. The independent production figure is somewhat artificial in that it had already reached 90 Bcm in 2004 and seemed relatively certain to rise to a minimum of 125 Bcm/year by 2020, so that the 125–210 Bcm suggested in Table 5.4 for potential independent production could be reduced to 0–85 Bcm.

Subtracting a minimum of 125 Bcm of independent production from the figures in Table 5.3 would leave a requirement of 124–353 Bcm from other sources (including additional independent production) in 2020. Given an additional requirement of only 124 Bcm in 2020, the lowest cost/lowest risk option for Gazprom would be to encourage more independent production and import the balance of its needs from Central Asia. Maximising independent production would leave around 50 Bcm to import from Central Asia which would provide Gazprom with significant market power in dealing with those suppliers, even if the proposed refurbished pipeline system bringing gas from Central Asia would be substantially under-utilised. There would be no need for any Yamal Peninsula production prior to 2020.

Table 5.4 shows that there is, at least in theory, the possibility to meet even the maximum additional requirement of 353 Bcm, but this would require urgent Gazprom action to develop all three sources in Table 5.4 if not to their maximum, then at least to a very considerable extent. Yamal Peninsula production of 175 Bcm would probably be necessary with the remaining 178 Bcm split between independent production and Central Asian imports both of which would need to supply close to their maximum potential. But such a scenario of meeting maximum additional requirements is not realistic because the price scenario from which it derives (Table 5.1) is too low to support either Yamal Peninsula development or higher price imports from Central Asia. In other words, even if these volumes of additional supply can be mobilised by 2020, they will not be commercially viable for sale to either domestic or export markets at 'low' domestic and export prices.

The actual outcome for 2020 almost certainly lies somewhere between the minimum and maximum requirements in Table 5.3. The aim of this section has been to lay out a framework within which readers can develop their own analysis as events unfold, and to stress that the correct methodological approach is to start with prices and demand, rather than resources and supply. The central problem for Gazprom on the supply side, however, is to take a position on the volumes and timing of gas required from the Yamal Peninsula fields because of the lead times involved in their development. For Gazprom to minimise risk and maximise revenue, higher prices with lower demand and hence lower supply requirements, would be the optimum market conditions. This is because, despite its massive resource wealth, future Russian gas supplies will be 'high cost' at the point of delivery to markets.

Reform and Restructuring

Gazprom will remain the dominant player in Russian gas production and sales for the foreseeable future, but that does not mean that no reform has taken place, or will take place in the gas sector. The advances in price reform were noted above. In terms of access to networks, in 2004 Gazprom carried nearly 112 Bcm of gas for 35 shippers, although more than 50 Bcm was Central Asian gas destined mainly for CIS countries. Despite the fact that probably only a handful of shippers accounted for the majority of the remaining 62 Bcm, this represented respectable progress. Nevertheless, much remains to be achieved in terms of non-discriminatory access to networks and the evolution of cost-related tariffs. In the reform environment of 2005, non-Gazprom producers – both oil companies and independent gas companies – could prosper as long as they did not provoke conflict with Gazprom management (and the Russian government) and stayed within the role determined by the latter which, for the foreseeable future, does not include exports to Europe. While this may not permanently condemn these producers to what the Head of the Federal Anti-Monopoly Service has termed 'vassal status' in respect of Gazprom, it does leave them somewhat short of operating as independent commercial entities in a non-discriminatory third party access regime.

In 2004, companies other than Gazprom accounted for around 14% of production and a similar percentage of gas sales. The speed with which the market share of non-Gazprom players will increase will depend on the development of:

- regulated prices;
- a transparent and enforceable regulatory regime for tariffs and access to networks and, in its absence, the interest of Gazprom in encouraging other suppliers to develop fields and move gas to market;
- the success of Gazprom in developing competitively priced supply from Central Asia (the more of this gas is available to Gazprom, the less independent gas will be required).

To the extent that Gazprom decides against, or is not successful in, importing supplies over which it has direct control, it will need to rely on other Russian producers who will take an increasingly large share of the Russian domestic market. Both Gazprom and the Russian government seem to be relatively comfortable with this prospect which would be positive for market reform. Less positive for reform would be a situation in which non-Gazprom production increased substantially, but those producers found their access to market blocked and were forced to sell their gas to Gazprom at the wellhead at regulated prices (minus transportation). But to be an independent producer, does not necessarily mean wishing to play a marketing role. Lukoil is to sell to Gazprom at the entrance to the transmission system, while Itera is playing a decreasing role in production and becoming a more important marketer; Novatek is becoming more important in both roles.

One of the most difficult developments to project is how far and how fast structural reform of Gazprom will develop. The creation of separate subsidiary companies for production, transmission, storage and other activities (legal unbundling) was well advanced in 2005. Break-up (ownership unbundling) of the company is politically unacceptable and this is unlikely to change even after the end of the second Putin presidency. As the 2000s unfolded, Minister of Economic Development and Trade (MEDT) Gref was clearly frustrated at the slowness of Gazprom reform and the lack of cost control, in an environment of sharply rising earnings from domestic and foreign markets. But MEDT was the only powerful government agency that has consistently expressed opposition both to the growing consolidation of the energy sector with Gazprom acquiring oil and electricity assets, and frustration with the slow pace of gas sector reform. The evolution of Gazprom's structure will depend significantly on a broader strategic vision of the company's future (see below).

Exports

Relatively bright prospects for liberalisation of domestic markets stand in sharp contrast to those of exports. Gazprom management, the government and the president are clear that the company will remain the 'single export channel' to Europe for the foreseeable future. The same policy has already been instituted for Asian pipeline exports, well in advance of any such exports actually happening.

In 2005, Gazprom re-established its position as sole exporter of Russian gas to CIS countries after a period in the late 1990s and early 2000s when it relinquished a large part of this role. Russian gas exports, especially to Ukraine, Belarus and Moldova, will remain extremely important for these countries and are intertwined with transit of Russian gas to Europe. Gazprom has commitments to supply around 90 Bcm/year to CIS countries in the mid to late 2000s, of which 60 Bcm/year will be to Ukraine (more than half of which should be re-exports from Turkmenistan) and up to another 20 Bcm/year to Belarus. Since 2003, Gazprom has progressively excluded other Russian suppliers from CIS markets, but to the extent that imports from Central Asian countries are constrained and CIS importers actively seek non-Gazprom supplies, other Russian producers and traders may retain an export role. Much will depend on the success or otherwise of the sales and transit agreements that Gazprom has painstakingly developed with its CIS trading partners in the 2000s.

Resolution of transit problems in Ukraine and Belarus (and to a lesser extent Moldova) will remain essential, and the North European Pipeline will not change that situation. Bilateral political relationships will continue to have a very important impact on gas supplies and commercial terms, but the era of supply to CIS countries at subsidised prices has ended and with it the era of ever-rising debts. These countries are expected to pay a minimum of Russian industrial prices plus additional transmission costs; debtors are placed under immediate and increasing pressure, and account is kept of their obligations.[5] Economic recovery and a change in the political orientation of key countries – such as Ukraine – towards Europe, suggests a progressive commercialisation of relationships, moving away from the post-Soviet bartering of gas supplies against transit services. If newly elected governments in these countries see political advantage in paying, and can afford to pay, 'market prices' for Russian gas, and charge cost of service tariffs for transit of Russian gas to Europe, this would fundamentally change gas relationships.[6]

Commercialising CIS trade in this way could revolutionise Gazprom's attitude towards exports to Europe. It would resolve the problem of physical deterioration of networks, since owners would have both the means and the incentive to carry out such work. Although this would significantly increase transit charges for Russian gas, it would mean that exporting gas to CIS countries would become as profitable for Gazprom as exports to Europe, a process similar to the post-1990 commercialisation of Russian gas exports to east European countries. Much needs to be resolved before this can become a reality, but a market in which exports to Ukraine were as profitable for Gazprom as exports to Germany, would create a very different future for Russian gas exports to CIS (and possibly European) countries in the 2010s.

In the Caucasus, new gas flows into the region in the late 2000s from Azerbaijan (to Georgia) and Iran (to Armenia and possibly also Georgia) mean that Russian (and Central Asian) gas will be competing with other suppliers for the first time. However, given the problematic security situation in the region, it is likely that a diversity of sources and pipeline routes will be needed to keep gas flowing to customers. Gazprom's drive to acquire equity in both networks and large gas-consuming companies in Caucasus countries – in cooperation with the Russian electricity conglomerate UES – signifies a determination to remain centrally involved in the region's energy sector. Such determination is probably not warranted by the profitability of sales and investments, and therefore owes much to Russian foreign policy towards the region.

In 2005, it was uncertain whether Gazprom's carefully constructed post-2002 commercial frameworks in the CIS countries would survive political changes in, and new commercial demands from, these countries. The most important of these were the election of the Yushchenko administration in the Ukraine, and the sharp increase in the price of Turkmen gas in 2005. These developments may unravel Gazprom's long-term import agreement of 2003 with Turkmenistan as well as its long-term agreement with Ukraine concluded in 2004 for sales, shipping of Turkmen gas, and transit of Russian gas to Europe. Inability to retain the basic price and volume aspects of these agreements would create significant uncertainty for Gazprom in the late 2000s. Lack of progress towards forming a consortium to refurbish the Ukrainian pipelines that transit gas to Europe, would be an equally bad omen.

Europe will remain the dominant export market for Russian gas in terms of volumes and revenues for at least the next two decades and probably much longer. Export capacity to European countries including Turkey was around 190 Bcm in the mid 2000s. Refurbishment of the Ukrainian network could add up to an additional 40 Bcm of capacity. The North European Pipeline (through the Baltic Sea to Germany) will add a minimum of another 20 Bcm. Gazprom's stated intention to complete the line by 2010 could be delayed, but will not affect marketing of additional Russian gas in Belgium and the UK, which can be achieved via the expanded capacity of Interconnector (IUK) and the new BBL pipeline, both of which should be completed by the end of 2006. Sales to these markets demonstrate another aspect of the future of Russian gas exports: confirmation that there is a role for short-term contracts based on gas-indexed prices, alongside the traditional long-term oil-indexed contracts. But the costs involved in serving these markets, particularly the UK, mean that they are highly price-sensitive and sales could disappear relatively quickly should prices fall from the levels of 2003−05.

There are substantial uncertainties for Russian gas sales to European markets over the next decade. These are related to the long-awaited development of gas to gas competition and pricing, anticipated as a consequence of liberalisation, which have yet to make a significant impact in Continental Europe. A growing surplus of supply over demand in the late 2000s, and increasing pressure from the second EU Gas Directive and the new Regulation on Access to be introduced in 2006, could give rise to gas to gas competition which would drive down European gas prices for a period of years. This would present substantial commercial difficulties for projects such as the North European Pipeline which might be commissioned around that time. With the possibility that European border gas prices, set by gas to gas competition might be in the range of $70−80/mcm (in 2004 dollars) in the late 2000s, European sales could become much less attractive if industrial customers in Moscow were by then paying $60/mcm, particularly with the growing convertibility of the ruble on international currency markets.

Under this scenario, given that Gazprom's current long-term contractual export commitments do not exceed 180 Bcm/year in the early 2010s − and that one-third of long-term contract volumes expire by

2008 and one half by 2012 – there might be a reduced incentive to expand exports through high cost infrastructure. On the other hand, should gas to gas competition fail to become a reality in Europe with prices remaining linked to those of oil (particularly at the oil price levels of 2003–05), additional sales through new infrastructure would remain attractive. But the outlook for increases in gas demand – and therefore increases in Russian exports – in a higher (oil-linked) price environment, would be significantly reduced.

Russian attitudes towards increasing European exports will be strongly influenced by political relationships with the European Union and major European countries, and commercial and regulatory conditions within these markets. As far as politics are concerned, Soviet and Russian gas exports have generally been able to surmount periodic concerns about 'security of supply' – a term used to denote concern about the degree of dependence on Russian gas supplies, rather than any specific threat or problem arising from this dependence. Nevertheless, should political relationships between Russia and European countries (and the European Union) deteriorate, individual countries might return to the concept of a limit on Russian gas as a percentage of total gas demand. Such a concept was often spoken about during the Cold War period, principally to placate conservative American Republican administrations during the 1980s, but nowhere written in an official document, and therefore not enforced in any major European market. Such market limitations made little sense in the past, and would make even less sense in a European market with greater gas trading, where it will become increasingly difficult to determine which gas is being burned in any particular country and by any specific customer.

On the commercial side, it is clear that Gazprom – in common with all other suppliers to the European gas market – will do nothing to jeopardise the very high gas prices of the post-2003 period which have resulted from correspondingly high oil prices. Russian receipts from European sales, which exceeded $19bn in 2004, have been boosted by sharply increased export volumes since 2002, and this has reduced much of the financial pressure for further rapid increases in exports. Indeed, given the risk that increased exports might jeopardise price levels by creating oversupply, Gazprom has a strong incentive to act prudently on export volumes.

The traditional explanation of Russian commercial gas behaviour has been that desperation to earn hard currency would always drive Gazprom to sell as much gas as possible in Europe. That explanation (with some qualifications) had considerable validity during the Soviet period, extending into the troubled years of economic transition, and the Russian and CIS non-payment crises of the 1990s. But over the next decade, the commercial context of Russian gas exports to Europe looks set to change in terms of supply availability and market attractiveness. Europe is still a highly attractive market for Russian gas but by 2005 it was no longer the only profitable market. In the late 2000s and certainly in the 2010s, a combination of,

- growing tightness in Gazprom's supply position;
- increasing domestic supply costs due to Yamal Peninsula development and higher prices for gas imports from Central Asia;
- higher domestic prices in Russia;
- higher CIS transit charges and sales prices in those countries;
- greater convertibility of the Russian ruble; and
- the possibility of falling European gas prices due to gas to gas competition,

could change the balance of profitability for Russian gas sales away from Europe and towards domestic and CIS customers. Should there be any suggestion that market limitations may be imposed from the European side for political and 'security' reasons, this would limit Russian incentives to increase deliveries to Europe just at the time when opportunities are opening up to expand exports to other foreign markets. Should any combination of these trends prove to be correct, a stagnation or slow increase in European export volumes in the late 2000s and early 2010s is much more likely than any rapid and substantial increase.

LNG exports to Asia and the west coast of North America will commence in 2007–08 with deliveries from the Sakhalin 2 (Sakhalin Energy) project. By early 2005, Sakhalin 2 had sold more than 90% of its capacity of more than 13 Bcm/year. Significantly, nearly 20% of that capacity will need to cross the Pacific Ocean to Mexico, when the natural geographical market for LNG from the Russian Far East is Asia. The fact that Sakhalin 2 has sold LNG in significant quantities to North America demonstrates a continuing problem of acceptability of Russian LNG in Asian countries; a problem which is even more acute when considering the prospects for pipeline gas.

Russian pipeline gas projects to Asia – in terms of both markets and financial requirements – require close political relationships between Russian and East Asian governments and, for some projects, between East Asian governments themselves. These political relationships, many of which were openly hostile during the Cold War period, have not sufficiently improved since. Indeed, the prospects for energy and natural gas cooperation in East Asia, after a largely positive decade in the 1990s, worsened in the 2000s due to deteriorating Sino-Japanese relations and mounting tensions on the Korean Peninsula. Lack of multinational institutional frameworks in Asia (akin to the EU in Europe or NAFTA in North America) mean that pipeline export projects need to be pursued as bilateral, rather than multilateral, initiatives. This imposes additional strain on bilateral political relations which, so far, they have been unable to bear.

In a domestic Russian context, Asian gas pipeline developments were complicated by the Russian government's decision to give Gazprom overall authority over East Siberian and Far Eastern gas develop-ment – domestic and export – despite the fact that the company had no equity stakes in any of the major projects. The collapse of the Gazprom-Rosneft merger, which would have brought Gazprom into all of the Sakhalin projects (with the exception of Sakhalin 2 where the company has conducted separate negotiations) has made this problem even more difficult. But the different options for pipelines to East Asian markets from Sakhalin, Kovykhta and Chayandinskoye (Sakha Repub-lic), and the need for Gazprom to negotiate simultaneously with both existing equity holders in those projects and gas buyers, suggested that a resolution of joint venture agreements, sales contracts and financing of projects were unlikely to be achieved quickly.

While the commercial problems within Russia are complex, the obstacles to pipeline gas development in East Asian markets in 2005 are also substantial. The centrally important Asian market for Russian gas is China which is capable of absorbing very large quantities of gas. Thus far, the Chinese government has preferred to concentrate on domestic gas development and LNG imports, and has yet to signal that it considers large-scale pipeline imports desirable commercially and acceptable in terms of energy security. The speed with which such perceptions change will depend on general Sino-Russian relations and specifically oil developments, where the replacement in 2005 of plans for a direct (Angarsk-Daqing) oil pipeline to China, by a pipeline to an export terminal on the Pacific coast, damaged Russia's image in Beijing as a reliable supplier of pipeline fuels.

Pipeline gas to South Korea from eastern Siberia (Kovykhta and Sakha Republic) will depend on the speed with which China is prepared to accept gas from these projects. The only possible direct supply of gas to South Korea (from Sakhalin via North Korea) would require a resolution of political problems on the Korean Peninsula to the satisfaction of the United States. That outcome appears extremely unlikely in 2005, but probably more likely than the prospects for pipeline gas exports to Japan which, for political and commercial reasons – connected with the difficulty of building a national pipeline network and obtaining the cooperation of electricity utilities – have made no progress over the past several decades.

The surprising conclusion therefore, given the market potential for gas in East Asia and especially China, is that large-scale pipeline exports of Russian gas to this region are at least ten, and probably closer to twenty, years in the future. A breakthrough in political and commercial relations with China would be needed to change that conclusion.

In Eastern Siberia and the Far East, the lack of established infrastructure and a limited domestic market mean that if the very large gas resources identified in those regions do not find export markets, they will remain stranded. The prospects for, and timing of, Russian pipeline gas and LNG exports to Asia and the west coast of North America are project-specific and largely disconnected from the western Russian, CIS and European issues with which this study has been principally concerned. For this reason, suggestions that Russia may not have enough gas for Europe because of its desire to supply Asian markets are completely wrong. Although West Siberian fields could supply markets further east, and East Siberian fields could supply markets west of the Urals, neither of these options make any commercial sense even if infrastructure would allow such physical flows. As far as gas is concerned, Russia will remain two different 'countries': Western Siberia – west, and Eastern Siberia – east.

The delivery of Russian LNG from the Sakhalin 2 project to Japan, Korea and the west coast of Mexico starting in 2007–08 has been noted above. While there are additional prospects for expanding Russian LNG supplies to Asia, since 2003 it has been to the east and gulf coasts of North America that Gazprom's LNG attention has been devoted. A liquefaction terminal at Murmansk – based on the Shtokman field –became Gazprom's flagship LNG project, and in 2005 was most advanced in terms of planning and partner selection. Despite the very ambitious intention to start deliveries by 2010, a somewhat longer time scale seemed more likely given the complexity of the project. Smaller volumes of LNG could arrive on North America's east coast from a liquefaction terminal planned at Ust Luga (near St Petersburg). The Ust Luga terminal will depend on the same gas supply as the North European Pipeline and its development will therefore depend critically on the latter's timing (and possibly the progress of the Shtokman project). A liquefaction plant at the Kharasevey field could grow in attractiveness depending on the timing of large-scale gas production on the Yamal Peninsula for pipeline supply to the Russian market. Gazprom is also seeking to swap pipeline gas supplies to Europe for LNG, enabling the company to establish an early presence in the US market.

Despite all these exciting prospects, Gazprom's pipeline and LNG export options in Asia and North America cannot reach significant proportions in comparison to European export levels until the late 2020s at the earliest. But by 2005, Russian and Gazprom gas export horizons had substantially expanded beyond pipeline exports to Europe and that will be a big change in the future of Russian gas, particularly in the 2020s and beyond.

Gazprom: from Russian gas utility to 'global gas company'?

An important task for those involved in the Russian energy sector is to determine President Putin's strategic vision for Gazprom and the Russian gas sector, and his ability to implement that vision during the remainder of his term of office. The vision emerging in 2004 appeared to be that Gazprom should become a multinational oil and gas (and possibly electricity) company, representing the interests of the government both domestically and internationally – a Russian equivalent to Saudi Aramco or ExxonMobil.[7] In June 2005, this vision was strengthened by a document on the Gazprom website stating that:

> The strategic goal of Gazprom is to become a global, vertically integrated energy company occupying a leading position on the world market, combining exploration, production, transportation, storage, sales and distribution of natural gas and liquid hydrocarbons, electricity, and also the production of a wide spectrum of high value final products.[8]

The Gazprom-Rosneft merger would have been the first step towards a major role for the company in the international oil market.

The years since 2003 have been a turbulent period for the Russian oil sector due to the state-orchestrated demise of Yukos, the largest Russian oil-producing company. The dramatic consequences of the Yukos episode raised major issues about President Putin's commitment to democracy, market reform and foreign investment. In September 2004, in order to give the state a majority equity share in Gazprom and allow the liberalisation of the company's share market, the Russian government announced a merger of Gazprom and the state-owned oil company Rosneft. However, in May 2005 the Gazprom-Rosneft merger was abandoned due to complexities in the financial architecture of the transaction, and resistance from Rosneft management and their sponsors within government, who saw a better future for themselves as an independent oil company, following the acquisition of Yuganskneftegaz (YNG) – the main producing asset of Yukos which the government had forced the latter to sell in order to meet tax liabilities.[9] The government decided to acquire majority shareholding in Gazprom, by selling part of the equity of the merged Rosneft/YNG. This decision left Gazprom as a majority state-owned gas company, and Rosneft/YNG as a majority state-owned oil company, although both companies will retain a strong interest in the main business area of the other.

The failure of the Gazprom-Rosneft merger raised serious questions both as to the president's commitment to any clear vision for the Russian energy sector, beyond majority state ownership, and his ability to enforce it. It is still not out of the question that Gazprom will be allowed to acquire significant oil assets, but with the Russian government having created a powerful national oil company, the rationale for such action appeared weaker.[10] It remains to be seen how much power the state will confer on newly created Rosneft/YNG and Gazprom in the oil sector in terms of the award of future licences. In any event, domestic and foreign companies operating in the Russian oil and gas sectors may increasingly need to ask themselves whether their commercial aspirations are consistent with (or at least not in opposition to) the wishes of Rosneft/YNG and Gazprom. These companies may be able to block any significant development which they believe – or the Russian government and president believe – to be against their corporate or national interests.

Gazprom's future prospects are immense, but so too are the tasks that its management faces over the next decade and beyond, both domestically and internationally. In addition to the ongoing gas business challenges of:

- corporatisation and legal unbundling of the company, in particular the development of subsidiaries in charge of the main business units with increased financial responsibilities and cost controls;
- maintaining the reliability of a very large, ageing high pressure pipeline network with significant refurbishment requirements;
- replacing gas production from declining fields with new production from the Yamal Peninsula and offshore fields;
- developing and maintaining reliable large-scale import relationships with Central Asian countries;
- maintaining stable sales and transit relationships with Ukraine, Belarus and Moldova;
- managing a very large European export portfolio during a period of potentially far-reaching change in the direction of liberalisation and competition,

the management have set themselves (or been set by the government) the following additional tasks, of which the first two are scheduled to be completed within the next five years:

- developing the North European Pipeline as the next major expansion of exports to Europe;
- developing LNG export projects aimed at the North American market, with a primary focus on the Shtokman field and a liquefaction terminal at Murmansk;
- a pipeline (and perhaps also an LNG) export business in east Asia as government-appointed coordinator – and in reality arbiter – of domestic and export projects in Eastern Siberia and the Far East.

Any one of these tasks would pose a significant challenge for the management of any company. The length and complexity of this list raises the question of just how much management time will be available for any individual task or project. There is a clear and urgent need for Gazprom (and the Russian government) to develop strategic priorities, and a significant risk that some of the export projects, despite being huge opportunities, could also prove to be significant distractions.

Domestic resource and export projects on Gazprom's agenda in 2005 will require investments of more than $100bn. Even with the increased capitalisation of the company following the liberalisation of its share market, borrowing on this scale will be well beyond its means. This will impose a further constraint on how quickly many of these projects will be able to proceed. In the mid 2000s, pressing priorities for domestic supply and transmission, high European gas prices and a considerable corporate enthusiasm for LNG exports to North America, suggest that the Asian market might be lower down Gazprom's priorities. But changes in international oil and gas prices, and political relationships between Russia and its current and potential gas trade partners in Europe, Asia (particularly China) and the United States, could alter those priorities over the next decade.

The future of Russian gas, and the success of Gazprom, is dependent on some hugely complex and risky supply and market calculations. Unlike market economies where investment choices are generally dictated by profitability, for many decades the Russian gas industry supplied gas unprofitably to a huge domestic and CIS market, and highly profitably to the European market. Gazprom's tightening supply situation in the late 2000s and early 2010s will require careful allocation between its three markets: domestic, CIS and European. To a much greater extent than in the past, allocation will depend on profitability which in turn will depend on prices and costs, especially transportation and transit costs. But narrow considerations of the 'bottom line' will always be tempered, and sometimes overturned, by the political requirements – both domestic and international – of the Russian government.

The Gazprom-Rosneft merger was an opportunity for Gazprom to make a decisive break with its past as a Russian gas utility with exports to Europe, to a future as a multinational gas and oil company. The failure of the merger was a major setback for the oil dimension of that vision, but whether that setback is temporary or permanent is not yet clear. In an important respect it may prove to have been a positive development given the company's long list of domestic and international gas priorities. With very substantial gas exports to Europe, a clear intention to export LNG to North America, aspirations to export both LNG and pipeline gas to Asian countries, and potential investments in a variety of other countries, Gazprom is clearly becoming a powerful multinational, even 'global', gas company. But even should it achieve this status, it would still be far from its stated strategic goal of becoming a global *energy* company. A key question for Gazprom's future is whether these international aspirations can continue to successfully coexist with a huge gas pipeline (including distribution) network and social responsibilities to supply gas to domestic customers – the legacy of its past as a Soviet, now Russian, gas utility. The vision and skills needed to manage domestic gas transmission and distribution networks and sales, are very different from those needed to develop a 'global gas business', and the contradiction between these two roles may give a clue to the next major phase of reform and restructuring within the Russian gas industry.

NOTES

Chapter 1

1 This section focuses on resource development in Western Siberia and western Russia for delivery westwards; resource development in Eastern Siberia and the Russian Far East for eastern Russian and Asian markets is dealt with in Chapter 3.

2 S. A. Orudzhev, *Gazovaya Promyshlennost' po Puti Progressa*, Moscow, 1976, pp.26–43.

3 *Russian Energy Strategy 2003*, p.57.

4 Figures from the Head of the Department of Fuel and Natural Resources, *Eastern Bloc Energy*, November 2003, p.24.

5 Appendix 1.1 contains definitions of $A+B+C_1$, and proven and probable reserves.

6 This is probably because most of the reserves are in the C_1 category which does not register as 'proven and probable'.

7 Victor Baranov, 'The Union of Independent Gas Producers', paper to the 18th Annual European Autumn Gas Conference, Prague, 18–19 November, 2003. For membership of the Union see note 38.

8 In several Tables these fields are referred to by their correct Russian names – Urengoiskoye, Yamburgskoye, etc. The text refers to all fields by their anglicised abbreviations – Urengoy, Yamburg, and so on.

9 Although Valenginian production at Urengoy and Yamburg is separate and could therefore be counted as separate fields.

10 *Russian Energy Strategy 2003*, p.73. Note that for Urengoy and Yamburg these figures are higher than those in Table 1.4 because the latter are % depletion of total reserves rather than the easy to access reserves.

11 *Russian Energy Strategy* 2003, p.75.

12 However, this is by no means an impossible task. Novatek's Yukharovneftegas (see below) is producing gas from Valengenian horizons.

13 *Loan Notes 2003*, pp.104–5.

14 The issue of customers and sources of gas in eastern Russia is dealt with separately in Chapter 3.

15 IEA, *Russian Energy Survey 2002*, Table 5.2, p.112.

16 The early history and cost estimates for Yamal are summarised in Jonathan Stern, *The Russian Natural Gas Bubble*, 1995, pp.15–27.

17 *VNIIgaz*. Gazprom refers to this as: 'Program for Comprehensive Development of Hydrocarbon Deposits on the Yamal Peninsula and under its Adjacent Waters'. A useful summary of the conclusions can be found in 'Gazprom's $69bn question – when to start developing Yamal gas?' *Gas Matters*, October 2004, pp.27–32.

18 *Eastern Bloc Energy,* June 2002, pp.23−4. However, the fact that these reserves have not been part of the DeGolyer and McNaughton independent assessment in Table 1.1 above means that a substantial amount of uncertainty needs to be attached to the Russian figures.
19 'Gazprom completes exploration drilling at Kara Sea section', *Interfax Petroleum Report,* September 1−7, 2000, pp.15−16. *Eastern Bloc Energy,* December 2003, p.22.
20 VNIIgaz, Table 4.4.19
21 Zapac karman ne tyanet, *Gazprom,* No. 6, June 2004, pp.18−19.
22 At mid-2002, Deputy Chairman Ryazanov suggested that the cost of producing Yamal gas would be $20/mcm which would give a delivered cost in central/western Russia of $40−50/mcm. *Interfax Petroleum Report,* July 12−18, 2002, p.18.
23 This fourth option is listed in the VNIIgaz study but does not appear to have been taken further.
24 Data from the VNIIgaz Institute cited in *Eastern Bloc Energy,* March 2004, p.7
25 'Yamal administration considers several gas transport options', *Interfax Petroleum Report,* November 4−10, 2004, p.25.
26 Press Conference with Alexander Ryazanov and Alexander Medvedev, March 2, 2004; *Gazprom's management committee examined paramount measures for the development of the Yamal Peninsula fields,* Press Release, November 27, 2003.
27 *Loan Notes* 2004, p.59.
28 See *Gas Matters Today,* June 22, 2004 quoting Deputy Chairman Ananenkov.
29 *Management committee reviews Gazprom's preliminary operating results for 2004 and main draft financial documents over 2005 to 2007,* Press Release, December 1, 2004; *Gazprom completes first phase of Bovanenko field investment planning,* Press Release, January 25, 2005.
30 David Tarr and Peter Thompson, *The Merits of Dual Pricing of Russian Natural Gas,* The World Bank, July 19, 2003.
31 *VNIIgaz*; the investment estimates in this paragraph can be assumed to be in 2002 dollars.
32 There is no reserve evaluation according to international classification.
33 See the section on LNG in Chapter 3.
34 Russia revives Shktokman ownership structure but leaves finance and marketing questions unanswered, *Gas Briefing International,* January 2003, pp.8−9.
35 Gazprom assumes management of Sevmorneftegaz, *Interfax Oil and Gas Report,* April 14−20, 2005, pp.24−5.
36 *Meeting on Yuzhno-Russskoye Development Held,* Gazprom Press Release, March 17, 2004.
37 *Gazprom stremitsa na gazovoy rinok SshA,* interview with Alexander Ryazanov in Eurasia Offshore, October 19, 2004, 'Pryamaya Rech', www.gazprom. ru

38 Soyuzgaz comprises 9 companies and production joint ventures: Artikgaz, Novatek, Northgas, Purneftegazgeologika, Sibneftegaz, Tarkosaleneftegaz, Khancheyneftegaz, Centrusgaz and National Oil and Gas Technologies. Itera is not a full member but is involved through its 70% ownership in Sibneftegaz.

39 Little information is available about Trans Nafta (which some have suggested is a Gazprom company); it appears to be a company managed by a small group of wealthy Russian individuals.

40 'Lukoil optimising oil production', *Interfax Petroleum Report*, April 4–10, 2003, pp. 9–10

41 *Gazprom i Lukoil podpicali dogovor po postavku gaza*, Gazprom Press release, October 22, 2003, *Lukoil and Gazprom enter into general agreement on strategic partnership over 2005 to 2014*, Gazprom Press Release, March 29, 2005.

42 We return to the question of Far East development in Chapter 3, *Ob itogakh rabochey vstrechi Alexei Miller c Sergeyem Bogdanchikovim I Vladimirom Bogdanovim*, Press Release November 21, 2003, www.gazprom.ru

43 TNK/BP buys Rospan from Yukos, *Interfax Petroleum Report*, August 12–18, 2004, p.14.

44 *Ob itogakh rabochey vstrechi Alexeya Millera i Sergeya Bogdanchikova*, Gazprom Press Release April 15, 2004, www.gazprom.ru

45 VNIIgaz 2002.

46 For details of Itera's CIS sales see Chapter 2. Brief details of the company's history and activities can be found on its website: www.itera.ru

47 IEA, *Russian Energy Survey 2002*, pp.116–17.

48 Marshall Goldman, *The Piratization of Russia*, 2003, p.111.

49 There were protests – in particular by Boris Fedorov of United Financial Group and representative of small shareholders on the Gazprom supervisory Board – that such investigations should be carried out by independent (rather than Gazprom's) auditors. Andrew Jack, 'Gazprom auditors to probe links with Itera,' *Financial Times*, March 15, 2001.

50 Andrew Jack, 'Link between Gazprom and Itera found,' *Financial Times*, March 14, 2001.

51 Andrew Jack, 'Auditors find no evidence of deals that aided Itera,' *Financial Times*, July 6, 2001. 'Audit Chamber does not uncover any infringements in Gazprom-Itera relations,' *Interfax Petroleum Report*, July 13–19, 2001, pp.18–19.

52 For details on Itera's purchase of 51% of Rospan International in January 2000 and subsequent bankruptcy of that company, sale of its shares to Yukos and continued accusations of impropriety, see 'Rospan International Declared Bankrupt, Yukos has net profit to GAAP of $3.47bn in 2001, State Duma member wants investigation of Rospan International privatisation,' *Interfax Petroleum Report*, August 18–4, 2000, pp.11–12; June 7–13, 2002, pp.12–13; August 22–8, pp.11–12.

53 Ownership of Itera remained mysterious with much of the equity being held by trusts. The company has published IAS accounts but the information on its website is rudimentary. It has repeatedly said that it intends to obtain

a stock exchange listing with a view to an IPO but has not done so in 2005. This allowed critics to place the worst possible construction on its activities. Nevertheless, in 2004 the company received an award from the *Euromoney* publication as a leader in Russian corporate governance. Andrew Jack and Robert Cottrell, 'Itera to publish list of owners,' *Financial Times*, March 30, 2001; Makarov, 'Oil and gas production grows harder each year,' *Interfax Petroleum Report*, November 14–20, 2003, pp.9–10; 'Itera recognised as leader in corporate governance', *Itera Press Release* April 27, 2004.

54 Gas Industry News, *Interfax Petroleum Report*, February 16–22, 2001, p.17.
55 *Loan notes* 2004, p.53.
56 'Itera becomes Russia's second largest gas producer,' *Interfax Petroleum Report*, June 4–10, 1999, pp.17–18.
57 *Gazprom Audit Report 2003*, Note 19.
58 'Gazprom to restrict Itera shipments to Azerbaidzhan, Kazakhstan, Ukraine'. *Interfax Petroleum Report*, November 22–8, 2002, pp.15–16.
59 'Uzbekistan to cut Russian gas company's transit,' BBC Monitoring Service, July 15, 2003.
60 'Gazprom offers Georgia gas,' *Interfax Petroleum Report*, January 23–9, 2004. p.15.
61 *Meeting of General Director of OOO Gazexport A.I. Medvedev with journalists from Azerbaidzhan*, Press conference February 9, 2004, www.gazprom.ru. Subsequently it was suggested that this would only be the case in the winter; in summer with lower demand, Itera would be able to supply Azerbaijan, but this did not happen. *Interfax Petroleum Report*, March 5–11, 2004, p.19.
62 'Sibneftegaz to get $13mln loan from Itera,' *Interfax Petroleum Report*, April 2–8, 2004, p.23.
63 'Itera loses stakes in Tarkosalneftegaz and Khancheyneftegaz,' *European Gas Markets*, January 14, 2005, p.12.
64 *Gazprom Audit Report 2003*, Note 9. (Note: the English translation of this document: Auditorskie Zakluchenie po Svodnoi Finansovoi (Bukhaltorskoi) Otchotnosti 2003 God, is somewhat unreliable, particularly in respect of the translation of units.
65 'Gazprom rekindles co-operation with rival Itera,' *European Gas Markets*, October 30, 2003, p.11.
66 The company appears to have arranged purchases of more than 14 Bcm/year for the period 2005–07, 'Itera IAS Profit up 29% I 2004,' *Interfax Oil and Gas Report*, December 2–8, 2004.
67 *'Itera invests into oil and gas projects in Kakmykia,'* Press Release 11/11/2004; 'President of Turkmenistan Sapamurat Niyazov received Igor Makarov, the Head of Itera Group,' *Press Release* 22/06/2004. www.itera.ru
68 www.novatek.ru; The 2003 figure is the total production from fields in which Novatek has an interest, the company's share of production was around 13.5 Bcm.
69 A.A. Koudrin, *Gas Business in Russia: the experience of an independent gas producing*

company, IEA 2003.

70 'Novatek to increase charter capital,' *Interfax Petroleum Report*, August 26—September 1, 2004, pp.5—6.

71 'Total plans to buy 25% of Novatek,' *Interfax Petroleum Report*, September 16—22, 2004, pp.5—6.

72 'Novatek and other Russian independents strengthen their position in Russian gas,' *Gas Matters Today*,October 28, 2004.

73 Nortgaz is the transliteration of the Russian name of the company; in its English-language publicity material, the company uses the name 'Northgas'.

74 'Northgas battles Gazprom to independent Russian producers' rights,' *Gas Briefing International*, February 2003, pp.1—2.

75 Northgas Russian Gas Company (publicity material) www.northgas.ru

76 'Northgas battles Gazprom to independent Russian producers' rights,' *Gas Briefing International*, February 2003, pp.1—2.

77 'Ministry to appeal cancellation of Northgas license,' *Interfax Oil and Gas Report*, May 5—11, 2005, pp.11-—12; 'Northgas says Gazprom trying to regulate independent production,' *Interfax Oil and Gas Report*, April 21—7, 2005, pp.26—7.

78 'Gazprom-Northgas agreement to be signed next week,' *Interfax Oil and Gas Report*, May 12—18, 2005, pp.27—8.

79 D.Yu. Kordunov, 'CentrRusgas: the role of an intermediary in the Russian gas business environment,' International Energy Agency/Union of Independent Gas Producers Conference on, Energy Security: The Role of Russian Gas Companies, November 2003. http://www.iea.org/dbtwwpd/textbase/work/2003/soyuzgaz/proceedings/Kordunov.pdf

80 *Loan notes* 2005, p.134.

81 *Loan notes* 2004, pp.120—21.

82 Voina I mir, *Gazprom*, December 2004, pp.14—15.

83 *Gazprom Audit Report 2003*, pp.25 and 29.

84 Voina i mir, *Gazprom*, No. 12, December 2004, pp.14—15. See IEA *Russia Energy Survey 2002*, p.122, for a range of alternative, not very attractive, investment options for oil companies in the late 1990s.

85 Vysokii Peredel, *Gazprom*, No. 3, March 2005, pp.6—9.

86 Voina i mir, *Gazprom*, No. 12, December 2004, pp.14—15; the title of this article 'War and Peace' is intended to show the shift in the relationship between Sibur and the oil producers.

87 http://www.novatek.ru/rus/our_business/processing

88 Interview with Viktor Gyrya, *Gazprom*, No. 12, December 2004, p.64.

89 Interview with Yosif Levinson, in *Neft I Kapital*, III 2004, special issue on Yamal, pp.3—10.

90 *Neft I Kapital*, Ibid., p.42.

91 This is likely to have been because Gazprom took back the South Russkoye field from Itera in the period between publication of the different versions of the Strategy. *Energeticheskaya Strategiya Rossii na Period do 2020 Goda*,May 22, 2003, figure 11, p.65.

92 *Gazprom uvelichivaet plani po dobycha gaza*, Press Release, October 23, 2003, www.gazprom.ru; *the Gazprom Annual Report 2003* (p.11) notes in its review of the year that 'new production targets of 580−590 Bcm in 2020 were established'.

93 *Ob itorakh vyesdnogo zasedaniya komissii gazovoi promysholennosti po razrabotke mestorozhdenii I ispolzovaniyu nedr*, Press Release, April 19, 2004, www.gazprom.ru

94 Prodolzhaem rasti, *Gazprom*, No 1−2, January−February 2005, pp.6−9.

95 VNIIgaz 2002.

96 Gazprom is projecting production around 547 Bcm in 2005, less than 2 Bcm above the 2004figure. 'Gazprom approves domestic gas quotes for 2005,' *Press Release*, November 10, 2004, www.gazprom.ru

97 See *Eastern Bloc Energy*, September 2004, pp.6−8 for a technical explanation of the problems. This gives details of the compression needed to produce the gas reservoirs as they enter the decline phase and concludes that: 'around 5% of the reserves can be produced very slowly and utilised by local consumers while 10% are irrecoverable. This means that in the reservoirs of Urengoy, Yamburg and Medvezhe alone, at least 1100 Bcm of gas could be left in the ground.'

98 Some of this independent production is from fields on the Yamal Peninsula which would require a transmission system to be established before production could begin. S.V. Gmyzin, 'Yamal-Nenets Autonomous Region: the core of Russian gas security', Paper to the 2nd International Conference on: Energy Security, the Role of Russian Gas Companies, International Energy Agency, Paris, November 2003.

99 During the Soviet period, the gas industry imported large quantities of large diameter pipeline and compressor stations from European and Japanese companies. These imports covered some – but by no means all – the requirements of the industry.

100 *Gazprom Annual Report 2003*, p.46.

101 *VNIIgaz*, Table 4

102 *Loan Notes 2004*, pp. 116−17.

103 See intervention of Pavel Zevalnie, in the round table discussion, in *Neft I Kapital*, III 2004, special issue on Yamal, p.32.

104 In fact, Table 1.3 shows that during the period 1999−2003 only in one year (2001) did withdrawals exceed injections.

105 'Zavicet' v trube stalo nevigono,' *Gazprom*, No 5, May 2004, pp.18−19.

106 *Loan Notes 2005*, p.128.

107 *Ibid.*

108 For details see IEA, *Energy Survey of Russia*, 1995, pp.164−5

109 IEA,*Russia Energy Survey 2002*, p.119

110 Mezhregiongaz is a shortened version of Mezhregionalnaya Kompaniya po Realizatsii Gaza (Interregional Company for Gas Sales), *OOO 'Mezhregiongaz': 7 let na rinke gaza Rossii*, Briefingi i press conferentsii, June 10, 2004. www.gazprom.ru

111 Decree No 328, May 22, 2002.

112 This margin is called a 'payment for supply/demand services' (PSSU in Russian).

113 There are differences in the figures from different sources as to the numbers of companies. *Loan Notes* 2005, p.147.

114 *Management Committee approved conception of the Gazprom group's asset consolidation in gas distribution sector, Press Release*, May 24, 2004. www.gazprom.ru

115 'Gazprom re-names core utility,' *Interfax Petroleum Report*, September 30–October 6, 2004, p.28.

116 Kirill Seleznev: *Seti prikhodit v negodnost'*, *a rolova bolit u Gazproma*, Interview in Vedemosti, August 5, 2004, Pryamaya Rech, www.gazprom.ru

117 *Ibid*, Udmurt and Krasnodar are regions where such agreements have been reached.

118 'Gosudarstvo nuzhno vernutsa v gazoraspredelenie,' *Gazprom*, No.12, December 2004, pp.10–11.

119 The majority of leakage in the Russian system is in the distribution network where metering has traditionally been so poor that accurate estimates are not possible.

120 For previous attempts to estimate Russian gas demand see Jonathan Stern, *The Russian Natural Gas Bubble*, 1995, pp.31–4; IEA *Energy Survey of Russia*, 1995, pp.171–3; IEA *Russian Energy Survey2002*, pp.124–6. The IEA data are particularly difficult to interpret in terms of consistency over time since they use OECD end-user classifications.

121 *OECD Economic Survey of the Russian Federation*, 2004, pp.132–7.

122 It is unclear whether the government has any influence over this allocation or whether Mezhregiongaz has total control over the process.

123 *OECD Economic Survey of the Russian Federation*, 2004, p.133.

124 For producers without access to customers, not wishing to take on the difficulties of access to Gazprom's network, there could be advantages in selling to Gazprom (as we saw above in the case of Lukoil) despite the potential price disadvantages.

125 'Drug drugu', *Gazprom*, No. 10, October 2004, pp.7–9.

126 'Nuzhno sozdat' yedinuyu skhemu razvitiya otryasl', *Gazprom*, No. 10, October 2004, pp.10–11.

127 This is a difficult judgement to make in the absence of temperature-corrected data; particularly in a country such as Russia where cold winters can add substantially to gas demand.

128 *Verbatim report of Alexander Ryazanov's speech given at the annual meeting with the RF President and Government's regional authorities' representatives*, April 2004, Pryamaya Rech, www.gazprom.ru

129 *West European gas consumption increased further in 2003*, Press Release February 2004, www.eurogas.be

130 Industrial prices in Zone 5 (around Moscow) are generally used as a proxy for Russian domestic gas prices.

131 Alexander Ryazanov's speech given at the annual meeting with the RF President and Government's regional authorities representatives, April 2, 2004, 'Spravochnyi Materiali', www.gazprom.ru

132 This statement of general agreement included Gazprom, Russian govern-
     ment ministries, the Federal Regulatory Commission and independent
     producers.
133 This consensus is not backed up by hard calculations demonstrating such
     profitability, but in 2004 it was a generally agreed figure.
134 'Tariff service says 11 gas price zones to remain until 2010,' *Interfax Petroleum
     Report*, November 11–17, 2004, p.11.
135 At the January 2005 exchange rate of $1 = RR28
136 *OECD Economic Survey of the Russian Federation*, 2004 Table 32, p.131.
137 Igor Bashmakov, *Energy Subsidies in Russia: the case of district heating*, in eds,
     Anna Von Moltke, Colin McKee and Trevor Morgan, *Energy Subsidies*,
     UNEP/Greenleaf Publishing, 2003, pp.68–75.
138 The figures given by Gazprom for 2004 were: the price of coal was 1.0,
     the price of gas was 0.88 and the price of fuel oil was 1.88. *Tarifnaya
     Politika*, presentation by Yelena Karpel', Brifingi I Press Conferentzii, June
     1, 2005.
139 M.P. Melnikova, 'Gas Sector Role in Energy Security,' Chart 12, IEA
     Conference on Energy Security, November 25, 2003.
140 RAO Gazprom, *IAS Consolidated Financial Statement*, December 31, 1996.
141 RAO Gazprom, *IAS Consolidated Financial Statement*, December 31, 1997; this
     compares with 29% and 12% respectively in Table 1.17.
142 *Government Resolution No 1*, January 5, 1998; *Government Resolution No 364*,
     May 29, 2002.
143 'Accounts Receivable' is defined as monies due for gas delivered including
     VAT but excluding late payment charges. *Loan Notes 2005*, p.147.
144 *Alexander Ryazanov's speech given at the annual meeting with the RF President and
     Government's regional authorities representatives*, April 2004; www.gazprom.ru; in
     2004 the worst of the remaining non-payment in the North Caucasus was
     in the Republics of Daghestan (payment 31% of receivables), Ingushetia
     (34%), Kabardino-Balkaria (55%) and North Ossetia (65%), Otklyuchim
     gaz, *Gazprom*, July–August 2004, pp.12–13.
145 Jonathan Stern, *The Russian Natural Gas Bubble*, 1995, Tables 2.6 and 4.2,
     pages 42 and 85. In this discussion, the definition of 'demand' is gas
     delivered to customers; it does not include pipeline fuel and losses in the
     production/transportation process.
146 The EBRD estimates that Russian GDP and industrial output fell in 1995,
     1996 and 1998, although both measures increased slightly in 1997 and
     strongly in 1999; thereafter both trends have been positive. European Bank
     for Reconstruction and Development, *Transition Report 2003*, p.187.
147 As noted above in Chapter 3, these are heroic (and not necessarily correct)
     assumptions.
148 Gas Industry News, *Interfax Petroleum Report*, May 2–15, 2003 p.16.
149 'V poiskakh elastichnost', *Gazprom*, No 12, December 2004, pp.22–3.
150 'Gazprom delaet yeshcho odun shag navstrechu nezavisimim proizvodite-
     lyam gaza,' *Gazprom* No. 5, May 2004, pp.20–21.
151 *Russian Energy Strategy 2003*, pp.31–2.

152 *Russian Energy Strategy 2003,* p.15
153 IEA, *World Energy Outlook 2004,* Paris: OECD, pp. 474–5.
154 Ibid., p.423.
155 It is traditional for Russian energy policies/strategies to project that coal and nuclear power will replace gas for power generation. In fact, it was largely the failure of those sectors in the 1970s and 80s that created such a large gas-fired power generation sector which was never intended by the Soviet authorities.
156 IEA, *Russian Energy Survey 2002,* Figure 21, p.230.
157 'Gazprom remains number one source of budget revenues,' *Interfax Petroleum Report,* June 5–11, 1998, p.13. 2003 figure from the presentation by Alexander Ryazanov, April 2004, loc. cit.
158 Reuters, July 2, 1998 reported Deputy Prime Minister Boris Nemtsov as saying that the government owed Gazprom RR13bn while Gazprom owed the government RR12bn. In October 1998 with the appointment of a new tax chief by the Primakov government, it was announced that Gazprom had overpaid 1.5bn rubles to the government. *Interfax Petroleum Report,* October 16–22, 1998, p.13.
159 Government institutions – known in Russia as 'budget organisations' – were very high on Gazprom's list of non-payers during the 1990s.
160 Gazprom's head office was continually being visited by regional political authorities and enterprises carrying the same message.
161 Gas Industry News, *Interfax Petroleum Report,* June 19–25, 1998, p.15.
162 Of the other taxes paid by Gazprom specific to the gas industry, road users' tax (abolished in 2003), mineral use tax (abolished in 2002), property tax and mineral restoration tax (replaced in 2002 by mineral extraction tax) have been the most significant. The company VAT and profits tax payments are itemised in the accounts as the largest payments aside from excise tax.
163 *Gazprom Financial Report 2003,* p.30. In addition, the taxation of gas condensate was changed from 16.5% to RR340/ton, and property tax was increased from 2% to 2.2%
164 This Appendix has been slightly amended from Loan Notes 2005, pp.104–6.

Chapter 2

1 With the exception of Turkmen exports to Iran which started in 1997 and were around 5–6 Bcm/year in 2003–04.
2 For example in the trades between Kazakhstan and Uzbekistan; Uzbekistan, Kyrgyzstan and Tajikistan, and Turkmenistan, Azerbaijan, Georgia and Armenia.
3 Similar agreements were signed with central and east European governments before the break-up of the Council for Mutual Economic Assistance

(Comecon) in 1991.

4 After 1993 it becomes impossible to determine precisely which gas was delivered from Russian sources and which from Central Asian although it is most likely that Gazprom gas was delivered exclusively from Russian fields while Itera's gas was predominantly from Central Asian sources, in particular Turkmenistan. It is doubtful that Itera could have profitably sold large quantities of Siberian gas to former republics given the transportation charges that would have been involved.

5 It is not possible to explain the statistical differences between the export breakdown in Table 2.4 and the detailed 2003 data in Table 2.5 – particularly since these are from the same source.

6 Although this mainly affects Table 2.4; Uzbek imports of gas, if they took place at all, would have been marginal and Table 2.5 does include Uzbek exports.

7 The quota reached a high of 15.6 Bcm in 1991 (although the high point of deliveries to former republics was reached the previous year at 78.7 Bcm). Akira Miyamoto, *Natural Gas in Central Asia*, 1998, pp.46–7.

8 Ibid., p.45.

9 Ibid., pp.49–51. Turkmenrosgaz was also intended to carry out exploration and pipeline construction although no details of any projects were ever made public. The failure of these initiatives was one of the reasons given by the Turkmen president for the winding up of the company.

10 'Ukraine resumes Turkmen gas imports as Itera clears some debt,' 'Chernomyrdin's visit ends in price deadlock,' *Gas Briefing International*, December 1997 p.XIV and February 1998, p.XI.

11 'Ukraine replaces Turkmen gas with Uzbek,' *Interfax Petroleum Report*, October 9–15, 1998, pp. 16–17.

12 'Chernomyrdin's Turkmen visit ends in price deadlock,' *Gas Briefing Europe*, February 28, 1998, p.11.

13 There is anecdotal evidence that Turkmen production wells suffered severe technical problems from being shut down and when the industry attempted to restart production, many could not be reopened. This added to Turkmen determination not to allow such a situation to recur.

14 'Turkmens desperately seeking exports while Turks gird themselves for power,' *Gas Matters*, November 1998, p.11.

15 'Blue Stream becoming foreign policy priority,' *Interfax Petroleum Report*, September 24–30, 1999, pp.10–11. For details of the Blue Stream pipeline see Chapter 3.

16 'Turkmen gas flows again to Ukraine,' *Gas Briefing Europe*, January 28, 1999, p.12; 'Turkmenistan to resume gas shipments to Ukraine,' *Interfax Petroleum Report*, January 8–14, 1999, pp.3–4.

17 The former Gazprom chairman can rarely have been required to humble himself in such a very public manner for saying that if the Turkmens did not want to accept the terms being offered for their gas they could 'eat sand'. A transcript of this meeting (which was also attended by the president of Itera, Igor Makarov) on December 17, 1999 was made avail-

able by WATAN TV News.

18 'Turkmenistan agrees sales to Russia, but not Ukraine,' *Interfax Petroleum Report*, December 24 1999–January 6 2000, pp.11–12.

19 Although it was unclear how future Turkmen imports would have resolved those problems.

20 'Vyakhirev: Gazprom may sign long term deal on Turkmen gas in April,' *Interfax Petroleum Report*, February 25–March 2, 2000, pp. 18–19.

21 'Russia to import more gas for Turkmenistan,' *Interfax Petroleum Report*, May 26–June 1, 2000, pp. 16–17.

22 In addition to those two companies with 25.5% each, the partners in Shah Deniz in late 2004 were: Socar, LukAgip and NICO, each with 10% and TPAO 9%. 'Lukoil to buy ENI out of Shah Deniz,' *Gas Matters Today*, June 30, 2004.

23 'Trans-Caspian gas pipeline project in jeopardy,' *Interfax Petroleum Report*, March 3–9, 2000, pp.14–15.

24 'PSG reduces staff as Trans-Caspian project falters,' *Gas Briefing International*, June 2000, p.1.

25 'Turkmenistan to resume gas exports to Ukraine,' *Interfax Petroleum Report*, August 4–10, 2000, pp.17–18.

26 'Turkmenistan and Ukraine sign agreement for natural gas supplies,' *Interfax Petroleum Report*, October 13–19, 2000, pp.14–15.

27 'Turkmenistan suspends gas exports to Russia in new price dispute,' *Gas Briefing Europe*, January 28, 2001, p.11; 'Turkmenistan celebrates 10 Bcm gas supply deal with Russia,' *Gas Matters Today*, February 18, 2001.

28 'Turkmenistan to supply 250 Bcm of gas to Ukraine in 2002–06,' *Interfax Petroleum Report*, May 18–24, 2001, p.21.

29 'Gazprom and Turkmenistan discuss long term supply contract,' *Gas Matters Today*, November 28, 2001.

30 'Turkmenistan signs contracts with Ukrainian, Russian firms,' BBC Monitoring Service, October 28, 2002.

31 'Russia, Turkmenistan presidents sign long-term gas agreement in Moscow,' *Interfax Petroleum Report*, April 18–24, 2003, pp.22–4. Russians and Turkmens put differences aside to sign 1.6Tcm trade deal, *Gas Matters*, April 2003, p.7.

32 We return in the section on Ukraine (below) to the shipping arrangements for Turkmen gas post-2004.

33 'Turkmenistan may increase gas prices for Russia, Ukraine,' *InterfaxOil and Gas Report*, December 2–8, 2004, p.35.

34 In some accounts the stoppage was said to be due to repairs on the Central Asia-Centre pipeline but much more likely is that while the gas was not flowing necessary repairs were indeed carried out.

35 *Ob itogakh vizita delegatsii OAO Gazprom v Turkmenistan*, Gazprom Press Release, April 15, 2005. Note: the English version of the press release contains much less information than the Russian version on the key issue of price; neither version acknowledges the key change to 100% cash which is contained in press reports.

36 Turkmenistan and Russia agree gas supply terms for 2005 and 2006, *Gas Matters Today*, April 26, 2005.
37 Marika S. Karayianni, 'Russia's foreign policy for Central Asia passes through energy agreements,' *Central Asia and the Caucasus*, No. 4, (22), 2003, pp. 90–96. The high import price relative to regulated Russian prices accounts for the small volumes actually imported by Gazprom prior to 2006. Itera was not required to sell at regulated prices.
38 For details see Najeeb Jung, 'Natural Gas in India,' in Ian Wybrew-Bond and Jonathan Stern (eds), *Natural Gas in Asia*, 2002, especially pp.79–85.
39 Marika S. Karayiannyi, 'Russia's foreign policy for Central Asia passes through energy agreements,' op.cit. pp.90–96. In April 2005, the Asian Development Bank declared the TAP project 'feasible and viable'. 'TAP dancing towards reality finally,' *Gas Matters*, April 2005, p.42.
40 'Gazprom declines Turkmen and Kazakh gas outlets to the West,' *Gas Briefing International*, September 1997, p.VIII.
41 'Lukoil/Gazprom in Kazakh Swap,' *International Gas Report*, July 5, 1996, p.9.
42 'Gazprom declines Turkmen and Kazakh gas outlets to the West,' *Gas Briefing International*, September 1997, p.VIII.
43 'Opportunism and Serendipity put Tractebel in a pivotal position in Central Asian gas,' *Gas Matters*, July 1998, p.13.
44 'Yet again Tractebel finds Kazakhstan intractable as assets and bank accounts are frozen,' *Gas Briefing International*, March 2000, p.14.
45 'Russia, Kazakhstan create gas joint venture,' *Interfax Petroleum Report*, May 26–June 1, 2000, p.15.
46 'Kazakhstan courts Russia in bid to increase gas exports,' *Gas Briefing International*, October 2001, pp. 3–14.
47 Although a Gazprom press release on Kazrosgaz states that it was formed in November 2001, it may be that this was only announced in June 2002. Initially Gazprom took only a 20% share in the joint venture but raised this to 50% in 2003. 'Directors' board of Gazprom approved acquisition of interest in Kazrosgaz,' Gazprom Press Release, July 21, 2003.
48 'Russia, Kazakhstan sign oil transit deal,' *Interfax Petroleum Report*, June 14–20, 2002, pp.6–7.
49 Raushan Nurshayeva, 'Kazakhstan, Gazprom to form European gas venture,' Reuters New Agency, May 17, 2002.
50 Alexander I Medvedev, *Press conference for Azerbaijan journalists*, February 9, 2004; subsequently these volumes have increased, see the section on Azerbaijan below.
51 *Results of meeting on cooperation between Gazprom and Republic of Kazakhstan in gas processing*. Gazprom Press Release, August 24, 2004; *Interfax Petroleum Report*, May 20–27, 2004, p.9.
52 *Ob itogakhk raboshey vstrechi Alexeya Millera i Timura Kulibaeva*, Gazprom Press Release, March 18, 2005.
53 Kazmunaigaz could start shipping gas to China by late 2008, *Interfax Oil and Gas Report*, February 3_9, 2005, p.30; Klara G. Rakhmetovo,

Transportation of Oil and Gas in Kazakhstan, Energy Charter Secretariat Conference on Energy Transit in Eurasia: challenges and perspectives, October 18-19, 2004; http://www.encharter.org//upload/9/668330802107360765343152272772074418117344441433f2468v1.pdf.

54 Kazakhstan has built additional pipelines in order to become independent of Uzbek gas in 2004.
55 'Ukraine replaces Turkmen gas with Uzbek,' *Interfax Petroleum Report*, October 9-15, 1998, pp.16-17.
56 Reuters, December 17, 2002.
57 'Gazprom signs pipeline deal with Kazakhstan and Uzbekistan and close to new deals in Italy,' *Gas Matters Today*, January 24, 2003.
58 'The Shakhpakhty field and fields in the Ust Yurt region; Uzbekneftegaz may sign 2nd PSA with Gazprom,' *Interfax Petroleum Report*, May 13-19, 2004, pp.28-9.
59 'Uzbekneftegaz, Lukoil sign PSA,' *Interfax Petroleum Report*, June 17-23, 2004, pp.29-30.
60 'On the outcomes of the meeting between Aleksey Miller and Akil Akilov,' *Gazprom Press Release*, April 24, 2003; 'The results of Aleksey Miller and Nikolay Tanaev's working meeting,' *Gazprom Press Release*, January 21, 2004.
61 For details see: Marika S. Karayianni, 'Russia's foreign policy for Central Asia passes through energy agreements,' *Central Asia and the Caucasus*, No. 4(22), 2003, pp.90-96.
62 *Central Asia Energy Monthly*, November 2004, p.12.
63 'Chechnya pipe break cuts off Russian gas supplies to Azerbaijan, and Gazexport agrees to increase supplies to Azerbaijan following supply interruption,' *Gas Matters Today*, July 7and September 2, 2004; *Caucasus Energy Monthly*, December 2004, p.7.
64 Alexander I Medvedev, *Press conference for Azerbaijan journalists*, February 9, 2004.
65 'Russia seeks involvement in Georgian gas market,' *European Gas Markets*, April 30, 2003, p.10.
66 Fiona Hill, *Energy Empire: oil and gas and Russia's revival*, London: The Foreign Policy Centre, September 2004, p.4.
67 'Makarov: oil and gas production grows harder each year,' *Interfax Petroleum Report*, November 14-20, 2003, pp.9-11.
68 'Gazprom offers Georgia gas,' *Interfax Petroleum Report*, January 23-29, 2004, p.15.
69 'Results of Alexey Miller and Zurab Zhvania's working meeting,' *Gazprom Press Release*, May 25, 2004.
70 'Georgia confident of reaching deal with Gazprom,' *Interfax Petroleum Report*, May 6-12, 2004, p.10.
71 Gas industry news, *Interfax Petroleum Report*, December 1-7, 2000, p.20.
72 *Caucasus Energy Monthly*, October 2004, Vol. II, No. 5, p.11.
73 'US Ambassador says Georgia should hold onto gas pipe,' *Interfax Oil and Gas Report*, March 17-25, 2005, p.33.

74 For details of the Shah Deniz project since the signing of the PSA in 1996, see 'Sanction of Shah Deniz opens door to corridor – but where will it lead?'; 'Whatever happened to Shah Deniz?' *Gas Matters*, March 2003, pp.8–12 and August 2004, pp.36–40. For technical details see 'Shah Deniz – Stage 1 becomes a reality,' IEA/ECS Seminar on Natural Gas in South East Europe, May 5–6, 2004. www.iea.org.

75 'Azerbaijan may stop importing Russian gas from 2007,' *Interfax Petroleum Report*, June 3–9, 2004, p.29.

76 'Armenian energy crisis caused by friction between other CIS states,' BBC Monitoring Service, SU/W0263, A/10-11, January 8, 1993.

77 Gas Industry News, *Interfax Petroleum Report*, August 21–27, 1998, p.18.

78 'Results of Alexey Miller and Robert Kocharyan's working meeting,' *Gazprom Press Release*, May 14, 2004.

79 Report on Armenian 'emergency' after destruction of pipeline, *Ibid*, SU 1597 C1/1, January 27, 1993.

80 'Desperate Armenia offers to pay for pipe from Iran,' *World Gas Intelligence*, June 1993, p.16; 'Gazprom is ready to fund Iran-Armenia pipeline,' BBC Monitoring Service, SU/W0616, WA/7, November 26, 1999.

81 'Iran agrees to supply gas to Armenia from 2007,' *Gas Matters Today*, May 14, 2004. There is a separate contract for Iran to supply the enclave of Nakhichevan.

82 *Basis for Investment in the Construction of the Iran-Armenia Gas Pipeline and Expansion of Gas Supply to Armenia Taking account of Agreements on the Exchange of Gas for Electricity*, Decree No. PR-875 May 28, 2004.

83 *Caucasus Energy Monthly*, March 2005, p.12.

84 Georgia has also suggested it could take Iranian gas via Azerbaijan – an idea that seems less likely given the latter's gas ambitions, 'Georgia interested in gas via Iran-Armenia pipeline,' *Interfax Petroleum Report*, July 22–8, 2004, p.22.

85 *Caucasus Energy Monthly*, December 2004, p.8; March 2005, p.7.

86 Ukrainian interruptions are worthy of a separate study in themselves, but an analysis of the problems in the early 1990s showed that: first, these episodes did not involve a *complete* interruption of deliveries to Europe, but rather a *reduction* of deliveries which (in one case) reached 50% of one importer's supplies. Second, these reductions were measured in terms of days; only one episode appears to have exceeded a week. Third, there was always ample warning of these reductions, allowing importers to make other arrangements. Jonathan Stern, *The Russian Natural Gas Bubble*, 1995, pp.60–61.

87 Tom Bukkvoll, 'Off the Cuff Politics – Explaining Russia's lack of a Ukraine Strategy,' *Europe-Asia Studies*, Vol. 53, No. 8, 2001, pp. 1141–57.

88 Charles Clover, 'Pipeline hope for Shell Ukraine deal,' *Financial Times*, February 21/22, 1998.

89 'Gazprom and Ukraine finally agree to trade 52 Bcm this year', *Gas Matters*, January 1998, pp.12–13.

90 Madame Timoshenko – who became prime minister in the 2005 government of President Yushchenko – was known as 'the gas queen'. Charles

Clover, 'Swiss investigate the profits from unaccountable Ukrainian gas trading,' *Financial Times*, December 9, 1998; Charles Clover, 'Sharp whiff of corruption threatens Ukraine sell-off,' *Financial Times*, October 20, 2000.

91 Gas Industry News, *Interfax Petroleum Report*, January 22–8, 1999, pp.11–12; the Gazprom Chairman said that this could lead to his company being fined by the European customers who had not received their full volume of gas, although there is no evidence that this did happen.
92 'Government approves energy stabilisation measures,' *Interfax Petroleum Report*, February 12–18, 1999, p.3.
93 'Moscow issues ultimatum to Ukraine,' *Interfax Petroleum Report*, December 17–23, 1999, p.5.Gazprom's insurers also filed for international arbitration for losses incurred due to siphoning and an International Arbitration Court at the Russian Chamber of Commerce found in Gazprom's favour, 'International Court rules Ukraine stole Russian gas,' *Interfax Petroleum Report*, August 25–30, 2000, pp.5–6.
94 Although the Ukrainian side claimed it was much less, \$0.36–0.38bn. Russia, Ukraine resume gas talks, *Interfax Petroleum Report*, January 14–20, 2000, p.14.
95 'Poland-Slovakia "Link" Line: would it solve Gazprom's Ukraine problem?' *Gas Matters*, October 2000, pp.9–11. Note that the bypass pipeline is not the same as 'Yamal 2' which is the second string of the Yamal pipeline and may or may not be built in the future, see Chapter 3.
96 A memorandum was signed in October 2000 by Gazprom, Gaz de France, Ruhrgas, Wintershall and ENI to form a consortium for the construction of the project. 'Gazprom makes significant progress in Ukraine bypass project,' *Interfax Petroleum Report*, October 27–November 2, 2000, pp.6–10.
97 'Moscow, Kiev clash over Ukraine-bypass gas pipeline plan,' *Interfax Petroleum Report*, July 28–August 3, 2000, pp. 12–13.
98 'Gazprom makes significant progress in Ukraine bypass project,' *Interfax Petroleum Report*, October 27–November 2, 2000, pp.6–10.
99 'Ukrainian, Russian politicians deny reports on unsanctioned removal of gas from pipeline,' *Interfax Petroleum Report*, June 22–28, 2001, pp. 17–18.
100 'New agreements by Moscow and Kiev yet to take effect,' *Interfax Petroleum Report*, December 8–14, 2000, pp.15–16.
101 'Russian government approves gas agreement with Ukraine for 2001'; 'Russian government approves Ukrainian transit agreement,' *Interfax Petroleum Report*, January 5–11 and 12–18, 2001, pp.20–21.
102 Despite the claims that Ukraine had exported 2 Bcm in 2001, in contravention of the agreement between the countries; 'Ukraine and Russia compromise on debt repayments and Ukrainian gas exports,' *Gas Briefing International*, October 2001, p.13.
103 'Russia approves Russian-Ukrainian gas agreement,' *Interfax Petroleum Report*, January 11–17, 2002, p.17. Nothing about export duty was specifically stated but it is believed that the \$140/mcm remained in force from the

2001 agreement.

104 'Russia, Ukraine sign deal on natural gas transit,' *Interfax Petroleum Report*, July 5–11, 2002, p.13

105 'Ukraine, Russia agree to increase gas transit,' *Interfax Petroleum Report*, July 1–7, 2004, p.22.

106 *Gazprom reshit voproc po truboprovody v obkhod Ukrainy*, Interview with Alexey Miller, March 4, 2002, *www.gazprom.ru*; 'Construction of Kobrin-Velke-Kapushany gas pipeline link postponed,' *Interfax Petroleum Report*, April 12–18, 2002, p.14.

107 'Putin hopes for investment in gas pipelines,' *Interfax Petroleum Report*, June 14–20, 2002, p.4.

108 'Ukrainian president requests gas consortium agreement,' *Interfax Petroleum Report*, June 21–27, 2002, pp.6–7.

109 'Russia, Ukraine confirm short term plan for gas consortium,' *Interfax Petroleum Report*, February 14–20, 2003, pp.12–13.

110 The legal complexities are explained further in the interview with Yuri Komarov, *It's a long time since we have been analysing gas market liberalisation in Europe*, Interviews, January 20, 2004.

111 'Settlement of Ukraine's debt for natural gas deliveries between 1997 and 2000,' *Gazprom Press Release*, August 11, 2004.

112 Ibid.

113 The information apparently comes from the Naftokhaz Ukraine press release, 'Ukraine pays entire gas debt to Gazprom,' *Interfax Petroleum Report*, August 12–18, 2004, p.7.

114 An anonymous Gazprom spokesman is quoted as saying: 'On the face of it, Gazprom is losing $180m from the debt settlement but there are advantages. In this way we avoid tax losses, settle the debt, fix transit conditions till 2009 and free up 2–6 Bcm previously used for payment in kind.' *European Gas Markets*, August 19, 2004, p.9.

115 'Gazprom, Ukraine transport deal is body blow for Itera,' *Gas Matters Today*, December 16, 2002. 'Ukraine to export 5 Bcm in 2003 – but there's a catch,' *European Gas Markets*, December 16, 2002, p.10.

116 The term of that contract coincided with the remainder of the bilateral Turkmen-Ukraine contract which also expires in 2006 (see above); 'Fresh Gazprom riddle over Turkmen gas intermediary,' *European Gas Markets*, March 14, 2003, p.10.

117 *Eural Trans Gas: an instant market force*, April 2004. A note at the beginning of the document reads: 'This document has been prepared with publicly-available information from sources in both OECD and CIS countries and cross-checked when possible. Nevertheless some information or facts of these sources may be inaccurate or false'.

118 Andras Knopp, 'Diversification – key to security: Central Asian gas coming to Europe', presentation to the 11th Central European Gas Conference, Bratislava, 7–9 June 2004.

119 ETG received 38% of the volume of gas shipped as a fee; this arrangement is the same as that enjoyed by Itera when it performed this role.

120 *ETG Press Release.*

121 Andras Knopp, op.cit.

122 *ETG Press Release.*

123 *Predlozhenie gaze zametno previshaet sproc,* Pryamaya Rech', June 24, 2004.

124 *Razyacneniya v Otnoshenie Poruchitel'stv za kompaniyu ETG,* Gazprom Press Release, November 21, 2003; Sergei Kuprianov quoted in 'Gazprom shareholder calls for better management,' *Wall St Journal,* May 28, 2003.

125 'Itera's return to the Ukrainian gas market unfeasible,' *Interfax Oil and Gas Report,* April 14–20, 2005, pp.28–9.

126 *Eural Trans Gas: an instant market force,* op.cit.

127 *Povyshayem kachestvo podgotovki otchotnosti,* Pryamaya Rech', June 24, 2004, www.gazprom.ru

128 'Ukraine pays entire gas debt to Gazprom,' *Interfax Petroleum Report,* August 12–19, 2004, p.7.

129 'Long-term agreements on Turkmen's gas supply to and transit via Ukraine signed,' *Press Release,* July 29, 2004, www.gazprom.ru.

130 The British company Centrica is reported as being interested in taking a share. 'Centrica signs up for LNG,' *UK Gas Report,* September 6, 2004, p.7.

131 'Russia, Ukraine announce strategic gas pipeline project,' *Interfax Petroleum Report,* August 19–25, 2004, p.18.

132 'Gazprom's management committee approves shifting over to implementation of investment phase by international consortium for Ukrainian gas transmission system operation and development'. *Gazprom Press Release,* August 31, 2004.

133 *Yuri Komarov: mi dabno gotovimsya k liberaliszatsiya rinka v Evrope,* Pryamaya Rech', January 20, 2004, www.gazprom.ru

134 This was the impression from the exchange between Presidents Yushchenko and Putin at their first official meeting in January 2005, http://www.president.gov.ua/eng/topics/prior_innov/319946070.html

135 'Naftokhaz Ukrayny claims to have secured a Euro 2bn loan from Deutsche Bank,' *Gas Matters Today,* March 10, 2005.

136 'On Alexey Miller's meeting with Ivan Plachkov and Alexey Ivchenko,' *Gazprom Press Release,* March 28, 2005.

137 'Ukraine to change gas payment only if expedient,' *Interfax Oil and Gas Report,* March 31–April 6, 2005, pp. 12–14.

138 *Central Asia Energy Monthly,* April 2005, p.8.

139 The most detailed available overview of Russia-Belarusian relations and the role of natural gas can be found in Chloe Bruce, *Fraternal Friction or Fraternal Fiction,* 2005.

140 Leyla Boulton, 'Former Soviet republics try to avert trade collapse,' *Financial Times,* January 22, 1993; Leyla Boulton, 'Belarusians look to ruble tie to save them,' *Financial Times,* Feburary 19, 1994; Leyla Boulton, 'Russia, Belarus agree on monetary union,' *Financial Times,* April 13, 1994.

141 No details of these intergovernmental agreements are available, and this account relies on fragmentary press reports. 'Minsk threatens Gazprom

over possible gas cutbacks', *Interfax Petroleum Report*, March 30, 1998; 'Belarus premier calls on governments to deal with Russian gas dispute,' BBC Monitoring Service, February 28, 2004.

142 BBC Monitoring citing Interfax News Agency, November 19, 2002.

143 *Interfax Petroleum Report*, October 23–29, 1998, p.19; 'Gazprom tax debts on January 1, 1999 totalled 17.5bn roubles,' *Interfax Petroleum Report*, March 19–25, 1999, pp.16–17.

144 'On the outcome of the visit of Gazprom's delegation to Belarus', *Press Release*, July 25, 2003, www.gazprom.ru

145 'Normal service appears to be resumed between Belarus and Russia,' *Gas Briefing International*, December 2002, p.11.

146 'Belarus risks gas cuts in row over Russian joint pipeline venture,' *Gas Briefing International*, October 28, 2002; 'Belarus House of Representatives approves Beltransgaz privatisation,' *Gas Matters Today*, November 21, 2002.

147 'On the outcome of the visit of Gazprom's delegation to Belarus,' *Gazprom Press Release*, July 25, 2003.

148 'Head of Russia's gas giant says not more talks with Belarus,' BBC Monitoring Service, September 15, 2003.

149 'Putin says Russia, Belarus should switch to market relations in the gas industry.' BBC Monitoring Service, September 15, 2003.

150 BBC Monitoring Service, January 20, 2004.

151 'Russia cuts off (and restores) gas supplies to Belarus,' *Gas Matters Today*, February 12, 2004.

152 A February 19 report from Bloomberg stated that supplies recommenced at 07.18 New York time which would have been 16.18 Moscow time, making the stoppage just over 22 hours.

153 Dmitri Zhdannikov, 'Gazprom stops gas transit to Europe via Belarus,' Reuters, February 18, 2004.

154 'Belarusian plants will grind to a halt, Russian gas executive warns', BBC Monitoring Service, February 18, 2004. The price of $26.58/mcm quoted in this report seems very low and if true, it is surprising that the Belarusian side was slow to agree, particularly since the price that Gazprom was demanding was so much higher.

155 *Verbatim report of the meeting of Alexey Miller, Gazprom's management committee chairman and Alexander Ryazanov, Deputy Chairman of Gazprom's management committee with Belarusian reporters*, held on 17 May, 2004.

156 *Gazprom Press Conference with Alexander Ryazanov and Alexander Medvedev*, (in Russian) March 2, 2004.

157 Pawel Kaminski (Polish Oil and Gas Company), 'Privatisation of POGC: facing the implementation of the enlarged EU gas market,' OME/University of Paris Dauphine, conference, June 16, 2004; 'Key challenges for POGC facing the introduction of the enlarged EU gas market,' 11th Central European Gas Conference, Bratislava, June 7–9, 2004.

158 This was possible because Gazprom is a joint venture partner in Latvias Gaze (see section in Chapter 3 on the Baltic countries) see: *Press Conference with Alexander Ryazanov and Alexander Medvedev*, (in Russian) March 2,

2004.

159 'Kaliningrad freezing as Russia cuts off gas supplies to Belarus,' BBC Monitoring Service, February 19, 2004.

160 Chernobyl is a reference to the 1986 nuclear accident in the Ukraine, the fall-out from which severely affected Belarusian territory and population. 'Belarus president calls Russia's cut-off "terrorism"', BBC Monitoring Service, February 19, 2004.

161 *Press Conference with Alexander Ryazanov and Alexander Medvedev*, (in Russian) March 2, 2004; *Verbatim report of the meeting of Alexey Miller, Gazprom's management committee chairman and Alexander Ryazanov, Deputy Chairman of Gazprom's management committee with Belarusian reporters*, held on 17 May, 2004.

162 It is somewhat bizarre to regard Sibur as an 'independent' company given that it is virtually 100% owned by Gazprom (see Chapter 1). 'Belarus signs new 1 Bcm gas deal with Russian company,' *Gas Matters Today*, March 11, 2004; 'Sibur and Belarus sign additional gas supply contract,' *Gas Matters Today*, March 24, 2004; 'Another short-term gas deal for Belarus, this time from Trans Nafta,' *Gas Matters Today*, March 31, 2004; 'Sibur and Beltranshaz sign new gas supply agreement,' *Gas Matters Today*, May 18, 2004.

163 'Outcomes of Gazprom's delegation's visit to Belarus,' *Gazprom Press Release*, June 8, 2004. The reason that a supply cut might have been imminent was that independents had already delivered the 8.8 Bcm of supplies which had been allotted to them.

164 'Gazprom plans to deliver 19.1 Bcm of gas to Belarus in 2005,' *Interfax Petroleum Report*, August 26–September 1, 2004, p.26. This has been confirmed by Gazprom, 'Gazprom approves domestic gas quotes for 2005,' *Gazprom Press Release*, November 10, 2004.

165 'Russia may let Belarus firms into its natural gas industry,' *Interfax Petroleum Report*, August 19–25, 2004, p.20.

166 'Belarus, Russia sign 2005 energy balance,' *Interfax Oil and Gas Report*, December 23–29, 2004, p.5.

167 'On working meeting between Alexey Miller and Dmitry Kazakov,' *Gazprom Press Release*, April 12, 2005.

168 'Results of Gazprom's delegations's visit to the Republic of Moldova,' *Gazprom Press Release*, April 15, 2004, www.gazprom.ru. These percentages may have slightly changed since the joint venture was created see: 'Moldova pays Gazprom with a half share in Moldova Gas', *Gas Briefing International*, November 1998, p.11.

169 Compared with $1.09/mcm/00km in Ukraine, 'Russian government has approved Russian-Moldovan gas agreement,' *Interfax Petroleum Report*, December 28–January 3, 2001/02, p.16.

170 Corruption alleged in the Moldovan market, *Gas Briefing International*, November 2002, p.8.

171 'Results of Gazprom's delegations's visit to the Republic of Moldova, *Gazprom Press Release*, April 15, 2004; 'Gazprom threatens to cut off Dnestr for non-payment of gas bills,' *Gas Matters Today*, June 28, 2004.

172 'Moldavia i Pridnestrov'e uregulirovali voproci po transitu gaza iz Rossii*, Gazexport Press Release, February 2, 2005.

173 Tom Warner and Stefan Wagstyl, 'Moldova polls take on orange and yellow hue,' *Financial Times*, March 4, 2005.

174 Richard Sakwa and Mark Webber, 'The Commonwealth of Independent States, 1991–1998: stagnation and survival,' *Europe-Asia Studies*, Vol. 51, No3, 1999, pp.379–415.

175 For a broader discussion see, Richard Sakwa, *Putin: Russia's Choice*, 2004, pp.229–33.

176 'Putin wants alliance of Eurasian gas producers,' *Interfax Petroleum Report*, January 25–31, 2002.

177 'Kasyanov urges Eurasian Economic Community to set up gas alliance,' *Interfax Petroleum Report*, February 21–2, 2003, p.3. The Eurasian Economic Community includes Belarus, Kazakhstan, Kyrgyzstan, Russia and Tajikistan, with Moldova and Ukraine as observers. Turkmenistan is not a member and has refused to participate in almost all regional initiatives of any sort. 'Turkmen government cool on regional gas alliance,' *Gas Briefing International*, August 2002, p. 12.

178 Sergey Kamenev, 'Turkmenistan: energy policy and energy projects,' *Central Asia and the Caucasus*, No. 4(22), 2003, pp. 117–25.

179 Roy Allison, 'Strategic reassertion in Russia's Central Asia Policy,' *International Affairs*, March 2004, pp.227–93.

180 Annette Bohr, 'Regionalism in Central Asia: new geopolitics, old regional order,' *International Affairs*, March 2004, pp.485–502.

181 It has been suggested to this author that the restriction of Itera's Turkmen exports by the Uzbek government in 2004 was strongly influenced by the deteriorating relationship between Presidents Niyazov and Karimov. Likewise, there is a strong Turkmen initiative to develop a new pipeline route closer to the coast of the Caspian Sea which would bypass Uzbekistan.

182 OAO Gazprom, *IFRS Consolidated Financial Statements*, 31 December 2003, p.20; Gazprom's 50% share in KazRosgaz is in the marketing joint venture not the pipeline company Kazmunaigaz.

183 For further discussion of the Energy Charter Treaty see Chapter 3.

Chapter 3

1 There is a detailed chronology (in Russian) of Soviet and Russian gas exports to Europe on the Gazexport website: http://www.gazexport.ru/history/?pkey1=00002

2 Yuri Komarov, 'It's A Long Time since We Have Been Analyzing Implications of Gas Market Liberalization in Europe,' *Interviews*, January 20 2004; Board of Directors examined Gazprom's export strategy, *Gazprom Press Release*, February 4, 2004.

3 *Loan Notes*, 2005, p.142.

4 See chapter 4 for a more detailed discussion on the organisation of exports. By 2004, ZGG had become a very important subsidiary with sales of 18.5 Bcm; http://www.zgg.de/english/press/press_details.php?newsid=77

5 The evolution of gas trade during the Soviet and early post-Soviet era and some of what follows here can be found in Jonathan Stern, *The Russian Natural Gas Bubble*, 1999.

6 It is worth pointing out that the relationship was forged more than a year before the break-up of the Union. Whether the joint venture would have prospered to the same extent if the Soviet Union had remained intact, can only be guessed.

7 WIEH was the original seller of gas to VNG in the eastern part of Germany, but otherwise came to act as a marketing company outside of the country. Wingas is the joint venture which both owns and builds pipelines, and which markets gas in the western part of Germany.

8 'Italy's Edison to buy North Sea Gas,' *International Gas Report*, May 29, 1998, p.4.

9 'Where do Gazprom's latest Rurhgas contracts leave Wintershall?', 'Ruhrgas and Gazprom kiss, make up and plan honeymoon in Europe,' *Gas Matters*, June 1998, p.6 and September 1998, pp.1–6.

10 'Ruhrgas goes back to the future by spending $1bn on long term relationship with Gazprom', 'Shrugging off risk, Ruhrgas ups Gazprom stake to 4%,' *Gas Matters*, January 1999, p.8 and May 1999, p.1.

11 The CEO of Ruhrgas has been a board member of Gazprom since 2000, *Ruhrgas Annual Report 2003*, p.34.

12 'Hungary's MOL to sell its 50% stake in Panrusgaz JV,' *European Gas Markets*, August 19, 2004, p.13.

13 The term 'world prices', which is completely meaningless, was used in the 1990s as a synonym for European (specifically German) border prices.

14 'Norway's Czech-Mate for Russian Gas,' *Gas Matters*, April 1997, pp. 1–7.

15 'Gas transit through Czech Republic to reach 30 Bcm,' *Interfax Petroleum Report*, October 23–29, 1998, p.17.

16 'Czechs remain reluctant to face the pain of liberalisation,' *Gas Matters*, July 1999, p.8.

17 The other bidders were E.ON, Gaz de France, Ruhrgas and Duke Energy, 'RWE triumphs in Czech Transgas tender,' *Gas Matters*, December 2001, p.19.

18 'Gazprom buys 37.5% of Gas-Invest for 200,000 Euros,' *Interfax Oil and Gas Report*, February 3–9, 2005, p.26.

19 Slovak transit capacity was 94 Bcm/year in 2004 and this may increase to 100 Bcm by 2010, 'Slovakia, Second-Largest Gas Transporter after Ukraine,' *Gas Matters*, March 2002, p.15; 'Slovakia publishes entry-exit system tariffs,' *European Gas Markets*, January 31, 2005, p.1.

20 'Slovakia gets cheapest gas in Europe but at a high political price,' *Gas Matters*, October 1997, pp. 6- 11.

21 Gazprom has until end 2005 to exercise its option. Milan Sedlacek, 'Slovakia: new ownership, new environment, new commercial approach,' 10th Central European Gas Conference, Zagreb, 28–30 April, 2003.

22 'Poland looks to Norway and Holland for supply diversity,' *Gas Matters*, January 1999, p.19.

23 'Poland looks for route for additional Norwegian gas imports,' *Gas Briefing Europe*, January 2000, p.9; 'Poland marks increase in import capacity from Germany,' *Gas Briefing Europe*, February 2001, p.12.

24 'Poland and Norway finally cancel long-term supply contract,' *Gas Matters*, December 2003, p.11.

25 Andras Knopp, 'Diversification – key to security', op.cit.; 'Poland issues 3.4 Bcm supply tender,' *Gas Matters Today*, April 19, 2005.

26 See for example Christopher Bobinski, 'Polish gas deal under attack,' *Financial Times*, September 25, 1996;

27 'Gazprom finally signs supply and transit contracts with Bulgaria,' *Gas Briefing International*, May 1998, p.1.

28 'Bulgaria's role as transit country helps stimulate interest in privatisation,' *Gas Matters*, March 2003, pp. 19–23.

29 Gazprom took part in the IX Meeting of the Intergovernmental Russia-Bulgaria Commission on Trade, Economic, Scientific and Technical Cooperation, *Gazprom Press Release*, October 2, 2004.

30 'Focus on the Romanian gas market, *European Gas Markets*, March 15, 2003, pp.3–6.

31 'Gazprom Delegation's Visit to Romania,' *Gazprom Press Release* July 13, 2004; 'Wintershall expands its Romania operations,' *Gas Matters*, August 2004, p.13; 'WIEH and Distrigaz Sud to invest jointly in Romanian grid,' *European Gas Markets*, March 15, 2004, p.13.

32 See the project section Yamal-Evropa on the Gazexport website: www. gazexport.ru.

33 In reality this meant from Germany to the Torzhok compressor station.'Yamal pipeline project drops gas fields,' *Gas Matters*, June 1994, p.3.

34 An Italian contract was originally conceived to be delivered through the Volta pipeline which was intended to connect to Yamal, but the Volta project was eventually abandoned (see above).

35 'On Working Meeting between Alexey Miller and Dmitry Kazakov,' *Gazprom Press Release*, April 12, 2005.

36 'Doubts cast over operator of Polish Yamal pipeline,' *European Gas Markets*, January 31, 2001, p.7; 'POGC losing control over destiny of Yamal-Europe pipeline,' *European Gas Markets*, April 12, 2001, p.6.

37 'The Miller's Tale: deal in sight between Gazprom and POGC,' *European Gas Markets*, April 15, 2002, p.1. 1996 projections from Janusz Tokarzewski, 'Prospects of Gas Industry Development in Poland,' 1996 Central/East European Gas Conference, May 29–30 1996, Warsaw, Figure 7.

38 'PGNiG finally signs revised and reduced Gazprom supply contract,' *Gas Matters Today*, June 24, 2003.

39 Vyborg is the starting point of the offshore section of NEP, but in early

2005 the offshore route had not yet been finalised. For details of the 917 km of NEP being built onshore, mostly in Leningrad Oblast, see 'On the results of the meeting between Alexey Miller and Valery Serdyukov,' *Gazprom Press Release*, October 8, 2004.

40 *Severniye Marshrut – Severo-Evropeiskii gazoprovod*, www.gazexport.ru; this conception of the pipeline also has a connection to Kaliningrad.

41 'Results of meeting on Yuzhno-Russkoye field project,' *Gazprom Press Release*, June 11, 2004.

42 'Andrey Kruglov named as project financing coordinator,' *Gazprom Press Release*, June 3, 2004.

43 'Gazprom acquires stake in Fortum and becomes 100% stockholder in North Transgas Oy,' *Gazprom Press Release*, May 17, 2005.

44 'Meeting on Yuzhno-Russskoye Development Held,' *Gazprom Press Release*, March 17, 2004.

45 The significance of Cenomanian gas is that it is shallow, relatively straightforward and low cost gas to produce (see Chapter 1); up to this time, other investors had only been offered the possibility of producing gas from deeper, more complex and costly geological horizons. 'E.ON and Gazprom deepen strategic cooperation and sign memorandum of understanding,' *Gazprom Press Release*, July 8, 2004.

46 'Gazprom, E.ON discuss asset swap,' *Interfax Petroleum Report*, July 8–14, 2004, p. 35; 'E.ON unwilling to allow Gazprom into Ruhrgas,' *Interfax Oil and Gas Report*, April 14–20, 2005, pp.23–4.

47 'BASF third contender for South Russkoye partnership,' *Interfax Oil and Gas Report*, February 10–16, 2005, pp.21–2.

48 The significance of the 'minus one share' provision relates to decision-making authority over the venture. 'Gazprom and BASF ink memorandum of understanding,' *Gazprom Press Release*, April 11, 2005.

49 'On Alexey Miller's working meeting with Wulf Bernotat and Burckhard Bergmann,' *Gazprom Press Release*, April 11, 2005.

50 But in late 2004, a Ruhrgas Board Member was guarded about the immediate prospects for the NEP, 'Long term contracts still crucial, but need to be adapted for gas-fired power,' *Gas Matters*, October 2004, pp.37–42.

51 http://president.kremlin.ru/eng/text/speeches/2004/05/26/1309_type70029_71650.shtml

52 'Russia's Blue Stream - Imminent Reality or Yamal Revisited?' *Gas Matters*, May 1998, pp.1–8.

53 In particular, competition from Turkmen gas through the Trans-Caspian pipeline which at the time, appeared to be a real competitor, see Chapter 2 for details.

54 International Energy Agency, *Energy Policies of IEA Countries, Turkey, 1997 Review*, Paris: OECD, 1997, p.72.

55 Technical description of these conditions and details of how the Blue Stream pipeline was laid can be found on the website of the company which carried out the project, www.saipem.it

56 In fact the contract stipulated a total of 365 Bcm to be delivered over

a 25-year period. Goluboi Potok, www.gazexport.ru

57 'Hello, Astrakhan: goodbye to gas from Central Asia?' *Gas Matters*, March 1998, pp.1−4.

58 'Blue Dream becomes reality,' *Gas Briefing International*, November 2002, p. 3.

59 For details of the general economic and political situation in Turkey during this period see Philip Robins, 'Confusion at home, confusion abroad: Turkey between Copenhagen and Iraq,' *International Affairs*, Vol. 79, No. 3, (2003), pp.547−66.

60 'Turkey ramps up gas ambitions to become east-west bridge,' *Gas Matters*, July 2002, pp.26-31; 'Turkey cuts back on Russian and Iranian gas imports,' *Gas Briefing International*, September 2002, p.8.

61 'Turkey interrupts Blue Stream supplies as energy shake-up continues,' *Gas Briefing International*, April 2003, pp.2−3.

62 Yuri Komarov: 'Mutually acceptable solution on Blue Stream will be found,' *Gazprom Press Release*, July 2, 2003; 'Blue Stream settlement pulls Turkey-Russia relations back from the brink,' *Gas Matters*, July 2003, pp. 27−29.

63 'Gazprom and Botas have completed negotiations on Russian gas supply to Turkey,' *Gazprom Press Release*, November 30, 2003.

64 'Whatever happened to Shah Deniz?' *Gas Matters*, August 2004, pp. 37−40. 'Gazprom to supply Israel, Syria,' Reuters, September 3, 2004.

65 'Results of Gazprom delegation's visit to Turkey,' *Gazprom Press Release*, July 30, 2004.

66 Although it would not have addressed the Turkish concern about security of transit, and might therefore have allowed Central Asian and Caspian supplies a larger share of the market in the longer run.

67 However, it is possible that 2003 was an unusual year. Latvia has major gas storages which are used to supply the entire Baltic region and Kaliningrad during the winter. The country therefore imports gas in excess of its domestic requirements.

68 'Estonia's gas supply is cut...then resumed,' *Gas Briefing International*, June 1993, p.5; 'Estonia and Latvia sign long(er)-term gas contracts with Gazprom,' *Gas Briefing Europe*, November 1999, p.11.

69 'Board of directors agrees on Gazprom's acquisition of Latvias Gaze's 9% stake,' *Gazprom Press Release*, October 29, 2004.

70 'Board of directors addresses Kaunas CHP's charter capital increase issue,' *Gazprom Press Release*, September 28, 2004.

71 'E.ON Ruhrgas and Gazprom increase stakes in Lietuvos Dujos,' *Gas Matters Today*, July 27, 2004.

72 Communication from the Commission to the Council, Kaliningrad Transit, COM(2002) 510, Final, Brussels 18/9/2002.

73 Annual progress reports can be found on the website of DG TREN, most recently: *EU Benchmarking Reports 2004 and 2005*. In early 2005, the Competition Directorate of the European Commission announced an investigation into the energy sector.

74 Much of the history prior to the agreement on the 1998 Directive can be found in Jonathan Stern, *Competition and Liberalisation in European Gas Markets*, 1998.
75 *EU Gas Directive 1998.*
76 *EU Gas Directive 2003.*
77 The ten new Member States were: Poland, Hungary, Czech Republic, Slovakia, Slovenia, Latvia, Estonia, Lithuania, Malta and Cyprus; the last two do not have gas markets.
78 This is Article 81 in the 1999 Maastricht Treaty; it was Article 85 under the previous Treaty.
79 Commission Decision of 29.09.1999 declaring a concentration compatible with the Common Market and the EEA Agreement, Case No IV/M.1383 – Exxon/Mobil, Brussels, 29.09.1999 C (1999) - 3093 final, Paras 89–93.
80 Michael Albers, 'Energy Liberalization and EC Competition Law,' paper submitted to the 28th Annual Conference of Antitrust Law and Policy, October 26, 2001.
81 Yuri Komarov's speech to the Offshore Northern Seas Conference, in Stavanger, Norway, 22–25 August 2000.
82 EU Russia Energy Dialogue, Synthesis Report, Brussels/Moscow September 2001, p.2.
83 Petr Rodionov, 'Liberalization of the Gas Market – Gazprom's Perspective,' European Gas Summit Conference, Paris, October 2001.
84 Council Directive 2004/67/EC of 26April 2004, concerning measures to safeguard security of natural gas supply. Recital 11. Article 2(2) of the Directive defines a long-term contract as 'a gas supply contract with a duration of more than 10 years.'
85 There have subsequently been indications that the Commission has relented on profit sharing mechanisms. 'Commission successfully settles GFU case with Norwegian gas producers,' Competition Directorate Press Release IP/02/1084, 17/07/2002.
86 Professor Mario Monti, 'Applying EU Competition Law to the newly liberalized energy markets,' speech to the World Forum on Energy Regulation, Rome, October 8, 2003.
87 'OMV links Russian supply contracts to Rotterdam,' *European Gas Markets*, May 14, 2004, p.5; 'Commission secures improvements to gas supply contracts between OMV and Gazprom,' DG COMP Press Release, IP/05/195, February 17, 2005.
88 'EU considers Gazprom-E.ON deal over destination clauses,' *European Gas Markets*, April 15, 2005, p.11.
89 'Russia's Gazprom aims to supply 10% of UK gas market by 2010,' *UK Gas Report*, November 29, 2004.
90 Eduard Gismatullin and Mathew Carr, 'Gazprom May Want to Expand U.K.-Dutch Natural Gas Pipeline,' Bloomberg, May 20, 2005.
91 Much of the information in this section has been taken from the EU website on the Dialogue: http://europa.eu.int/comm/energy/russia/overview/in-

dex_en.htm

92 The Dialogue named two 'sole interlocutors': Francois Lamoureux – Director General of the European Commission, and Viktor Khristenko – Vice Prime Minister of the Russian Federation.

93 Green Paper, *Towards a European strategy for the security of energy supply*, 29 November 2000 COM (2000) 769 final, p.74.

94 'Trans-European Energy Networks: TEN-E priority projects,' EU Directorate General for Energy and Transport, June 2004.

95 EU-Russia Energy Dialogue, Fifth Progress Report, Moscow, Brussels, November 2004; EU-Russia Energy Dialogue, para 3.1.

96 EU-Russia Energy Dialogue, para 3.0.

97 Ibid.

98 EU-Russia Energy Dialogue, Fourth Progress Report, Moscow/Brussels, November 2003, p.3.

99 Ibid., para 3.4c

100 EU-Russia Energy Dialogue, Fifth Progress Report, Moscow/Brussels, November 2004.

101 There is a wealth of material on all aspects of the Treaty on the Charter Secretariat website: http://www.encharter.org

102 For the early history of the Treaty see Julia Dore and Robert de Bauw, *The Energy Charter Treaty: origins, aims and prospects*, London: RIIA, 1995. For a comprehensive legal appraisal of the Charter see: Thomas W. Walde (ed.), *The Energy Charter Treaty: an East-West Gateway for Investment and Trade*, London: Kluwer Law International, 1996.

103 For a full list see Energy Charter Secretariat, *Annual Report 2004*, p.5; the Charter Conference also has 18 states and 10 international organisations with observer status.

104 In addition, Australia, Iceland and Norway had not ratified; USA and Canada had not signed.

105 This is because all parties lose revenue from transit disruptions so there is no cost-free disruption option; most will also lose gas supplies in the event of a disruption.

106 Another approach, sponsored by the EU, is the Interstate Oil and Gas Transport to Europe (INOGATE) initiative which is a more limited regional, project-based initiative. www.inogate.org

107 Energy Charter Secretariat, *Annual Report 2003*, p.16. The draft of the Protocol at December 2003 can be found at: http://www.encharter.org//upload/9/759402917116997827317310529151983625821751198806f1813v1.pdf

108 For an assessment of these issues in late 2004, see Andrey Konoplyanik, *Transit Provisions of the Energy Charter Treaty and the draft Transit Protocol, Energy Transit in Eurasia: challenges and perspectives*, Brussels, October 2004. http://www.encharter.org//upload/9/966438503801773293695530051153416820420585731212444v1.pdf

109 Press Conference given by the Russian Deputy Prime Minister Viktor Khristenko at the Russian EU Mission in Brussels, 23 June 2003.

110 Deputy Prime Minister Khristenko quoted in *RIA-Novosti*, December 1, 2003.
111 Gazprom IFRS Consolidated Financial Statements, 31 December 2003; Management Discussion and Analysis of Financial Conditions and Results of Operations, p.17.
112 Some of the detail of CIS transit tariffs has been noted in Chapter 2.
113 *Loan Notes 2004*, p.57.
114 Aside from press releases, it is very difficult to find any official source to confirm the content of the WTO negotiations; information filtered out through press reports. Gas issues were by no means the only ones requiring resolution.
115 Gazexport's monopoly on Russian gas exports to Europe had – as we have seen above – already been breached by Eural Transgas.
116 'Russia-WTO: EU-Russia deal brings Russia a step closer to WTO membership,' *EU Press Release*, IP/04/673, Brussels, May 21, 2004. For a general discussion of the WTO agreement see David Kernohan and Yevgeny Vinokurov, *The EU-Russia WTO deal: balancing mid-term and longer-term growth prospects?* Centre for European Policy Studies, October 2004.
117 Francis Williams and Andrew Jack, 'Lamy defends Brussels over WTO entry deal with Russia,' *Financial Times*, May 26, 2004.
118 Nick Paton-Walsh, 'Putin throws lifeline to Kyoto as EU backs Russia joining WTO,' *The Guardian*, May 22, 2004.
119 The only official document referred to 'avoiding undue dependence on a single source of supply' and was not specific to either Soviet/Russian gas or European countries. International Energy Agency, *Energy Policies and Programmes of the IEA Countries, 1983 Review*, Paris: OECD, Appendix A, Annex 1, pp.72–3. For a complete account of this episode see Bruce Jentleson, *Pipeline Politics: The Complex Political Economy of East-West Energy Trade*, Cornell University Press: 1986, especially pp. 202–03.
120 For a general overview of natural gas security see International Energy Agency, *Security of Gas Supply in Open Markets: LNG and power at a turning point*, Paris: OECD, 2004. For a specific evaluation of the European context see Jonathan Stern, *Security of European Natural Gas Supplies*, 2002.
121 Stern ibid. Hadi Hallouche, 'Will There Be an Effective Organisation of Gas Exporting Countries? Potential Regional Groupings and Market Power,' OIES forthcoming 2005.
122 'Gasunie opens new markets to Gazprom,' *Gas Matters*, June 1996, pp.1–2.
123 The Energy Dialogue between the European Union and the Russian Federation between 2000 and 2004, Brussels, December 2004, COM (2004) final, paras 3.1 and 3.3a.
124 Kevin Morrison et al, 'Europe too dependent on Russian gas, says IEA,' *Financial Times*, December 3, 2004.
125 This section draws on Jonathan Stern in *Natural Gas in Asia*, ed. Ian Wybrew-Bond and Jonathan Stern, 2002, pp.230–76.
126 Robert E. Ebel, *Communist Trade in Oil and Gas*, Praeger Publishers, 1970, p.

151 has a map of three pipeline proposals for Sakhalin exports to Japan dating from the late 1960s, clearly showing options currently under consideration. An early history of all the East Siberian and Far Eastern projects can be found in, Peter Egyed, *Western Participation in the Development of Siberian Energy Resources,* Case Studies: East-West Commercial Relations Series Report 20, Institute of Soviet and East European Studies, Carleton, Ottawa, May 1983.

127 The islands are Habomai, Shikotan, Etorofu and Kunashiri.

128 For an overview of developments in the Russian Far East in the post-Soviet period see Michael Bradshaw (ed.) *The Russian Far East and Pacific Asia,* 2001, especially Introduction and Part 1.

129 Some of the project details in this section are taken from Michael Bradshaw, 'Sakhalin Oblast', in G.P. Herd and A. Aldis (eds), *Russian Regions and Regionalism: Strength through weakness?* Richmond: Curzon, 2002.

130 For a detailed post-Soviet history, see Michael J. Bradshaw, 'Going Global: the political economy of oil and gas development offshore of Sakhalin,' *Cambridge Review of International Affairs,* Summer/Fall 1998, Vol. XII, No. 1, pp. 147–76.

131 Information about Sakhalin 2 can be found on the website: www. sakhalinenergy.com; a detailed timeline can be found at: http://www. sakhalinenergy.com/project/prj_timeline.asp

132 Sakhalin Energy Investment Company, Press Release, Yuzhno-Sakhalinsk, July 17, 2001.

133 1 million tons of LNG is approximately equal to 1.38 Bcm of gas.

134 'Kyushu Electric signs first Sakhalin 2 PSA,' *Gas Matters,* June 2004, p.13; 'Shell consortium poised to reveal Sakhalin II cost overruns to Russian government,' *Gas Matters Today,* September 9, 2004.

135 TEPCO still has an option to purchase an additional 0.5mt/year. 'TEPCO speeds up and tops up its Sakhalin LNG volumes,' *Gas Matters Today,* April 23, 2004.

136 A chronology of presidential, prime ministerial and ministerial visits up to 2000 can be found in Victor Pavliatenko and Alexander Shlindov, 'Russian-Japanese Relations: Past Achievements and Future Prospects at the Start of the 21ˢᵗ Century', *Far Eastern Affairs,* No. 4, 2000, pp.3–32.

137 'First Russian gas for North America as Sakhalin Energy signs 37 million tonne deal,' *Gas Matters Today,* October 14, 2004.

138 ''Sakhalin LNG seals North America "first" for Russia,' *International Gas Report,* 22 October 2004, pp.1–5; 'Sakhalin Energy to sell entire LNG output from Sakhalin II by end-2005,' *Gas Matters Today,* March 31, 2005.

139 'Sakhalin Energy to sell entire LNG output from Sakhalin II by end 2005,' *Gas Matters Today,* March 31, 2005.

140 Pacific Basin LNG trade showed almost no growth in the late 1990s and early 2000s, especially in comparison to other regions of the world. James Jensen, *The Development of a Global LNG Market,* 2004, pp.38–9.

141 'Shell in "intense" talks with Gazprom over Sakhalin 2,' *Interfax Petroleum Report,* October 7–13, 2004, p.27; 'Results of the meeting between Alexey

Miller and Jeroen van der Veer,' *Gazprom Press Release*, April 7, 2005.

142 *Sakhalin 1 Consortium Press Release*, Yuzhno-Sakhalinsk, October 30, 2001. This press release and many other details of the project including the sources which follow can be found at: www.sakhalin1.ru

143 Jack King, 'Sakhalin 1 Gas Marketing Update,' Presentation to the Sakhalin Oil and Gas Conference, November 18–19, 2003

144 David Pilling and Enid Tsui, 'Japan risks missing out on Russian island's gas,' *Financial Times*, November 3, 2004.

145 For details of Korean initiatives see Keun-Wook Paik, *Pipeline Gas Introduction to the Korean Peninsula*, 2005.

146 David Pilling and Enid Tsui, 'Exxon rethinks natural gas delivery options,' *Financial Times*, November 5, 2004.

147 'Sakhalin 1 Consortium to start early oil production in summer,' *Interfax Oil and Gas Report*, March 10–16, 2005, p.19

148 'Sakhalin 1 project participants sign letters of intent for gas sales to Khabarovsk Krai partners,' *Sakhalin 1 Press Release*, June 10, 2004. http://www.sakhalin1.ru/en/index.htm

149 G.N. Pavlova, 'Sakhalin Projects: results and issues,' a paper to the Sakhalin Oil and Gas 5th Annual Conference, 13–14 November 2001.

150 'Companies mull response after government annuls rights to Sakhalin-3,' *Interfax Petroleum Report*, February 6–12, 2004, pp.4–5.

151 'BP, Rosneft rents drilling section for first Sakhalin 5 well,' *Interfax Petroleum Report*, June 10–16, 2004, pp.12–13; 'Rosneft-BP strikes gas and oil in Sakhalin V,' *Gas Matters Today*, October 6, 2004.

152 http://www.sakhalinenergy.com/project/prj_overview.asp; http://www.sakhalin1.ru/en/index.htm.

153 Keun-Wook Paik, *Tarim Basin Energy Development: implications for Russian and Central Asian oil and gas exports to China*, RIIA, CACP Briefing, No. 14, November 1997.

154 An account of the BP/Sidanco affair and some details of what followed can be found in: Andrew Jack, *Inside Putin's Russia*, 2004, pp.187–91.

155 'TNK-BP may lend Kovykta operator 1.49 bn rubles,' *Interfax Petroleum Report*, August 12–18, 2004, p.22.

156 Keun-Wook Paik, *Pipeline Gas Introduction to the Korean Peninsula*, 2005; Table 5 refers to these as Manzhouli Route 1 and 2.

157 Ibid.

158 These figures are taken from, Luvsandorj Sukhbuyan, 'Why western route of natural gas pipeline from Kovykta?' Proceedings of the 7th International Conference on Northeast Asian Natural Gas Pipelines, Tokyo, December 3–5, 2001.

159 'BP to offer Gazprom various forms of participation in Kovykta project', *Interfax Petroleum Report*, November 2–8, 2001, p.4.

160 'Results of the meeting between Alexei Miller and Victor Vekselberg,' May 13, 2003; 'Outcomes of the working meeting between Alexei Miller and Victor Vekselberg,' June 3, 2004; 'Results of Alexei Miller and Vladimir Potanin's working meeting,' July 21, 2004, *Gazprom press releases*.

161 'TNK-BP, Irkutsk region sign agreement establishing East Siberian gas company,' *Interfax Petroleum Report*, March 12–18, 2004, p.10

162 'TNK-BP May join East Siberia Consortium,' *Interfax Petroleum Report*, May 20–27, 2004, pp.12–13. The three companies signed a Consortium Agreement in January 2004, 'Working meeting of the consortium for Eastern Siberia held,' *Gazprom Press Release*, May 14, 2004.

163 'Trutnev doubts TNK-BP can correct Kovykta violations on time,' *Interfax Petroleum Report*, September 23–9, 2004, p.26.

164 James Boxell, 'Gazprom losing interest in BP's Siberia field,' *Financial Times*, September 24, 2004; Arkady Ostrovsky and Andrew Jack, 'TNK-BP holds talks with Gazprom,' *Financial Times*, September 28, 2004.

165 The alliance was set up in 2002. 'Results of Alexei Miller's and Vyacheslav Shtyrov's working meeting,' *Gazprom Press Release*, March 23, 2004.

166 'Russia to auction Chayandinskoye oil and gas field in May,' *Interfax Oil and Gas Report*, March 10–16, 2005, pp.9–10.

167 For more details of the Sakha Republic projects see Keun-Wook Paik, *Pipeline Gas Introduction to the Korean Peninsula*, 2005.

168 Jonathan Stern in Ian Wybrew-Bond and Jonathan Stern (eds), *Natural Gas in Asia*, especially pp.230–4.

169 Keun-Wook Paik and Jae-Yong Choi, *Pipeline gas in Northeast Asia: recent developments and regional perspective*, RIIA, Energy and Environmental Programme Briefing Paper No. 39, January 1998, date Gazprom's interest from February 1997 and note a reference to exporting a proportion of Yamal Peninsula gas to Asia.

170 Rem Vyakhirev, 'The Perspectives of Russian Natural Gas. Role in the World Gas Market,' World Gas Conference, Copenhagen, June 1997.

171 'The North East Asia Energy and Environmental Cooperation: Russian Approach,' Tokyo: *NIRA Research Output*, Vol. 13, No. 1, 2000, p.47

172 Rem Vyakhirev, 'Russian Gas Industry in the 21st Century,' World Gas Conference, Nice, 2000.

173 'Vostokgazprom celebrated 5-year anniversary of commercial gas production,' *Gazprom Press Release*, May 20, 2004.

174 Spravka k brifingu 'Komplekcnoe osvoenie mestorozhdenie Vostochnoy Sibiri I Dalnevo Vostoka', Briefing June 3, 2004.

175 *Russian Energy Strategy 2003*, p.55.

176 Alexey B. Miller, 'Euroasian Direction of Russia's Gas Strategy,' 22nd World Gas Conference, Tokyo, June 4, 2003.

177 This was in sharp contrast to the map presented by the previous Gazprom Chairman at the previous World Gas Conference in which Sakha and Krasnoyarsk gas travelled through Irkutsk with the Kovykta field being the focal point of development. Rem Vyakhirev, 'Russian Gas Industry in the 21st Century,' World Gas Conference, Nice, 2000.

178 Earlier versions of the pipeline to the coast had proposed Angarsk to Nakhodka as the start and finish points.

179 Murad D. Muzhamedzhanov and Sergey S. Skaterschikov, 'Transneft: new heights – new horizons,' March 2005; http://www.indexatlas.com/Tran-

sneft_presentation_March_2005_Eng.pdf; 'Khristenko says Russia will deliver oil to China,' *Interfax Oil and Gas Report*, January 20−26, 2005, pp.5−7.

180 Alexander Ananenkov's report theses delivered at 4th All-Russian Oil and Gas Week, *Gazprom Press Release*, October 26, 2004. (Translated from the Russian by the author; the English press release talks about 'supplying targeted markets on an uncompetitive basis'.)

181 Pavel A. Minakir, 'The Economic Situation in the Russian Far East: contemporary problems and prospects for the future,' in Michael J. Bradshaw (ed.), *The Russian Far East and Pacific Asia*, 2001, pp.32−50; Jonathan Stern in Ian Wybrew Bond and Jonathan Stern (eds), op.cit., 2002, pp.254−6.

182 'Agreement on cooperation between Gazprom and the Kogas corporation (South Korea),' *Gazprom Press Release*, May 12, 2003.

183 'Outcomes of Alexey Miller and Jong Tae Ick's working meeting,' *Gazprom Press Release*, June 4, 2004.

184 'Outcomes of Alexey Miller and Victor Vekselberg's working meeting,' *Gazprom Press Release*, June 3, 2004.

185 See the map on eastern routes for Russian gas in Rem Vyakhirev, 'Russian Gas Industry in the 21st Century,' World Gas Conference, Nice, 2000.

186 Reports on the withdrawal of Shell, ExxonMobil and Gazprom did not make clear whether the companies had withdrawn from the project (given that the pipeline was virtually completed and no agreement had been signed), or whether Petrochina had told them that they were surplus to requirements. Carola Hoyos and Richard McGregor, 'PetroChina ends talks on pipeline venture with foreign companies, and Pipeline pullout embarrasses Petrochina,' *Financial Times*, August 4, 2004.

187 'Gazprom, CNPC ink strategic gas cooperation deal,' *Interfax Petroleum Report*, October 14−20, 2004, p.28.

188 'Ministry puts $16bn price tag on eastern pipeline,' *Interfax Oil and Gas Report*, March 3−9, 2005, pp.10−11.

189 'TNK/BP hopes for increased cooperation with Gazprom,' *Interfax Petroleum Report*, September 16−22, 2004, p.27.

190 Jonathan Stern in Robert Mabro and Ian Wybrew-Bond (eds), *Gas to Europe*,1999, especially pp.153−4.

191 For an overview of all these issues see James Jensen, *The Development of a Global LNG Market*, 2004, op.cit.

192 American Chamber of Commerce in Russia, Development of Russian-American Trade and Economic Relations I the Framework of the Commercial Energy Dialogue. http://www.usrbc.org/pdfs/ced_may2003_eng.pdf

193 Alexey B. Miller, 'Eurasian Direction of Russia's Gas Strategy', 2003, World Gas Conference, Tokyo, 2003.

194 These discussions should be regarded as separate from the Pacific LNG business which was discussed above in the section on the Asian market.

195 Both options are shown in Alexander Medvedev, 'Outlook for Russian Natural Gas Exports,' Presentation to the European Gas Summit Confer-

ence, Paris, October 21, 2004.

196 *Gazprom stremitsa na gazovoy rinok SshA*, Interview with Alexander Ryazanov in Eurasia Offshore, Pryamaya Rech, October 19, 2004. Given Ryazanov's position as a Deputy Chairman of the company and his participation in Gazprom's Coordinating Committee for LNG Production and Transportation, his views can be regarded as official company policy. Much of what follows in this section is based on this interview.

197 'Outcomes of Alexey Miller and Eivind Reiten's Working Meeting,' *Gazprom Press Release*, June 3, 2004; 'Gazprom, Rosneft and Statoil sign memorandum of understanding,' *Gazprom Press Release*, September 9, 2004.

198 'On working meeting between Alexey Miller and Jim Mulva,' *Gazprom Press Release*, April 14, 2005.

199 'On Alexey Miller and Rex Tillerson's working meeting,' *Gazprom Press Release*, October 22, 2004; 'Results of Alexey Miller and Alfonso Cortina's working meeting,' *Gazprom Press Release*, October 22, 2004; 'Gazprom and ChevronTexaco sign memorandum of understanding,' *Gazprom Press Release*, September 22, 2004; 'Gazprom and Sempra Energy signed the memorandum of understanding,' *Gazprom Press Release*, April 25, 2005.

200 'Sakhalin seals North America "first" for Russia,' *International Gas Report*, October 22, 2004, pp.1–5.

201 Quote from Alexander Medvedev, General Director of Gazexport, 'Sakhalin LNG seals North America "first" for Russia,' *International Gas Report*, 22 October 2004, pp.1–5.

202 'Results of Alexey Miller and Lord Browne's working meeting,' *Gazprom Press Release*, October 22, 2004.

203 *Loan Notes 2005*, p.121; 'Gazprom to consider Shtokman investment proposals in May,' *Interfax Oil and Gas Report*, March 17–23, 2005, p.29.

204 'Gazprom and PetroCanada signed a memorandum of understanding,' *Gazprom Press Release*, October 12, 2004

205 'Medvedev replaces Komarov on Gazprom managing board,' *European Gas Markets*, April 25, 2005, p.12.

206 'Sakhalin LNG seals North America "first" for Russia,' *International Gas Report*, 22 October 2004, pp.1–5.

207 Alexander Medvedev: '"Gazprom" nameren ne tolko sokhanit', no I ucilit' svoy positsii na Evropeiskom rinke,' Pryamaya Rech, December 21, 2004.

208 'Gazprom's management committee addresses corporate gas export strategy implementation in Europe,' *Press Release*, December 16, 2004.

209 'Focus on Gazprom Marketing and Trading,' *European Gas Markets*, November 30, 2004, p.12.

210 *Russian Energy Strategy 2003*, Chart 8, p.51.

211 IEA, *World Energy Outlook 2004*, p.313.

212 'South Korea's privatisation plans crumble,' *Gas Matters*, June 2004, p.15.

213 IEA, *World Energy Outlook 2004*, p.313.

Chapter 4

1 For an authoritative account of Gazprom's creation see Valery Kryukov and Arild Moe, *Gazprom: Internal structure, management principles and financial flows*, 1996. The company was established by Presidential Decree No 1333 of November 5, 1992, *On the Transformation of the State Gas Concern Gazprom into Russian Joint Stock Company Gazprom*; and by the Resolution of the Council of Ministers of the Government of the Russian Federation No. 138 *On the Establishment of the Russian Joint Stock Company Gazprom* (Order No. 138) of February 17, 1993.

2 *Loan Notes 2005*, p.101.

3 *Gazprom Annual Report 2003*, p.14 has a chart which shows how these percentages changed from year to year during the period 1999–2003.

4 *Loan Notes 2004*, p.152.

5 *Loan Notes 2004*, p.152; Presidential Decree No 529 of May 28, 1997 limited foreign ownership to 9% of the company and Presidential Decree No 943 of August 10, 1998 allowed the sale of another 5%.

6 During the period 1997–2004, the discount ranged from 30–90% with the gap narrowing in the later years as the promise of share liberalisation neared. *Renaissance Capital*, 'Gazprom: Don't miss it!' 2004.

7 In most companies with many thousands of individual shareholders it would be considered that a '50% plus one share' holding was not necessary to maintain control but perhaps this is an indication of the importance of Gazprom in the eyes of the Russian government.

8 'Gazprom makes first step towards liberalising share market,' *Interfax Petroleum Report*, 14–20 March 2003, p.16.

9 Valery Kryukov and Arild Moe,*Gazprom: internal structure, management principles and financial flows*, 1996, p.39.

10 Richard Sakwa, *Putin: Russia's* Choice, 2004, p.200. Because of Victor Chernomyrdin's links with the company, the party was widely known in Russia as 'Nash Dom, Gazprom' (Our Home is Gazprom).

11 A biography of Alexey Miller can be found on the Gazprom website: http://www.gazprom.com/eng/articles/article8603.shtml

12 Victor Ilyushin (regions), Vasily Podiuk (production of gas, gas condensate and oil) and Bogdan Budzulyak (transportation, storage and use). For an analysis of the management in 2005 see 'Inside the Gazprom management team,' *Gas Matters*, April 2005, pp.5–12.

13 http://www.gazprom.ru/subjects/groups/sovet.shtml. The others were two members of Gazprom's management committee, the head of Gazprom's economic analysis division, and two representatives of shareholders, domestic and foreign.

14 'Our goal is a free market'. Interview with Alexei Ryazanov in *Mirovaya Energetika*, January 12, 2004.

15 A better indicator than the average across all zones is the average across zones 5–11 where the majority of the gas is consumed, which was RR1086

(nearly \$39)/mcm.

16 *Russian Energy Strategy 2003*, p.69.

17 The nominal increases were 2005 – 20%, 2006 – 11%; 2007 – 8%, 'O Senarnikh Usloviyakh Sotsialno-Ekonomicheskovo Razvitiya Rossiskoy Federatsii no 2005 god i na period do 2007 goda' – presentation and text, MEDT Press Service March 25, 2004, www.economy.gov.ru.

18 Alex Fak and Caroline McGregor, 'EU Backs Russia's Bid to Join WTO,' *Moscow Times*, May 24, 2004, p.1; 'EU Wants More WTO Concessions,' *Ibid*, May 26, 2004, p.7.

19 The survey was based on 390 responses (out of 744 enterprises surveyed) in 61 of Russia's 89 regions. *OECD Economic Survey of the Russian Federation 2004*, Annex 3.2, pp.150–53.

20 'Gazprom management makes corporate decisions on internal, external operations,' *Interfax Petroleum Report*, June 20–6, 2003, p.18.

21 Note the distinction between allowing Gazprom to sell at unregulated prices, and Gazprom's sales of 'above quota' gas to customers at higher than regulated prices, where it is not known whether regulatory authorities have any oversight.

22 'Russian Gas exchange could be formed soon,' *Interfax Petroleum Report*, 30 August–5 September, 2002; 'Gazprom board to discuss share liberalisation mid-November,' *Interfax Petroleum Report*, November 8–14, 2002, pp.21–2.

23 'Resolution to free gas prices should be first step in liberalisation,' *Interfax Petroleum Report*, January 31–February 6, 2003, p.7.

24 Kirill Seleznev, *Seti prikhodit v negodnost', a rolova bolit u Gazproma*, Interview in Vedemosti, August 5, 2004.

25 In early 2005, twelve other companies were listed as participants http://www.mbnk.ru/002memb/0201memb.htm

26 'Our goal is a free market'. Interviews, www.gazprom.ru; January 12, 2004.

27 'The statement of Alexey Miller, Chairman, Gazprom Management Committee about natural gas pricing regulation,' April 2005, www.gazprom.ru

28 *Ibid*.

29 Many would argue that even 50% is too great a market share to allow self-sustaining competition to develop.

30 It was noted in Chapter 3 that in 2002–03, transit charges accounted for 13–16% of Gazprom's total operating costs.

31 Government Decree 858, June 14, 1997.

32 For progress of gas to gas competition in EU member states see *EU Benchmarking Reports*.

33 The FEC's other responsibilities were transferred to the Energy Regulatory Agency under MEDT.

34 The tariff for Russian and CIS customs Union countries came into force on October 1, 2004; it is assumed that the tariff for customers outside those countries remained the same. 'Independent producers' gas transport tariff

hiked 17%,' *Interfax Petroleum Report,* September 16–22, 2004, p.29–30.
35 The 'economic radius' is the distance from the point of production within which gas sales to customers are commercially viable.
36 'Board of Directors examined gas production and transmission subsidiaries pricing policy,' *Gazprom Press Release,* February 2, 2004.
37 Third party users of a network must 'balance' – i.e. ensure that the volumes they inject into the network equate to the volumes they withdraw – over a period of time which should be defined by regulation.
38 'Gas market coordinator wants new method for setting transport rates,' *Interfax Petroleum Report,* July 25–31, 2003, pp.14–16.
39 The GMC is a self-regulated body comprising the 17 largest consumers and producers in Russia. Gazprom and UES are co-founders; other participants include TNK/BP, Yukos, Lukoil, Russian Gas Company, Severstal, Novolipetsk Metallurgical Combine, Evrokhim, Sibur, Comprehensive Energy Systems, International Union of Metallurgists, FosAgroAG, Blagodar, Russian Public Works Systems, MetalEnergo Finance, and Mechtel Trading House. 'Gazprom and govt announce domestic gas price liberalisation proposals,' *Interfax Oil and Gas Report,* March 31–April 5, 2005, pp. 6–10.
40 This 'entry/exit' tariff design is considered best practice in the European Union, see the discussion of the Madrid Forum of Regulators http://europa.eu.int/comm/energy/gas/madrid/index_en.htm
41 This refers to the share of *naselenie* – population, which would include district heating supplies as well as direct gas sales. Alexander Ryazanov, *Razvitiye Rinka Gaza v Rossii,* Briefingi i Press Konferentzii, June 1, 2005.
42 See the *istoria* section of the Gazexport website, www.gazexport.ru
43 Resolution No. 39 of the RAO Gazprom Board dated April 9, 1997, and Resolution No.53 of OAO (Joint-Stock Company) Gazprom Board of Directors of February 12, 1998. See the 'about' section of the Gazexport website, www.gazexport.ru
44 There is a chart showing these relationships and shareholdings on the ZGG website, http://www.zgg.de/english/company/konzern.php
45 Presidential Decree No 1333 of November 5, 1992, *On the Transformation of the State Gas Concern Gazprom into Russian Joint Stock Company Gazprom.*
46 Press Conference with Deputy Chairman Alexander Ryazanov and General Director of Gazexport Alexander Medvedev (in Russian), *Postavki Rossiskovo gaza k otechestvennim i zarubezhnim p otrebitelyam,* Brifingi I Press Konferentsii, March 2, 2004.
47 'Our goal is a free market', interview with Deputy Chairman Alexander Ryazanov, January 12, 2004.
48 Arild Moe, 'The Reorganisation of Gazprom: Scope and Impact,' and Valery Kruykov, 'Gazprom – Financial Flows and Management: the need for internal transparency', proceedings of the Conference, Reform in the Russian Gas Industry: Regulation, Taxation, Foreign Investment and New Export Prospects, RIIA, London 20–21, November 1997.
49 *Presidential Decree No 426,* April 28 1997.

50 'Accounting unbundling' is a term from the first European Gas Directive which requires the separation of accounts of different business units within a vertically integrated utility. This is the most modest form of separation compared with 'ownership unbundling' which is the most radical separation.

51 *Strategy of development of the Russian Federation through 2010, Social and Economic Aspect*, Centre for Strategic Research, submitted to the government of the Russian Federation on 25 May 2000, Section 3.5.1.

52 This originally appeared at: www.gazeta.ru/2002/09/16/gazpromvseta. shtml but only for a few weeks; there is a useful summary of it in 'Leaked Conception sets out radical agenda for Russia's gas future,' *Gas Matters*, October 2002, pp.5–10.

53 See the criticism by the Federal Energy Commission in 'Economics Minister, Gazprom settle differences on gas market development,' *Interfax Petroleum Report*, December 13–19, 2002, p.18.

54 'Economic development ministry not calling for Gazprom division,' *Interfax Petroleum Report*, February 28–March 6, 2003, p.3.

55 'Natural monopoly reforms needed in three years,' *Interfax Petroleum Report*, August 29–September 4, 2003, p.3; 'Liberalisation of Gazprom share market tied to loss of state control,' *Interfax Petroleum Report*, August 1–7, 2003, p.14.

56 'Russia to keep control over pipeline system, Gazprom,' *Interfax Petroleum Report*, October 17–23, 2003, p.4.

57 'Putin calls for transparent Gazprom share structure, slow reform,' *Interfax Petroleum Report*, March 19–25, 2004, p.5.

58 'Our goal is a free market,' interview with Deputy Chairman Alexander Ryazanov, January 12, 2004. *Aleksander Ananenkov, zamestitel' predsedatelya pravleniya Gazproma: 'Vse kompanii po dobiche, transportirovke i prodazhe gaza ostanutsa stoprotsentnimi dochkami Gazproma'*, Pryamaya Rech', April 14, 2004.

59 *Ibid.*

60 'Miller discusses Gazprom development prospects with Putin,' *Interfax Petroleum Report*, August 5–11, 2004, p.13.

61 'Sharonov says govt to consider Gazprom spin-offs eventually,' *Interfax Petroleum Report*, October 11–17, 2004, p.7. 'Gref wants pipelines set apart during gas industry reforms,' *Interfax Petroleum Report*, October 14–20, 2004, p.33.

62 'FAS studying discrimination claim against Gazprom,' *Interfax Petroleum Report*, August 12–18, 2004, p.8.; 'FAS tells Gazprom to stop discrimination in pipeline access,' *Interfax Petroleum Report*, October 28–November 3, 2004, p.25.

63 A summary of power sector reform up to 2004 can be found in *OECD Economic Survey of the Russian Federation 2004*, Chapter 4. For a survey of future developments see: International Energy Agency, *Russian Electricity Reform: emerging challenges and opportunities*, OECD/IEA: Paris, 2005.

64 'Fradkov notes difficult of parallel gas, electricity reform,' *Interfax Petroleum Report*, August 26–September 1, 2004, p.7.

65 *Loan Notes 2005*, p.154.

66 In May 2003 Gazprom acquired a 15.76% interest in Mosenergo (which press reports have subsequently suggested has been increased to 25%) and in 2004 a 5.3% share in RAO UES. *Loan Notes 2004*, p.53.

67 *Gazprom Annual Report 2003*, p.49.

68 *OECD Economic Survey of the Russian Federation 2004*, p.140.

69 This is, of course, not the meaning of the term 'natural monopoly' in traditional economic literature.

70 'Over 10% of the French market switches away from GDF,' *European Gas Markets*, November 2004, p.4

71 Hans-Joachim Zeising, 'The E.ON/Ruhrgas Merger and Competition,' *Oxford Energy Forum*, November 2002, pp. 12–14.

72 Anders Aslund, *Building Capitalism*, 2002, p.183.

73 Marshall Goldman, *The Piratization of Russia*, 2003, p.108.

74 In particular *Ibid.*, pp.105–16.

75 For details of the resulting political storm see Andrew Jack, *Inside Putin's Russia*, 2004, pp.131–73.

76 For a review of the many books on Enron's demise see *The Energy Journal*, Vol. 25, No. 4, 2004, pp. 115–35.

77 Richard Sakwa, *Putin: Russia's Choice*, 2004, pp.200–01 (but no substantiation of this allegation is provided). The fact that certain members of that management subsequently moved to jobs at Itera may have suggested inappropriate relations with that company during their tenure at Gazprom, but also suggested that these individuals were not sufficiently rich to retire as a result of their time on the Gazprom board.

78 *Loan Notes 2004*, pp.53–4.

79 Renaissance Capital, 'Gazprom: Don't Miss it!' 2004, p.12.

80 OAO Gazprom, *Notes to the Consolidated Financial Statements* – 31 December 2003, p.37; Marshall Goldman, op.cit., p.109 shows the role of Gazprom board members and their families in Stroytransgaz's management.

81 OAO Gazprom, *Audit Report on Statutory Consolidated Financial (Accounting) Reports 2003*, p.26.

82 OAO Gazprom, *Notes to the Consolidated Financial Statements* – 31 December 2003, p.37. A fuller account of the Stroytransgaz and Interprocom episodes can be found in *Loan Notes 2004*, pp. 154–5.

83 OAO Gazprom, *Notes to the Consolidated Financial Statements* – 31 December 2003, p.39.

84 *Ibid.* The table shows guarantees for Itera of RR3.1bn in 2002 and RR2.7bn in 2003.

85 Andrew Jack, *Inside Putin's Russia*,op.cit., p.317.

86 The subject of 'cosy deals with obscure companies' in the previous reference.

87 Dmitry Butrin, 'Gazprom cast the net,' *Kommersant*, March 19, 2004.

88 Interview with Alexander Ananenkov, *Vce kompanii po dobyche, transportirovke i prodazhe gaza ostanutsa stoprotsentnimi dochkami Gazproma*, April 14, 2004, Pryama Rech.

89 'Gazprom decides on companies to be established during restructuring,' *Interfax Petroleum Report*, March 17–23, 2005, pp.28–9.

90 'Management committee reviews Sibur's development strategy issue,' *Gazprom Press Release*, November 12, 2004.

91 'Alexey Miller convenes meeting on Gazprom's restructuring,' *Gazprom Press Release*, January 29, 2005.

92 *OAO Gazprom IFRS Consolidated Financial Statements*, 31 December 2003, p.7 and 30.

93 It was suggested by the Commission that 'The Community acquis could become a reference framework for a reform of the energy sector to be implemented in Russia,' *EU-Russia Energy Dialogue*, para 4.

94 *EU Gas Directive 1998*. Article 13.

95 *EU Gas Directive 2003*, Article 9.

96 Common position adopted by the Council with a view to the adoption of a *Regulation of the European Parliament and of the Council on Conditions of Access to the Gas Transmission Networks*. Brussels, 12 November 2004. http://europa.eu.int/comm/energy/gas/legislation/doc/gas_regulation/cp_en.pdf

97 'Regulator said gas market monopoly growing,' *Interfax Oil and Gas Report*, March 17–23, 2005, p.11.

98 In October 2004, the Commission served formal notice on 18 member states which had not transposed the second directive into law. 'Opening up of energy markets, 18 member states still have to transpose the new EU rules,' *EU Press Release, IP/04/1216*, October 13, 2004. The Commission's assessment of progress of gas liberalisation can be found in *EU Benchmarking Reports 2004 and 2005*.

99 An increase in production from 10.2mt in 2001 and 10.6mt in 2002. *Gazprom Annual Report 2003*, p.8; 'Gazprom reports its major interim operating results over 2004,' *Gazprom Press Release*, January 25, 2005.

100 Estimates by DeGolyer and McNaughton at 31/12/04, *Loan notes 2005*, Appendix A, p.A4.

101 http://www.rosneft.ru/english/operations/extraction.html

102 'Gazprom to set up oil company,' *Interfax Petroleum Report*, April 9–15, 2004, pp.23–4.

103 Arkardy Ostrovsky, 'Curtain falls on final act of Yukos farce,' *Financial Times*, December 20, 2004; Patti Waldemeir, 'US ruling opens "barrel of worms"', *Financial Times*, December 20, 2004; Arkardy Ostrovsky, 'Putin defends Rosneft purchase of Yukos unit,' *Financial Times*, December 23, 2004.

104 Svetlana Savateyeva, 'Gazpromneft: small company with great ambitions,' *Interfax Oil and Gas Report*, December 2–8, 2004, pp.13–16.

105 'Board of directors addresses upcoming shareholders' annual general meeting issues,' *Gazprom Press Release*, May 17, 2005. Neil Buckley and Isabel Gorst, 'Russia scraps energy merger and plans to open up shares,' *Financial Times*, May 18, 2005.

106 *Loan Notes 2005*, p.9.

107 'On the meeting of Alexey Miller and Sergey Bogdanchikov,' *Gazprom Press*

Release, April 15, 2004.

108 'On Alexey Miller and Zhoiu Jiping's Meeting,' *Gazprom Press Release*, December 12, 2004; Arkardy Ostrovsky, 'Putin hint at China alliance on Yukos oil,' *Financial Times*, December 22, 2004.

109 For example the 2004 visits to India, Brazil and Venezuela, see Gazprom press releases: 'Gazprom delegation completes visit to Venezuela,' December 13, 2004; 'On Alexey Miller and Dilma Rousseff's working meeting,' November 24 2004; 'On Gazprom delegation's visit to India,' December 4, 2004.

110 Anders Aslund, *Building Capitalism*, 2002, p.111.

111 *Ibid*, p.184.

112 Clifford Gaddy and Barry Ickes, *Russia's Virtual* Economy, 2002, pp.5–6.

113 In the 2000s, this is being replaced by the general explanation of authoritarian government presided over by President Putin that 'they are all from the security services' (*siloviki*).

Chapter 5

1 For example the *BP Statistical Review of World Energy 2004*, p.20, gives a reserve to production figure for 2003 of 81 years.

2 Profitability will depend to a significant extent on the tax regime for Yamal gas.

3 All prices in this section assume real 2004 US dollars at 2004 dollar/ruble exchange rates. There is a growing problem in denominating prices in dollars given the fall in that currency both against the Ruble and the Euro post-2003, and the fact that European gas prices are mostly denominated in Euros.

4 They do not include: domestic demand in Eastern Siberia and the Far East, pipeline exports to Asia or LNG exports to any destination (i.e. future production from Shtokman). This is because of the project-specific nature of these developments and their lack of connection with western Russian gas supplies and exports.

5 In early 2005, the possible exception to this conclusion seemed to be the trans-Dnestr region of Moldova.

6 Exactly how to define 'market prices' will continue to be a problem until other sources of gas become available to these countries.

7 At a press conference announcing the Gazprom/Rosneft merger, Gazprom Chairman Alexey Miller said that it would help Gazprom to become 'one of the largest gas-oil-power companies in the world,' Zayavlenie predsedatelya OAO Gazprom Alexeya Millera i presidenta OAO NK Rosneft Sergeya Bogdanchikova or pricoyedinenii Rosnefti i Gazproma, Broadcast on Channel 1, NTV, March 2, 2005; Spravochnie Materiali, www.gazprom.ru

8 *Gazprom v Voprosakh*, p.9, www.gazprom.ru; note that in the English version,

Gazprom in Questions and Answers, the chapter on strategy from which this quote is taken, does not appear.

9 The establishment of YNG under the control of the Rosneft management, while Rosneft's assets would be transferred to Gazprom without their management, was never a convincing corporate model.

10 Immediately following the collapse of the Rosneft merger, there were rumours that Gazprom had entered into negotiations for a takeover of Sibneft.

SELECT BIBLIOGRAPHY

Aslund, Anders, *Building Capitalism: the Transformation of the former Soviet Bloc*, Cambridge University Press, 2002.

Bashmakov, Igor, *Energy Subsidies in Russia: the case of district heating*, in (eds), Anna Von Moltke, Colin McKee and Trevor Morgan, *Energy Subsidies*, UNEP/ Greenleaf Publishing, 2003.

Bradshaw, Michael J. (ed.), *The Russian Far East and Pacific Asia: unfulfilled potential*, Curzon Press, 2001.

Dore, Julia and Robert de Bauw, *The Energy Charter Treaty: origins, aims and prospects*, London: RIIA, 1995

Bruce, Chloe, *Fraternal Friction or Fraternal Fiction? The Gas Factor in Russian-Belarusian Relations*, Oxford Institute for Energy Studies, April 2005; http://www.oxfordenergy.org/pdfs/NG8.pdf

Ebel, Robert E., *Communist Trade in Oil and Gas*, Praeger Publishers, 1970.

ETG, *Eural Trans Gas chooses Cedric Brown as Chairman-elect*, Press Release, March 29, 2004; http://www.etg.hu/pressroom.asp?rel=1087

EU Benchmarking Report 2004: DG TREN Commission Staff Working Paper, *Third benchmarking report on the implementation of the internal electricity and gas market*, Brussels 01/03/2004.

EU Benchmarking Report 2005: Report from the Commission: *Annual Report on the Implementation of the Gas and Electricity Internal Market*, COM(2004) 863 final, Brussels 5/1/2005.

EU Gas Directive 1998: Directive 98/30/EC of the European Parliament and of the Council of 22 June 1998 concerning common rules for the internal market in natural gas, *Official Journal* L204, 21/07/1998 pp.0001-0012.

EU Gas Directive 2003: Directive 2003/55/EC of the European Parliament and the Council Concerning Common Rules for the Internal Market in Natural Gas and Repealing Directive 98/30/EC", Brussels 26 June 2003, *Official Journal* L176, 15/07/2003, pp. 57-78.

EU-Russia Energy Dialogue: Communication From the Commission to the Council and the European Parliament, *The Energy Dialogue between the European Union and the Russian Federation between 2000 and 2004*, Brussels, December 2004, COM (2004) final. http://europa.eu.int/comm/energy/russia/issues/gas_en.htm

http://europa.eu.int/comm/energy/russia/overview/index_en.htm

Gaddy, Clifford G. and Barry W. Ickes, *Russia's Virtual Economy*, Brookings Institution: 2002.

Gazprom: Annual Reports, Press Releases, Interviews, Press Conferences; all available on the company's website www.gazprom.ru (see notes on sources).

Gazprom Audit Report 2003: Open Joint Stock Company Gazprom, *Audit Report on Statutory Consolidated Financial (Accounting) Reports 2003.* www.gazprom.ru

Goldman, Marshall I., *The Piratization of Russia,* Routledge: 2003.

Hill, Fiona, *Energy Empire: oil and gas and Russia's revival,* London: The Foreign Policy Centre, September 2004.

International Energy Agency (IEA), *Energy Survey of Russia,* Paris: OECD, 1995.

International Energy Agency, *Russia Energy Survey 2002,* Paris: OECD, 2002.

International Energy Agency, Conference on: *Energy Security: the Role of Russian Gas Companies,* November 25, 2003, http://www.iea.org/textbase/work/2003/soyuzgaz/proceedings/programme.htm

International Energy Agency, *World Energy Outlook 2004,* Paris: OECD, 2004.

Jack, Andrew, *Inside Putin's Russia,* London: Granta Books, 2004, pp. 187–91.

Jensen, James T., *The Development of a Global LNG Market: is it likely and if so when?* Oxford Institute for Energy Studies, September 2004.

Jentleson, Bruce, *Pipeline Politics: The Complex Political Economy of East-West Energy Trade,* Cornell University Press, 1986.

Kernohan, David and Yevgeny Vinokurov, *The EU-Russia WTO deal: balancing mid-term and longer-term growth prospects?* Centre for European Policy Studies, October 2004.

Knopp, Andras, *Diversification – key to security: Central Asian gas coming to Europe,* presentation to the 11th Central European Gas Conference, Bratislava, 7–9 June 2004.

Koudrin, A.A., *Gas Business in Russia: the experience of an independent gas producing company,* Paris: IEA 2003.

Kryukov, Valery and Arild Moe, *Gazprom: internal structure, management principles and financial flows,* London: RIIA, 1996.

Loan Notes 2003: *Open Joint Stock Company Gazprom, Loan Participation Notes due 2013,* Dresdner Kleinwort Wasserstein/Morgan Stanley, 2003.

Loan Notes 2004: *Open Joint Stock Company Gazprom, US$5,000,000,000 Programme for the Issuance of Loan Participation Notes,* Deutsche Bank/UBS Investment Bank, April 26, 2004.

Loan Notes 2005: *Open Joint Stock Company Gazprom, US$5,000,000,000 Programme for the Issuance of Loan Participation Notes,* Gaz Capital S.A. May 15, 2005.

Miller, Alexey B., 'Euroasian Direction of the Russia's Gas Strategy', 22nd World Gas Conference, Tokyo, June 4, 2003.

Miyamoto, Akira, *Natural Gas in Central Asia: industries, markets and export options of Kazakhstan, Turkmenistan and Uzbekistan,* RIIA: London 1998,

Organization of Economic Cooperation and Development (OECD), *OECD Economic survey of the Russian Federation,* Volume 2002/5, Paris: OECD, 2002.

—— *OECD Economic Survey of the Russian Federation,* Paris: OECD, July 2004.

Orudzhev, S.A., *Gazovaya Promyshlennost' po Puti Progressa,* Moscow, 1976.

Paik, Keun-Wook, *Pipeline Gas Introduction to the Korean Peninsula,* Project on Energy and Environmental Cooperation on the Korean Peninsula, Chatham House, January 2005. http://www.chathamhouse.org.uk/viewdocument.php?documentid=5579

Renaissance Capital, *Gazprom: don't miss it!* April 2004.

264

Russian Energy Strategy 2003, *Energeticheskaya Strategiya Rossiya na period do 2020 goda*; confirmed by the Russian Government on August 28, 2003.

Sakwa, Richard, *Putin: Russia's Choice*, London: Routledge, 2004.

Stern, Jonathan P., *The Russian Natural Gas Bubble: consequences for European gas markets*, London:RIIA, 1995.

Stern, Jonathan P., *Competition and Liberalisation in European Gas Markets: a diversity of models*, London: RIIA. 1998.

Stern, Jonathan P., 'The origins and evolution of Gazprom's export strategy', in Robert Mabro and Ian Wybrew-Bond (eds), *Gas to Europe, the strategies of the four major suppliers*, Oxford University Press, 1999, pp. 135–200.

Stern, Jonathan P., *Security of European Natural Gas Supplies: the impact of import dependence and liberalisation*, Royal Institute of International Affairs, 2002, http://www.riia.org/pdf/research/sdp/Sec_of_Euro_Gas_Jul02.pdf

Stern, Jonathan P., 'Russian and Central Asian Gas Supply for Asia,' in Ian Wybrew-Bond and Jonathan Stern (eds), *Natural Gas in Asia: the challenges of growth in China, India, Japan and Korea*, Oxford University Press, 2002.

Tarr, David and Peter Thompson, *The Merits of Dual Pricing of Russian Natural Gas*, The World Bank, July 19, 2003.

VNIIgaz, *Programma Kompleksnoi Promyshlennogo Osvoeniya Mestorozhdeniay Poluostrova Yamal*, Moscow: 2002.

Vyakhirev, Rem, *Russian Gas Industry in the 21ˢᵗ Century*, World Gas Conference, Nice, June 2000.

Walde, Thomas W. (ed.), *The Energy Charter Treaty: an East-West Gateway for Investment and Trade*, London: Kluwer Law International, 1996.

INDEX